~~THE~~ SURVIVAL GUIDE:

HOME REMODELING

PLESSET'S PRINCIPLES FOR AN ALMOST-PERFECT PROJECT

Diane Plesset, ASID, CBD/CKD, CCIDC

Illustrations by: Janis Emerson

D. P. Design Publishing
P. O. Box 305, 9610 SE 82nd Ave.
Portland, OR 97266

Library of Congress #2003106312
ISBN #0-9729627-0-0

In the preparation of this book, every effort has been made to offer the most current and correct information possible. Nonetheless, inadvertent errors can occur. Estimates and pricing may be affected by region, the time of year, normal increases, and economic situations. Illustrations contained in this book are not meant to represent any particular person living or dead, except the characters defined as "Ms. Designer" and "Mr. Homeowner." Any resemblance of other characters is purely coincidental. Examples given in the text are extrapolated from real situations. In many cases, situations have been altered slightly to protect the privacy of homeowners, contractors, and design professionals.

The information in the text is intended to afford general guidance to homeowners. If legal, accounting, tax, investment, or other expert advice is required, readers are encouraged to consult with professional advisers who are familiar with local codes and pricing. The author and publisher disclaim any responsibility for positions taken by homeowners in their individual cases or for any misunderstanding on the part of readers.

This publication is designed to provide accurate and authoritative information in regard to the subject matter covered. It is sold with the understanding that the publisher is not engaged in rendering legal, accounting, or other professional service and that the author is not offering such advice in this publication. If legal advice or other expert assistance is required, the services of a competent professional person should be sought.

PREFACE

I have been a bath-kitchen design specialist for over 20 years. Eight years ago, I began teaching seminars for homeowners, helping them to understand the remodeling process. After hearing most of them suggest that I write a book based on my class handouts, I embarked on the five-year journey of compiling and composing "THE Survival Guide" for homeowners.

My goals are clear:

> To educate homeowners about the remodeling process, so they will become informed consumers, able to talk knowledgeably with contractors, design professionals, and suppliers about what they want, when they want it, and how much they want to invest.

> To help homeowners develop more realistic expectations, which in turn will help contractors, design proessionals, and suppliers be more efficient (and more profitable).

> To become a better businesswoman -- more assertive and confident.

> To help everyone appreciate the importance of the remodeling team and to respect all team members.

> To help everyone have fun, to enjoy the building-remodeling process. To take what they *do* more seriously than who they *are*.

ACKNOWLEDGEMENTS

So many people have helped to make this book possible. Every former client, instructor, professional peer, and student has given me many opportunities to learn and grow professionally. I thank every one of you for your generosity. Two women have paved the road for the rest of us. They have been instrumental in my development as a bath and kitchen design specialist. A world of thanks to Martha Kerr, CMKBD/CR, and Ellen Cheever, CMKBD.ASID.

Particular professionals who have helped with technical information for this book:

> Glenda McAdam
> Brendon Murphy
> Paul Slattery
> Gary Sellers

A very special "Thank You" to Dr. "S" In San Carlos, Dr. "S" in Oregon City, Laurel and Dana in San Mateo, Peg and Melinda in Oregon City, who have worked so hard to keep this ol' body limber and strong, despite my long hours at the computer writing this book.

Three very important people have played a key role in my life. They have been inspirational role models for me (and millions of other people). Following their examples, I have given myself permission to <u>dream it</u> and <u>do it</u> -- with humor, faith, and perseverance.

       Emeril Lagasse
       Dr. Robert Schuller
       Oprah Winfrey

Janis Emerson, whose patience and wit made our collaboration on the book so much fun.

It would be unfair to omit Frank Lloyd Wright from these acknowledgements. His creative genius, courage, humor, and determination have been my professional inspiration. Learning more about Mr. Wright has opened many doors that I could never have imagined 35 years ago. Special appreciation is offered to individual and collective members of The Frank Lloyd Wright Building Conservancy, the wonderful staff at Taliesen West, the Oregon Garden, and the Gordon House Conservancy Board.

My dear family and friends, who have given their love and support in every way possible:

       Gert Darneal
       Liz Greene
       Elke Janker
       Polly Plesset
       JoAnn Rees
       Kuni Sunada
       Rosanne Wolf

This book is dedicated to my friend, partner, soulmate; the president of my fan club. Thank you, Jay, for being you.

CONTENTS

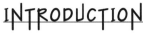
CHAPTER 1

Hello. I'm Diane Plesset.

INTRODUCTION

I wrote this book to help you understand the remodeling process, to help you get through your remodeling project successfully. The process is broken down into logical steps. If you follow the steps outlined, you will survive one of life's most emotionally trying experiences, remodeling your home.

Step Zero is obvious: You've decided to remodel your home. You may have been thinking about remodeling for several years (the average is five years). Like most other homeowners, you've probably had several false starts: Looking at magazines, visiting showrooms, attending home shows, and talking with contractors. You lost interest for one reason or another, and now more time has passed and you <u>need</u> to remodel because you need more space, or want to update the appearance and function of your home. Your home may have more serious problems, like dry rot or leaks, that are your motivation to remodel.

"**When you hear the toilet flush and the words 'Uh-oh,' it's already too late.**"

You may have just purchased a nice home that needs upgrading and improving, but you're so overwhelmed with the process you've just been through, you don't have the energy to tackle another major event.

Don't despair! Remodeling is a complex process, but you're going to learn how to take it in logical steps, to make decisions one at a time in logical order. Whenever you remodel, with the information you'll gather from this book, you'll be prepared to make the <u>hundreds</u> of decisions necessary to achieve the remodeled home you desire. You've already made the first good decision: You bought this book!

There is one main theme, my inspiration for writing this book; it's my advice to EVERY client, every homeowner: Be active in your project, from today to the end of your project.

Don't assume that others will take care of you, read your mind or make the best decisions for you. You are the most important member of a team. The team should work together to achieve your (realistic) goals. The best, most successful projects are the ones where everyone takes their role more seriously than they take themselves.

> **"People who want milk should not seat themselves on a stool in the middle of a field in hope that the cow will back up to them."** (Elbert Hubbard)

Step One (Chapter 1). If you are planning to invest over $150,000 in your home, you've probably weighed the pro's and con's of remodeling versus buying a new(er) home. The first survey will help you define, in writing, why you prefer to remodel.

Step Two (Chapter 2). Fill out the short survey as honestly as possible; it's going to be the foundation for everything else you do. Then fill out the longer survey, to help you define what you want most in your newly-remodeled home. This survey is very useful for your whole family. It's also useful for the design professional, the contractor, and product suppliers who are members of your team. The survey will be a good communication aid, to remind everyone of your priorities as you go through design and construction.

> **"Informed consumers make the best consumers."**

In **Step Three (Chapter 4)**, you will learn how product choices affect your project. The same hypothetical project is presented in "good-better-best" format to emphasize the importance of informed decisions. **Step Four (Chapter 5)** explains how to compile product pricing information to help confirm or change the preferences you defined earlier (Step Two). **Step Five (Chapter 6)** clarifies how to estimate your budget and affirms the importance of a simple spreadsheet to help you.

Step Six (Chapter 8) will help you choose a design professional, and **Step Seven (Chapter 9)** will explain the design process in detail, which includes getting preliminary labor estimates to verify what you want is affordable.

If you are thinking about being your own contractor, you will take a test to determine your qualifications. In **Step Eight (Chapter 11)**, you'll get information about how to hire and work with a contractor. If you've completed Steps One through Seven, you will be able to talk knowledgeably with contractors about your project. Don't be surprised if they're surprised; most homeowners <u>aren't</u> "armed" with good information.

When you have determined your project is feasible, **Step Nine (Chapter 12)** will define the construction process. It will help you understand how long it will probably take to complete your project.

So, now you really understand all of the steps involved in your remodeling project. Please, don't stop reading.......

"Read a little, dream a little. Live, love, laugh, and learn a little." (Compendium Books)

Chapters 13 and 14 talk about the plans that translate your desired results into reality. You will understand why permits are necessary for most projects. You will learn how and why the building department and building inspectors are needed to help you achieve good results.

Chapter 15 talks honestly about something of critical importance to a successful project: Remodeling Etiquette. Not the stodgy, Emily Post-type etiquette, but everyday courtesy that makes everyone feel better. There's also a list of hints in Chapter 16 to make your project better for everyone.

Chapter 17 is full of information about the products you'll be choosing for your whole house: Appliances, electrical and lighting, countertops, plumbing, flooring, wall finishes, etc. Chapter 18 is an example of a remodeling project that went well from beginning to end. It's included to provide inspiration that your home remodeling can be enjoyable! Chapter 19 contains a glossary of terminology that's used in the design and construction industry.

You are at the beginning of your remodeling process, where all of the information can be general, often scrambled and confusing. Think of a funnel. You are at the top, working towards the neck. The scrambled information will become solid information, like building blocks. It will be the foundation of informed decisions, as you read this book.

I hope you enjoy "THE Survival Guide," and hope that it helps you. Your feedback is very important to me. Please contact me through my website (www.dp-design.com); be sure to complete the feedback form to let me know how the book helped you, and make suggestions about information that will help future readers. Your personal examples are definitely welcome! Good luck with your project!

"There are two things to aim at in life: First to get what you want; and after that, to enjoy it. Only the wisest of mankind achieve the second." (Logan Pearsall Smith)

TO MOVE -- OR -- TO REMODEL?

"The status quo sucks." (George Carlin)

Remodeling (and building) is all about options, and important decisions. The first question you should answer is: Do I/we want to remodel our existing home, or would it be better if I/we invest the same amount and get a new(er) home?

The following survey will help you define, in writing, what will be best for you. It will help you make an important decision, based on information. The final decision is YOURS.

HINTS: USING THE SURVEY FORMS

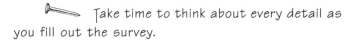

GET THE POINT?

📌 Make copies for everyone in the family.

📌 Take time to think about every detail as you fill out the survey.

📌 After everyone has filled out the survey, family members should discuss their priorities and make a decision about what will and will not be included in the project.

📌 If you re-take the surveys, use different color ink every time. **DON'T use a fountain pen or soft-tip pen; the ink will bleed through.**

📌 Take the completed surveys with you when you go shopping.

WEIGHING THE FACTS

How long have you lived in your home?   _____

What did you pay for your home?   _____

What is your home <u>really</u> worth?   _____
    (If it's been more than five years since you had it appraised professionally, get it appraised now!)

How old is your home?   _____

Is your home:
- [ ] Older than most homes in the neighborhood;
- [ ] The same age as most homes in the neighborhood;
- [ ] Newer than most homes in the neighborhood.

How does the value of your home compare with other homes in your neighborhood?
- [ ] Considerably less
- [ ] A little less
- [ ] About the same
- [ ] A little more
- [ ] Considerably more

Do you like the size of your property, or do you secretly wish for more garden?
- [ ] The property suits our needs.
- [ ] I/we would really like a larger garden (or patio).
- [ ] I/we will be unhappy if an addition takes away some of our garden.

How many homes in your neighborhood have been remodeled in the past two years?

A:_____

What percentage of the remodeled neighborhood homes were large projects?

A: _____

(A call or visit to your local building department will help you get the answer to the two questions above.)

What is the target budget for your project?

A: _____

If you invested the same amount of money to purchase a new(er) home, would you achieve everything on your wish list?

[ ] Yes   [ ] No

How much is your current monthly mortgage?

A: _____

How much will your monthly mortgage be if you borrow equity to remodel?

A: _____

How much will your monthly mortgage be if you buy a new(er) home?

A: _____

What are your current yearly property taxes?

A: _____

What will your yearly property taxes be if you buy a new(er) home?

A: _____

(This is really important in California, and possibly other states that have laws freezing property taxes.)

A family in California were trying to decide whether to buy a new home or remodel their existing home. They had lived there for over 20 years, and their yearly property tax was frozen by "Proposition 13" to $1,300. They calculated that an additional $250,000 investment would increase their taxes to approximately $2,000 a year, but if they bought a new home, they'd lose their "Proposition 13" protection. Their yearly tax bill would be over $8,000!

Do you like your neighborhood?
[ ] Yes   [ ] No   [ ] Neutral

Do you like your neighbors?
[ ] Yes   [ ] No   [ ] Neutral

Do you live in a well-established neighborhood?
[ ] Yes   [ ] No

Does your neighborhood have mature trees?
[ ] Yes   [ ] No

Do you like the style of homes in your neighborhood?
[ ] Yes   [ ] No   [ ] Neutral

Do you like the gardens in your neighborhood?
[ ] Yes   [ ] No   [ ] Neutral

What do you like about your neighborhood?

1. _____

2. _____

3. _____

4. _____

5. _____

What do you dislike about your neighborhood?

1. _____

2. _____

3. _____

4. _____

5. _____

Some reminders to consider:

➤ Remodeling allows you to customize your home to meet your needs and desires. The only similar, but much more costly alternative, is to have a brand new custom home designed and built.

➤ Remodeling means that you don't have to give up a familiar neighborhood and schools.

➤ Remodeling is a more efficient use of your financial resources. According to the American Homeowner Foundation, selling your home and moving typically costs about 8-10 percent of the value of your current home. And much of this goes into moving expenses, closing costs, and broker commissions - items that have no direct impact on your home's quality.

➤ Remodeling can be stressful, but few experiences are more stressful than moving.

➤ Whatever your decision is, you have concrete reasons written down to support your decision. There's no guarantee that you won't second-guess (or regret) your decision in the future. You're not a fortune-teller; if you were, you'd play the lottery and could afford several homes!

"Don't worry about what's ahead. Just go as far as you can go -- from there you can see farther."

The rest of this book is based on your decision to stay in your current home and remodel it to fit your needs. The next two surveys will help you define why you want to remodel your home, what you want to achieve, how much you want to invest, and when you want to start/finish your project.

"Any change, even a change for the better, is always accompanied by drawbacks and discomforts." (Arnold Bennett)

7

DATE:_____

PERSON:_____   ROOMS/AREAS:_____

─── CHAPTER 3: HOMEOWNER SURVEY #2 ───

"What would you attempt to do if you knew you could not fail?" (Dr. Robert Schuller)

TANGIBLE REASONS FOR REMODELING

[ ] House not large enough
[ ] Plumbing leaks
[ ] Need more and better storage
[ ] Layout not satisfactory
[ ] Style outdated/color scheme outdated
[ ] Dry rot/termite damage

[ ] Need more space for:_____

_____

_____

[ ] Want more space for:_____

_____

_____

[ ] House is expensive to heat
[ ] Lighting is poor (i.e., have to turn on lights during the day, glare at certain times of the year)
[ ] Ventilation is poor (old windows, no exhaust fans)

[ ] Other: _____

[ ] Other: _____

Target completion date: _____

Target budget for entire project:_____

INTANGIBLE REASONS FOR REMODELING

[ ] Need to improve function
[ ] Need to improve safety
[ ] Want our home to fit our lifestyle
[ ] Want to remodel for an important occasion
[ ] Company coming; want to impress them
[ ] *Neighbor, friend, family member just remodeled their home; I/we deserve just as
    good as they got
[ ] *If we remodel, it will improve:
    [ ]   Our family relationship
    [ ]   Our social life
    [ ]   Our status in the community

    [ ]   Our _____

If you feel uncomfortable with the last two reasons (*), you may want to re-think your remodeling project. Remodeling will not magically improve anything (except your home); remodeling your home will not mend a difficult relationship, or automatically guarantee a different lifestyle. The investment may put a strain on the family income.

"Change is inevitable, except from vending machines."

NOTES

REMODELING IS AN EMOTIONAL ROLLER COASTER

The best, smoothest remodeling projects can test the strongest relationships. During the process, your lifestyle will change dramatically. Your project will be challenging for everyone in your immediate family, including pets. Everyday quirks that you accept as part of your partner's personality may turn into ugly monsters.

One couple are nesters, especially the husband. They love to stay home evenings and weekends -- puttering, reading, enjoying hobbies. The thought of packing up all of his possessions made the husband withdraw emotionally, which added stress to his wife. She had to make all the design decisions, and took total responsibility for communication with the designer, contractors, and suppliers.

Remodeling will probably affect every aspect of your life, including your interaction with working associates, friends, neighbors, and extended family members. You will discover many things about yourself and everyone around you. New differences of opinion will arise, which may cause conflicts you never imagined.

*"A great marriage is not when the perfect couple come together.
It's when an imperfect couple learns to enjoy their differences."*
(David Meure)

To avoid potential problems, it's best to include everyone in open discussion about your proposed remodeling project.   Family members will have different priorities and goals. It's best to explore as many of these as possible, before remodeling begins. Product and project decisions should be made jointly; no one should have the right to line-item veto. Open communication is key: Talking <u>and</u> Listening. Effective communication <u>NOW</u> is the only way to avoid future problems during design and construction.

When the designer asked the husband and wife why their teenage daughters hadn't been included in the Survey for their bathrooms, the husband stated emphatically, "This is MY house. My daughters will only be here until they go to college. I pay the bills. MY word is final in MY house. It's not a democracy."

"WISH LIST"

"Turn the problem into a project." (Dr. Robert Schuller)

PERSON:_____ DATE:_____

PROJECT WILL INCLUDE:

[ ] Master Bedroom/Bathroom   [ ] Powder Room
[ ] Another bedroom   [ ] Garage/Storage
[ ] Another Bathroom   [ ] Media Room
[ ] Family Room

[ ] _____

[ ] _____

[ ] _____

AREAS/FEATURES TO BE ADDED:
[ ] Swimming Pool   [ ] Poolhouse   [ ] Deck
[ ] Patio   [ ] Barbecue   [ ] Fireplace(s)

[ ] _____ [ ] _____ [ ] _____

ROOM(S) TO BE REMODELED:
[ ] Kitchen/Eating Area   [ ] Living Room   [ ] Dining Room
[ ] Master Bedroom/Bathroom   [ ] Other Bedroom/Bathroom

[ ] _____   [ ] _____

ADJACENT AREAS AFFECTED:
[ ] Hallway(s)   [ ] Closet(s)   [ ] Living Room
[ ] Dining Room   [ ] Bathroom

[ ] _____   [ ] _____

HOUSE STATISTICS:
[ ] Area
    [ ] Lot size: _____ sq.ft.

    [ ] Existing space: _____ sq.ft.

    [ ] Addition: _____ sq.ft.

(NOTE: 5 = VERY IMPORTANT
0 = NOT IMPORTANT)

	5	4	3	2	1	0	INFO. PG./NOTES
ARCHITECTURAL FEATURES:							
[ ] Door(s)							132-133
Entry	[ ]	[ ]	[ ]	[ ]	[ ]	[ ]	
Patio (Quantity:_____)	[ ]	[ ]	[ ]	[ ]	[ ]	[ ]	
French (Quantity:_____)	[ ]	[ ]	[ ]	[ ]	[ ]	[ ]	
[ ] Grids	[ ]	[ ]	[ ]	[ ]	[ ]	[ ]	
Garage	[ ]	[ ]	[ ]	[ ]	[ ]	[ ]	
Interior (Quantity:_____)	[ ]	[ ]	[ ]	[ ]	[ ]	[ ]	134
[ ] Windows							134-135
[ ] Double-hung	[ ]	[ ]	[ ]	[ ]	[ ]	[ ]	
[ ] Casement	[ ]	[ ]	[ ]	[ ]	[ ]	[ ]	
[ ] Awning	[ ]	[ ]	[ ]	[ ]	[ ]	[ ]	
[ ] Picture	[ ]	[ ]	[ ]	[ ]	[ ]	[ ]	
[ ] Bay/Bow	[ ]	[ ]	[ ]	[ ]	[ ]	[ ]	
[ ] Grids	[ ]	[ ]	[ ]	[ ]	[ ]	[ ]	
[ ] Skylight(s)	[ ]	[ ]	[ ]	[ ]	[ ]	[ ]	
[ ] Openable	[ ]	[ ]	[ ]	[ ]	[ ]	[ ]	
[ ] Heating/Cooling							
Forced Air	[ ]	[ ]	[ ]	[ ]	[ ]	[ ]	
Radiant	[ ]	[ ]	[ ]	[ ]	[ ]	[ ]	
Air Conditioning	[ ]	[ ]	[ ]	[ ]	[ ]	[ ]	
Other:_____	[ ]	[ ]	[ ]	[ ]	[ ]	[ ]	
[ ] Roofing material							137-139
[ ] Composition	[ ]	[ ]	[ ]	[ ]	[ ]	[ ]	
[ ] Shake	[ ]	[ ]	[ ]	[ ]	[ ]	[ ]	
[ ] Tile	[ ]	[ ]	[ ]	[ ]	[ ]	[ ]	
[ ] Concrete	[ ]	[ ]	[ ]	[ ]	[ ]	[ ]	
[ ] Membrane	[ ]	[ ]	[ ]	[ ]	[ ]	[ ]	
Other:_____	[ ]	[ ]	[ ]	[ ]	[ ]	[ ]	
[ ] Exterior Walls							
[ ] Wood Siding	[ ]	[ ]	[ ]	[ ]	[ ]	[ ]	
[ ] Stucco	[ ]	[ ]	[ ]	[ ]	[ ]	[ ]	
[ ] Brick	[ ]	[ ]	[ ]	[ ]	[ ]	[ ]	
[ ] Stone	[ ]	[ ]	[ ]	[ ]	[ ]	[ ]	
Other:_____	[ ]	[ ]	[ ]	[ ]	[ ]	[ ]	

ENERGY-EFFICIENT DESIGN [ ] [ ] [ ] [ ] [ ] [ ]

"GREEN" DESIGN/CONSTRUCTION

[ ] [ ] [ ] [ ] [ ] [ ]

INITIALS/DATE:_____

MASTER BATHROOM SURVEY and "WISH LIST"

PERSON:_____ DATE:_____

	5	4	3	2	1	0	INFO. PG./NOTES

PLUMBING FIXTURES/FITTINGS:

	5	4	3	2	1	0	INFO. PG./NOTES
[ ] Plumbing fittings:							
[ ] Chrome	[ ]	[ ]	[ ]	[ ]	[ ]	[ ]	
[ ] Brass	[ ]	[ ]	[ ]	[ ]	[ ]	[ ]	
[ ] Other:	[ ]	[ ]	[ ]	[ ]	[ ]	[ ]	
[ ] Single lavatory*	[ ]	[ ]	[ ]	[ ]	[ ]	[ ]	170-171
[ ] Pedestal	[ ]	[ ]	[ ]	[ ]	[ ]	[ ]	
[ ] Double lavatories*							
[ ] Pedestal	[ ]	[ ]	[ ]	[ ]	[ ]	[ ]	
[ ] Countertop on cabinet	[ ]	[ ]	[ ]	[ ]	[ ]	[ ]	
[ ] Lavatory height							
[ ] Standard (31"+/-)	[ ]	[ ]	[ ]	[ ]	[ ]	[ ]	
[ ] Kitchen (36" +/-)	[ ]	[ ]	[ ]	[ ]	[ ]	[ ]	

(*Lavatory = Bathroom sink)

	5	4	3	2	1	0	INFO. PG./NOTES
[ ] Lavatory faucet(s)	[ ]	[ ]	[ ]	[ ]	[ ]	[ ]	171-174
[ ] Single-lever	[ ]	[ ]	[ ]	[ ]	[ ]	[ ]	
[ ] Two-lever	[ ]	[ ]	[ ]	[ ]	[ ]	[ ]	

INITIALS/DATE:_____

	5	4	3	2	1	0	INFO. PG./NOTES

PLUMBING FIXTURES/FITTINGS (CONT'D.):

	5	4	3	2	1	0	INFO. PG./NOTES
[ ] Separate Shower	[ ]	[ ]	[ ]	[ ]	[ ]	[ ]	174-178
[ ] One person	[ ]	[ ]	[ ]	[ ]	[ ]	[ ]	
[ ] Two persons	[ ]	[ ]	[ ]	[ ]	[ ]	[ ]	
[ ] With steam	[ ]	[ ]	[ ]	[ ]	[ ]	[ ]	
[ ] Single-lever valve	[ ]	[ ]	[ ]	[ ]	[ ]	[ ]	
[ ] Stationary shower head	[ ]	[ ]	[ ]	[ ]	[ ]	[ ]	
[ ] Separate Diverter	[ ]	[ ]	[ ]	[ ]	[ ]	[ ]	
[ ] Adjustable personal shower	[ ]	[ ]	[ ]	[ ]	[ ]	[ ]	
[ ] Separate Tub	[ ]	[ ]	[ ]	[ ]	[ ]	[ ]	179-180
[ ] One person	[ ]	[ ]	[ ]	[ ]	[ ]	[ ]	
[ ] Two persons	[ ]	[ ]	[ ]	[ ]	[ ]	[ ]	
[ ] Standard	[ ]	[ ]	[ ]	[ ]	[ ]	[ ]	
[ ] Whirlpool	[ ]	[ ]	[ ]	[ ]	[ ]	[ ]	180-181
[ ] Tub valve	[ ]	[ ]	[ ]	[ ]	[ ]	[ ]	
[ ] Tub filler	[ ]	[ ]	[ ]	[ ]	[ ]	[ ]	
[ ] Waste/overflow	[ ]	[ ]	[ ]	[ ]	[ ]	[ ]	
[ ] Toilet (1.6 gal.)	[ ]	[ ]	[ ]	[ ]	[ ]	[ ]	169-170
[ ] One-piece "lowboy"	[ ]	[ ]	[ ]	[ ]	[ ]	[ ]	
[ ] Two-piece	[ ]	[ ]	[ ]	[ ]	[ ]	[ ]	
[ ] Bidet	[ ]	[ ]	[ ]	[ ]	[ ]	[ ]	
[ ] Bidet faucet	[ ]	[ ]	[ ]	[ ]	[ ]	[ ]	

INITIALS/DATE:_____

	5	4	3	2	1	0	INFO. PG./NOTES
VENTILATION:							
[ ] Improved ventilation	[ ]	[ ]	[ ]	[ ]	[ ]	[ ]	
[ ] Quiet fan	[ ]	[ ]	[ ]	[ ]	[ ]	[ ]	
[ ] Heat lamp	[ ]	[ ]	[ ]	[ ]	[ ]	[ ]	
BATHROOM ELECTRICAL/LIGHTING:							
[ ] Improved lighting	[ ]	[ ]	[ ]	[ ]	[ ]	[ ]	
[ ] General	[ ]	[ ]	[ ]	[ ]	[ ]	[ ]	
(Fluorescent required)							
[ ] Task	[ ]	[ ]	[ ]	[ ]	[ ]	[ ]	
[ ] "Mood"	[ ]	[ ]	[ ]	[ ]	[ ]	[ ]	
[ ] More outlets	[ ]	[ ]	[ ]	[ ]	[ ]	[ ]	
(GFI required)							
[ ] Inside cabinets	[ ]	[ ]	[ ]	[ ]	[ ]	[ ]	
(for rechargeables)							
[ ] In backsplash	[ ]	[ ]	[ ]	[ ]	[ ]	[ ]	
[ ] Dimmer switches	[ ]	[ ]	[ ]	[ ]	[ ]	[ ]	164
[ ] Telephone	[ ]	[ ]	[ ]	[ ]	[ ]	[ ]	
BATHROOM HEATING:							
[ ] Furnace duct(s)	[ ]	[ ]	[ ]	[ ]	[ ]	[ ]	
[ ] Radiant area pads	[ ]	[ ]	[ ]	[ ]	[ ]	[ ]	
(under the floor)							
[ ] Radiator/towel warmer	[ ]	[ ]	[ ]	[ ]	[ ]	[ ]	
COUNTERTOPS:							
[ ] Laminate	[ ]	[ ]	[ ]	[ ]	[ ]	[ ]	182-185
[ ] Cultured Composite Stone	[ ]	[ ]	[ ]	[ ]	[ ]	[ ]	
[ ] Solid Surface	[ ]	[ ]	[ ]	[ ]	[ ]	[ ]	
("Corian" or equiv.)							
[ ] Ceramic Tile	[ ]	[ ]	[ ]	[ ]	[ ]	[ ]	
[ ] Limestone	[ ]	[ ]	[ ]	[ ]	[ ]	[ ]	
[ ] Marble	[ ]	[ ]	[ ]	[ ]	[ ]	[ ]	
[ ] Granite	[ ]	[ ]	[ ]	[ ]	[ ]	[ ]	
[ ] Other:_____	[ ]	[ ]	[ ]	[ ]	[ ]	[ ]	
CABINETS:							45; 140-147
[ ] Face-frame	[ ]	[ ]	[ ]	[ ]	[ ]	[ ]	140
[ ] European 32-mm	[ ]	[ ]	[ ]	[ ]	[ ]	[ ]	
[ ] Traditional	[ ]	[ ]	[ ]	[ ]	[ ]	[ ]	142
[ ] Contemporary	[ ]	[ ]	[ ]	[ ]	[ ]	[ ]	
[ ] Laminate	[ ]	[ ]	[ ]	[ ]	[ ]	[ ]	143
[ ] Wood	[ ]	[ ]	[ ]	[ ]	[ ]	[ ]	
[ ] Maple	[ ]	[ ]	[ ]	[ ]	[ ]	[ ]	
[ ] Cherry	[ ]	[ ]	[ ]	[ ]	[ ]	[ ]	
[ ] Oak	[ ]	[ ]	[ ]	[ ]	[ ]	[ ]	
[ ] Other:_____	[ ]	[ ]	[ ]	[ ]	[ ]	[ ]	INITIALS/DATE:_____

CABINETS (Continued):
[ ] "Standard" height   [ ] [ ] [ ] [ ] [ ] [ ]
[ ] Kitchen height   [ ] [ ] [ ] [ ] [ ] [ ]

STORAGE:
[ ] Linens   [ ] Brushes/Combs   [ ] Blow Dryer   [ ] CurlingIron
[ ] Elec. Shaver   [ ] Elec. Floss   [ ] Elec. Toothbrush   [ ] Skin Care

[ ] Medication   [ ] Toiletries   [ ] Shoe care   [ ] _____

[ ] _____   [ ] _____   [ ] _____   [ ] _____

BATHROOM WALL SURFACES: 177-178
[ ] Cultured Composite Stone   [ ] [ ] [ ] [ ] [ ] [ ]
[ ] Solid Surface   [ ] [ ] [ ] [ ] [ ] [ ]
     ("Corian" or equiv.)
[ ] Ceramic Tile   [ ] [ ] [ ] [ ] [ ] [ ]
[ ] Limestone   [ ] [ ] [ ] [ ] [ ] [ ]
[ ] Marble   [ ] [ ] [ ] [ ] [ ] [ ]
[ ] Granite   [ ] [ ] [ ] [ ] [ ] [ ]

[ ] Other:_____ [ ] [ ] [ ] [ ] [ ] [ ]

BATHROOM FLOORING: 187-190
[ ] Vinyl   [ ] [ ] [ ] [ ] [ ] [ ]
[ ] Tile   [ ] [ ] [ ] [ ] [ ] [ ]
   [ ] Ceramic*   [ ] [ ] [ ] [ ] [ ] [ ]
   [ ] Limestone*   [ ] [ ] [ ] [ ] [ ] [ ]
   [ ] Marble*   [ ] [ ] [ ] [ ] [ ] [ ]
   [ ] Granite*   [ ] [ ] [ ] [ ] [ ] [ ]

[ ] Other:_____ [ ] [ ] [ ] [ ] [ ] [ ]

(*NOTE: FOR SAFETY REASONS, TILE SHOULD NOT BE
POLISHED OR SHINY; MATTE OR ROUGH RECOMMENDED)

ACCESSORIES & SAFETY: 175-179
[ ] Towel bar(s)   [ ] [ ] [ ] [ ] [ ] [ ]
[ ] Towel ring(s)   [ ] [ ] [ ] [ ] [ ] [ ]
[ ] Robe hook(s)   [ ] [ ] [ ] [ ] [ ] [ ]
[ ] Medicine cabinet(s)   [ ] [ ] [ ] [ ] [ ] [ ]
[ ] Shampoo/soap   [ ] [ ] [ ] [ ] [ ] [ ]
   [ ] Niche(s)   [ ] [ ] [ ] [ ] [ ] [ ]
   [ ] Shelf/Shelves   [ ] [ ] [ ] [ ] [ ] [ ]
[ ] Rinse glass(es)   [ ] [ ] [ ] [ ] [ ] [ ]
[ ] Glass shelf/shelves   [ ] [ ] [ ] [ ] [ ] [ ]

[ ] Other:_____ [ ] [ ] [ ] [ ] [ ] [ ]

INITIALS/DATE:_____

	5	4	3	2	1	0	INFO. PG./NOTES

ACCESSORIES & SAFETY (Continued):

INFO. PG./NOTES
175-179

	5	4	3	2	1	0
[ ] Other:	[ ]	[ ]	[ ]	[ ]	[ ]	[ ]
[ ] Tub seat	[ ]	[ ]	[ ]	[ ]	[ ]	[ ]
[ ] Shower seat	[ ]	[ ]	[ ]	[ ]	[ ]	[ ]
[ ] GRAB BAR(S)*	[ ]	[ ]	[ ]	[ ]	[ ]	[ ]

(*NOTE: HIGHLY RECOMMENDED FOR EVERY BATHROOM PROJECT)

COLOR PREFERENCE:

	5	4	3	2	1	0
[ ] Warm	[ ]	[ ]	[ ]	[ ]	[ ]	[ ]
[ ] Cool	[ ]	[ ]	[ ]	[ ]	[ ]	[ ]

Favorite Color(s): _____

Least Favorite Color(s): _____

STYLE PREFERENCE:
- [ ] Traditional:
  - [ ] Louis IV [ ] Empire [ ] French Country [ ] 18th Century
  - [ ] American Federal [ ] Greek Revival [ ] Victorian
- [ ] Modern:
  - [ ] Art Noveau [ ] Art Deco [ ] European
- [ ] Contemporary:
  - [ ] Post-Modern [ ] European [ ] Japanese

[ ] Other: _____

OTHER:

[ ] _____

[ ] _____

[ ] _____

"A house is where you store all your stuff while you're out buying new stuff." (George Carlin)

INITIALS/DATE: _____

BATHROOM SURVEY and "WISH LIST"

PERSON:_____ DATE:_____

[ ] Existing (to be remodeled)   [ ] New (to be added)
[ ] Purpose/Use:
    [ ] Family only   [ ] Family/guests   [ ] Guests only

	5	4	3	2	1	0	INFO. PG./NOTES
ARCHITECTURAL FEATURES:							
[ ] Door(s)	[ ]	[ ]	[ ]	[ ]	[ ]	[ ]	
[ ] Window(s)	[ ]	[ ]	[ ]	[ ]	[ ]	[ ]	
[ ] Skylight(s)	[ ]	[ ]	[ ]	[ ]	[ ]	[ ]	
PLUMBING FIXTURES/FITTINGS:							
[ ] Single lavatory*							*14; 170-171
[ ] Pedestal	[ ]	[ ]	[ ]	[ ]	[ ]	[ ]	
[ ] Countertop	[ ]	[ ]	[ ]	[ ]	[ ]	[ ]	
[ ] Double lavatories*	[ ]	[ ]	[ ]	[ ]	[ ]	[ ]	
[ ] Pedestal	[ ]	[ ]	[ ]	[ ]	[ ]	[ ]	
[ ] Countertop	[ ]	[ ]	[ ]	[ ]	[ ]	[ ]	
(over cabinet)							
[ ] Lavatory faucet(s)							171-174
[ ] Single-lever	[ ]	[ ]	[ ]	[ ]	[ ]	[ ]	
[ ] Two-lever	[ ]	[ ]	[ ]	[ ]	[ ]	[ ]	
[ ] Tub+Shower							
[ ] One person	[ ]	[ ]	[ ]	[ ]	[ ]	[ ]	
[ ] Two persons	[ ]	[ ]	[ ]	[ ]	[ ]	[ ]	
[ ] Tub valve	[ ]	[ ]	[ ]	[ ]	[ ]	[ ]	
[ ] Tub filler	[ ]	[ ]	[ ]	[ ]	[ ]	[ ]	
[ ] Waste/overflow	[ ]	[ ]	[ ]	[ ]	[ ]	[ ]	
[ ] Diverter	[ ]	[ ]	[ ]	[ ]	[ ]	[ ]	
[ ] Shower Only							174-178
[ ] One person	[ ]	[ ]	[ ]	[ ]	[ ]	[ ]	
[ ] Two person	[ ]	[ ]	[ ]	[ ]	[ ]	[ ]	
[ ] With steam	[ ]	[ ]	[ ]	[ ]	[ ]	[ ]	
[ ] Shower Valve	[ ]	[ ]	[ ]	[ ]	[ ]	[ ]	
[ ] Fixed Showerhead	[ ]	[ ]	[ ]	[ ]	[ ]	[ ]	
[ ] Personal Shower	[ ]	[ ]	[ ]	[ ]	[ ]	[ ]	
[ ] Toilet (1.6 gal.)	[ ]	[ ]	[ ]	[ ]	[ ]	[ ]	169-170
[ ] One-piece "lowboy"	[ ]	[ ]	[ ]	[ ]	[ ]	[ ]	
[ ] Two-piece	[ ]	[ ]	[ ]	[ ]	[ ]	[ ]	

INITIALS/DATE:_____

	5	4	3	2	1	0	INFO. PG./NOTES

PLUMBING FITTINGS FINISH:

	5	4	3	2	1	0	INFO. PG./NOTES
[ ] Chrome	[ ]	[ ]	[ ]	[ ]	[ ]	[ ]	
[ ] Brass	[ ]	[ ]	[ ]	[ ]	[ ]	[ ]	
[ ] Other:_____	[ ]	[ ]	[ ]	[ ]	[ ]	[ ]	

VENTILATION:

	5	4	3	2	1	0	
[ ] Improved ventilation	[ ]	[ ]	[ ]	[ ]	[ ]	[ ]	
[ ] Quiet fan	[ ]	[ ]	[ ]	[ ]	[ ]	[ ]	
[ ] Heat lamp	[ ]	[ ]	[ ]	[ ]	[ ]	[ ]	

BATHROOM HEATING:

	5	4	3	2	1	0	
[ ] Furnace duct(s)	[ ]	[ ]	[ ]	[ ]	[ ]	[ ]	
[ ] Radiant area pads (under the floor)	[ ]	[ ]	[ ]	[ ]	[ ]	[ ]	
[ ] Radiator/towel warmer	[ ]	[ ]	[ ]	[ ]	[ ]	[ ]	

BATHROOM ELECTRICAL/LIGHTING:

	5	4	3	2	1	0	
[ ] Improved lighting	[ ]	[ ]	[ ]	[ ]	[ ]	[ ]	
[ ] General (Fluorescent required)	[ ]	[ ]	[ ]	[ ]	[ ]	[ ]	
[ ] Task	[ ]	[ ]	[ ]	[ ]	[ ]	[ ]	
[ ] "Mood"	[ ]	[ ]	[ ]	[ ]	[ ]	[ ]	
[ ] More outlets (GFI required)	[ ]	[ ]	[ ]	[ ]	[ ]	[ ]	
[ ] Inside cabinets (for rechargeables)	[ ]	[ ]	[ ]	[ ]	[ ]	[ ]	
[ ] In backsplash	[ ]	[ ]	[ ]	[ ]	[ ]	[ ]	
[ ] Dimmer switches	[ ]	[ ]	[ ]	[ ]	[ ]	[ ]	164
[ ] Telephone	[ ]	[ ]	[ ]	[ ]	[ ]	[ ]	

COUNTERTOPS: 182-185

	5	4	3	2	1	0	
[ ] Laminate	[ ]	[ ]	[ ]	[ ]	[ ]	[ ]	
[ ] Cultured Composite Stone	[ ]	[ ]	[ ]	[ ]	[ ]	[ ]	
[ ] Solid Surface ("Corian" or equiv.)	[ ]	[ ]	[ ]	[ ]	[ ]	[ ]	
[ ] Ceramic Tile	[ ]	[ ]	[ ]	[ ]	[ ]	[ ]	
[ ] Limestone	[ ]	[ ]	[ ]	[ ]	[ ]	[ ]	
[ ] Marble	[ ]	[ ]	[ ]	[ ]	[ ]	[ ]	
[ ] Granite	[ ]	[ ]	[ ]	[ ]	[ ]	[ ]	
[ ] Other:_____	[ ]	[ ]	[ ]	[ ]	[ ]	[ ]	

INITIALS/DATE:_____

	5	4	3	2	1	0	INFO. PG./NOTES

CABINETS:
	5	4	3	2	1	0	INFO. PG./NOTES
[ ] Face-frame	[ ]	[ ]	[ ]	[ ]	[ ]	[ ]	140-147
[ ] European 32-mm	[ ]	[ ]	[ ]	[ ]	[ ]	[ ]	140-147
[ ] Traditional	[ ]	[ ]	[ ]	[ ]	[ ]	[ ]	140-147
[ ] Contemporary	[ ]	[ ]	[ ]	[ ]	[ ]	[ ]	
[ ] Laminate	[ ]	[ ]	[ ]	[ ]	[ ]	[ ]	143
[ ] Wood	[ ]	[ ]	[ ]	[ ]	[ ]	[ ]	
[ ] Maple	[ ]	[ ]	[ ]	[ ]	[ ]	[ ]	
[ ] Cherry	[ ]	[ ]	[ ]	[ ]	[ ]	[ ]	
[ ] Oak	[ ]	[ ]	[ ]	[ ]	[ ]	[ ]	
[ ] Other: _____	[ ]	[ ]	[ ]	[ ]	[ ]	[ ]	

STORAGE:

[ ] Linens	[ ] Brushes/Combs	[ ] Blow Dryer	[ ] Curling Iron
[ ] Elec. Shaver	[ ] Elec. Floss	[ ] Elec. Toothbrush	[ ] Skin Care
[ ] Medication	[ ] Toiletries	[ ] Shoe care	[ ]_____
[ ]_____	[ ]_____	[ ]_____	[ ]_____

WALL SURFACES: 177-178
	5	4	3	2	1	0
[ ] Cultured Composite Stone	[ ]	[ ]	[ ]	[ ]	[ ]	[ ]
[ ] Solid Surface ("Corian" or equiv.)	[ ]	[ ]	[ ]	[ ]	[ ]	[ ]
[ ] Ceramic Tile	[ ]	[ ]	[ ]	[ ]	[ ]	[ ]
[ ] Limestone	[ ]	[ ]	[ ]	[ ]	[ ]	[ ]
[ ] Marble	[ ]	[ ]	[ ]	[ ]	[ ]	[ ]
[ ] Granite	[ ]	[ ]	[ ]	[ ]	[ ]	[ ]
[ ] Concrete	[ ]	[ ]	[ ]	[ ]	[ ]	[ ]
[ ] Other: _____	[ ]	[ ]	[ ]	[ ]	[ ]	[ ]

BATHROOM FLOORING: 175-177
	5	4	3	2	1	0
[ ] Vinyl	[ ]	[ ]	[ ]	[ ]	[ ]	[ ]
[ ] Tile	[ ]	[ ]	[ ]	[ ]	[ ]	[ ]
[ ] Ceramic*	[ ]	[ ]	[ ]	[ ]	[ ]	[ ]
[ ] Limestone*	[ ]	[ ]	[ ]	[ ]	[ ]	[ ]
[ ] Marble*	[ ]	[ ]	[ ]	[ ]	[ ]	[ ]
[ ] Granite*	[ ]	[ ]	[ ]	[ ]	[ ]	[ ]
[ ] Other:_____	[ ]	[ ]	[ ]	[ ]	[ ]	[ ]

(*NOTE: For safety reasons, tile should NOT be polished or shiny; matte or rough recommended)

INITIALS/DATE:_____

21

	5	4	3	2	1	0	INFO. PG./NOTES

ACCESSORIES & SAFETY:

	5	4	3	2	1	0
[ ] Towel bar(s)	[ ]	[ ]	[ ]	[ ]	[ ]	[ ]
[ ] Towel ring(s)	[ ]	[ ]	[ ]	[ ]	[ ]	[ ]
[ ] Robe hook(s)	[ ]	[ ]	[ ]	[ ]	[ ]	[ ]
[ ] Medicine cabinet(s)	[ ]	[ ]	[ ]	[ ]	[ ]	[ ]
[ ] Shampoo/soap	[ ]	[ ]	[ ]	[ ]	[ ]	[ ]
[ ] Niche(s)	[ ]	[ ]	[ ]	[ ]	[ ]	[ ]
[ ] Shelf/Shelves	[ ]	[ ]	[ ]	[ ]	[ ]	[ ]
[ ] Rinse glass(es)	[ ]	[ ]	[ ]	[ ]	[ ]	[ ]
[ ] Glass shelf/shelves	[ ]	[ ]	[ ]	[ ]	[ ]	[ ]
[ ] Other:_____	[ ]	[ ]	[ ]	[ ]	[ ]	[ ]
[ ] Other:	[ ]	[ ]	[ ]	[ ]	[ ]	[ ]
[ ] Tub seat	[ ]	[ ]	[ ]	[ ]	[ ]	[ ]
[ ] Shower seat	[ ]	[ ]	[ ]	[ ]	[ ]	[ ]
[ ] GRAB BAR(S)*	[ ]	[ ]	[ ]	[ ]	[ ]	[ ]

(*NOTE: HIGHLY RECOMMENDED FOR EVERY BATHROOM PROJECT)

COLOR PREFERENCE:

	5	4	3	2	1	0
[ ] Warm	[ ]	[ ]	[ ]	[ ]	[ ]	[ ]
[ ] Cool	[ ]	[ ]	[ ]	[ ]	[ ]	[ ]

Favorite Color(s): _____

Least Favorite Color(s): _____

STYLE PREFERENCE:

[ ] Traditional:
    [ ] Louis IV [ ] Empire [ ] French Country [ ] 18th Century
    [ ] American Federal [ ] Greek Revival [ ] Victorian

[ ] Modern:
    [ ] Art Noveau   [ ] Art Deco   [ ] European   [ ] Contemporary:

    [ ] Post-Modern   [ ] European   [ ] Japanese

[ ] Other:_____

OTHER:

	5	4	3	2	1	0
[ ]_____	[ ]	[ ]	[ ]	[ ]	[ ]	[ ]
[ ]_____	[ ]	[ ]	[ ]	[ ]	[ ]	[ ]
[ ]_____	[ ]	[ ]	[ ]	[ ]	[ ]	[ ]

INITIALS/DATE:_____

KITCHEN SURVEY and "WISH LIST"

PERSON: _____ DATE: _____

ROOM(S) TO BE REMODELED:
[ ] Kitchen   [ ] Laundry room   [ ] Family room   [ ] Garage

[ ] Other: _____

ADDITION(S) TO:
[ ] Kitchen   [ ] Laundry room   [ ] Family room   [ ] Garage

[ ] Other: _____

ARCHITECTURAL FEATURES:	5	4	3	2	1	0	INFO.PG./NOTES
[ ] Patio door	[]	[]	[]	[]	[]	[]	132-133
[ ] Window(s)	[]	[]	[]	[]	[]	[]	134-135
[ ] Skylight(s)	[]	[]	[]	[]	[]	[]	

FUNCTION/USE:
[ ] One person for cooking and cleaning
[ ] One person for cooking, different person for cleaning
[ ] Shared cooking, two or more persons
[ ] Shared cleanup, two or more persons
[ ] Regular entertaining, family (10 people max.)
[ ] Regular entertaining, 10+ people
[ ] Entertaining less than 4 times yearly, 10 people
[ ] Entertaining less than 4 times yearly, 10+ people

[ ] Other: _____

[ ] Other: _____

"If you want to get rid of stinking odors in the kitchen, stop cooking." (Erma Bombeck)

INITIALS/DATE: _____

23

ERGONOMICS:

Main user:_____

    [ ] Right-handed   [ ] Left-handed   Height:_____

    Duties:_____

Other user:_____

    [ ] Right-handed   [ ] Left-handed   Height:_____

    Duties:_____

Other user:_____

    [ ] Right-handed   [ ] Left-handed   Height:_____

    Duties:_____

APPLIANCES:

	5	4	3	2	1	0	INFO.PG./NOTES
[ ] Water Purification*	[ ]	[ ]	[ ]	[ ]	[ ]	[ ]	159
Finish Preferred:							
[ ] Stainless	[ ]	[ ]	[ ]	[ ]	[ ]	[ ]	
[ ] Black	[ ]	[ ]	[ ]	[ ]	[ ]	[ ]	
[ ] White	[ ]	[ ]	[ ]	[ ]	[ ]	[ ]	
[ ] Other:	[ ]	[ ]	[ ]	[ ]	[ ]	[ ]	
[ ] Single oven(s)	[ ]	[ ]	[ ]	[ ]	[ ]	[ ]	152-153
[ ] Gas	[ ]	[ ]	[ ]	[ ]	[ ]	[ ]	
(continuous cleaning)							
[ ] Electric	[ ]	[ ]	[ ]	[ ]	[ ]	[ ]	
(self-cleaning)							
[ ] Convection	[ ]	[ ]	[ ]	[ ]	[ ]	[ ]	
[ ] Steam	[ ]	[ ]	[ ]	[ ]	[ ]	[ ]	
[ ] Double ovens	[ ]	[ ]	[ ]	[ ]	[ ]	[ ]	152-153
[ ] Gas	[ ]	[ ]	[ ]	[ ]	[ ]	[ ]	
(continuous cleaning)							
[ ] Electric	[ ]	[ ]	[ ]	[ ]	[ ]	[ ]	
(self-cleaning)							
[ ] Convection	[ ]	[ ]	[ ]	[ ]	[ ]	[ ]	
[ ] Micro-thermal	[ ]	[ ]	[ ]	[ ]	[ ]	[ ]	
[ ] Steam	[ ]	[ ]	[ ]	[ ]	[ ]	[ ]	
[ ] Dishwasher	[ ]	[ ]	[ ]	[ ]	[ ]	[ ]	154
(Quantity:_____)							

(*NOTE: Separate appliance, or whole-house system? If separate appliance under kitchen sink, water line should also go to your icemaker)

INITIALS/DATE:_____

KITCHEN APPLIANCES (Cont'd):

	5	4	3	2	1	0	INFO.PG.
[ ] Refrigerator and Freezer (Separate units)	[ ]	[ ]	[ ]	[ ]	[ ]	[ ]	
[ ] Refrigerator/Freezer	[ ]	[ ]	[ ]	[ ]	[ ]	[ ]	154-156
[ ] Built-in	[ ]	[ ]	[ ]	[ ]	[ ]	[ ]	
[ ] Standard	[ ]	[ ]	[ ]	[ ]	[ ]	[ ]	
[ ] With ice maker	[ ]	[ ]	[ ]	[ ]	[ ]	[ ]	
[ ] Side-by-side	[ ]	[ ]	[ ]	[ ]	[ ]	[ ]	
[ ] Top freezer	[ ]	[ ]	[ ]	[ ]	[ ]	[ ]	
[ ] Bottom freezer	[ ]	[ ]	[ ]	[ ]	[ ]	[ ]	
[ ] Wine refrigerator (#Bottles:)	[ ]	[ ]	[ ]	[ ]	[ ]	[ ]	161
[ ] Ice maker	[ ]	[ ]	[ ]	[ ]	[ ]	[ ]	

	5	4	3	2	1	0	INFO.PG.
[ ] Separate microwave	[ ]	[ ]	[ ]	[ ]	[ ]	[ ]	156-158
[ ] Cooktop - "Standard"							149-150
[ ] Gas - 30" (4 burners)	[ ]	[ ]	[ ]	[ ]	[ ]	[ ]	
[ ] Gas - 36" (5+ burners)	[ ]	[ ]	[ ]	[ ]	[ ]	[ ]	
[ ] Electric 30" (4 burners)	[ ]	[ ]	[ ]	[ ]	[ ]	[ ]	
[ ] Electric 36" (5+ burners)	[ ]	[ ]	[ ]	[ ]	[ ]	[ ]	

INITIALS/DATE:_____

KITCHEN APPLIANCES (Cont'd):

	5	4	3	2	1	0	INFO.PG./NOTES
[ ] Cooktop - "Professional"							149-150
[ ] All gas burners	[ ]	[ ]	[ ]	[ ]	[ ]	[ ]	
[ ] Burners +	[ ]	[ ]	[ ]	[ ]	[ ]	[ ]	
[ ] B-B-Q	[ ]	[ ]	[ ]	[ ]	[ ]	[ ]	
[ ] Griddle	[ ]	[ ]	[ ]	[ ]	[ ]	[ ]	
[ ] Wok	[ ]	[ ]	[ ]	[ ]	[ ]	[ ]	
[ ] Range - "Standard"							153
[ ] All Gas	[ ]	[ ]	[ ]	[ ]	[ ]	[ ]	
[ ] All Electric	[ ]	[ ]	[ ]	[ ]	[ ]	[ ]	
[ ] Combination	[ ]	[ ]	[ ]	[ ]	[ ]	[ ]	
[ ] Convection	[ ]	[ ]	[ ]	[ ]	[ ]	[ ]	
[ ] Range - "Professional"							
[ ] All Gas	[ ]	[ ]	[ ]	[ ]	[ ]	[ ]	
[ ] Combination	[ ]	[ ]	[ ]	[ ]	[ ]	[ ]	
[ ] Convection	[ ]	[ ]	[ ]	[ ]	[ ]	[ ]	
[ ] Exhaust fan							150-151
[ ] Hood	[ ]	[ ]	[ ]	[ ]	[ ]	[ ]	
[ ] Downdraft	[ ]	[ ]	[ ]	[ ]	[ ]	[ ]	
[ ] Barbecue/grill							159
[ ] Gas	[ ]	[ ]	[ ]	[ ]	[ ]	[ ]	
[ ] Electric	[ ]	[ ]	[ ]	[ ]	[ ]	[ ]	
[ ] Garbage disposal	[ ]	[ ]	[ ]	[ ]	[ ]	[ ]	158
[ ] Trash compactor	[ ]	[ ]	[ ]	[ ]	[ ]	[ ]	158
[ ] Hot water dispenser	[ ]	[ ]	[ ]	[ ]	[ ]	[ ]	
[ ] Cold water dispenser	[ ]	[ ]	[ ]	[ ]	[ ]	[ ]	
[ ] Water filter	[ ]	[ ]	[ ]	[ ]	[ ]	[ ]	159
[ ] Other:_____	[ ]	[ ]	[ ]	[ ]	[ ]	[ ]	
[ ] Other:_____	[ ]	[ ]	[ ]	[ ]	[ ]	[ ]	

KITCHEN PLUMBING:

	5	4	3	2	1	0	INFO.PG./NOTES
							167-168
[ ] Main Sink							
[ ] Large single bowl	[ ]	[ ]	[ ]	[ ]	[ ]	[ ]	
[ ] Two bowls (large+small)	[ ]	[ ]	[ ]	[ ]	[ ]	[ ]	
[ ] Two bowls - equal	[ ]	[ ]	[ ]	[ ]	[ ]	[ ]	
[ ] Stainless steel	[ ]	[ ]	[ ]	[ ]	[ ]	[ ]	
[ ] Cast iron	[ ]	[ ]	[ ]	[ ]	[ ]	[ ]	
[ ] Quartz	[ ]	[ ]	[ ]	[ ]	[ ]	[ ]	
[ ] Solid-surface	[ ]	[ ]	[ ]	[ ]	[ ]	[ ]	
[ ] Other:_____	[ ]	[ ]	[ ]	[ ]	[ ]	[ ]	

"If you can organize your kitchen, you can organize your life."
(Louis Parrish)

INITIALS/DATE:_____

KITCHEN PLUMBING (CONT'D):
INFO.PG./NOTES: 167-168

	5	4	3	2	1	0	INFO.PG./NOTES
[ ] Main Faucet							
[ ] Single lever	[ ]	[ ]	[ ]	[ ]	[ ]	[ ]	
[ ] With spray	[ ]	[ ]	[ ]	[ ]	[ ]	[ ]	
[ ] Integral	[ ]	[ ]	[ ]	[ ]	[ ]	[ ]	
[ ] Separate	[ ]	[ ]	[ ]	[ ]	[ ]	[ ]	
[ ] Dual controls	[ ]	[ ]	[ ]	[ ]	[ ]	[ ]	
[ ] With spray	[ ]	[ ]	[ ]	[ ]	[ ]	[ ]	
[ ] Auxiliary Sink*							167
[ ] Stainless steel	[ ]	[ ]	[ ]	[ ]	[ ]	[ ]	
[ ] Cast iron	[ ]	[ ]	[ ]	[ ]	[ ]	[ ]	
[ ] Quartz	[ ]	[ ]	[ ]	[ ]	[ ]	[ ]	
[ ] Solid-surface	[ ]	[ ]	[ ]	[ ]	[ ]	[ ]	
[ ] Other:_____	[ ]	[ ]	[ ]	[ ]	[ ]	[ ]	

*NOTE: Should be larger than a bar sink, with drain to accommodate a garbage disposal

	5	4	3	2	1	0	INFO.PG./NOTES
[ ] Auxiliary Faucet							
[ ] Single lever	[ ]	[ ]	[ ]	[ ]	[ ]	[ ]	
[ ] With spray	[ ]	[ ]	[ ]	[ ]	[ ]	[ ]	
[ ] Dual controls	[ ]	[ ]	[ ]	[ ]	[ ]	[ ]	

COUNTERTOPS/BACKSPLASH:
INFO.PG./NOTES: 182-186

	5	4	3	2	1	0	INFO.PG./NOTES
[ ] Granite	[ ]	[ ]	[ ]	[ ]	[ ]	[ ]	183
[ ] Laminate	[ ]	[ ]	[ ]	[ ]	[ ]	[ ]	183
[ ] Marble	[ ]	[ ]	[ ]	[ ]	[ ]	[ ]	184
[ ] Solid Surface ("Corian" or equiv.)	[ ]	[ ]	[ ]	[ ]	[ ]	[ ]	185
[ ] Stainless	[ ]	[ ]	[ ]	[ ]	[ ]	[ ]	185
[ ] Ceramic Tile	[ ]	[ ]	[ ]	[ ]	[ ]	[ ]	185
[ ] Wood	[ ]	[ ]	[ ]	[ ]	[ ]	[ ]	182
[ ] Concrete	[ ]	[ ]	[ ]	[ ]	[ ]	[ ]	182
[ ] Other:_____	[ ]	[ ]	[ ]	[ ]	[ ]	[ ]	

CABINETS:
INFO.PG./NOTES: 140-147

	5	4	3	2	1	0	INFO.PG./NOTES
[ ] Face-frame	[ ]	[ ]	[ ]	[ ]	[ ]	[ ]	140
[ ] European 32-mm	[ ]	[ ]	[ ]	[ ]	[ ]	[ ]	
[ ] Traditional	[ ]	[ ]	[ ]	[ ]	[ ]	[ ]	141-142
[ ] Contemporary	[ ]	[ ]	[ ]	[ ]	[ ]	[ ]	
[ ] Laminate	[ ]	[ ]	[ ]	[ ]	[ ]	[ ]	143
[ ] Wood	[ ]	[ ]	[ ]	[ ]	[ ]	[ ]	
[ ] Maple	[ ]	[ ]	[ ]	[ ]	[ ]	[ ]	
[ ] Cherry	[ ]	[ ]	[ ]	[ ]	[ ]	[ ]	
[ ] Oak	[ ]	[ ]	[ ]	[ ]	[ ]	[ ]	
[ ] Other:_____	[ ]	[ ]	[ ]	[ ]	[ ]	[ ]	

INITIALS/DATE:_____

CABINETS (Continued):

[ ] Better storage   45; 145-147

	5	4	3	2	1	0
[ ] Pantry	[ ]	[ ]	[ ]	[ ]	[ ]	[ ]
[ ] Corner lazy susan(s)	[ ]	[ ]	[ ]	[ ]	[ ]	[ ]
[ ] Pull-out shelves (aka rollouts)	[ ]	[ ]	[ ]	[ ]	[ ]	[ ]
[ ] Recycling bins	[ ]	[ ]	[ ]	[ ]	[ ]	[ ]
[ ] Tray dividers	[ ]	[ ]	[ ]	[ ]	[ ]	[ ]
[ ] More drawers	[ ]	[ ]	[ ]	[ ]	[ ]	[ ]
[ ] Appliance garage(s)	[ ]	[ ]	[ ]	[ ]	[ ]	[ ]
[ ] Chopping board	[ ]	[ ]	[ ]	[ ]	[ ]	[ ]
[ ] Menu-message ctr.	[ ]	[ ]	[ ]	[ ]	[ ]	[ ]
[ ] Baking prep. center	[ ]	[ ]	[ ]	[ ]	[ ]	[ ]
[ ] Other:_____	[ ]	[ ]	[ ]	[ ]	[ ]	[ ]
[ ] Other:_____	[ ]	[ ]	[ ]	[ ]	[ ]	[ ]
[ ] Other:_____	[ ]	[ ]	[ ]	[ ]	[ ]	[ ]
[ ] Other:_____	[ ]	[ ]	[ ]	[ ]	[ ]	[ ]
[ ] Other:_____	[ ]	[ ]	[ ]	[ ]	[ ]	[ ]
[ ] Other:_____	[ ]	[ ]	[ ]	[ ]	[ ]	[ ]

FLOORING: 187-190

	5	4	3	2	1	0
[ ] Stone	[ ]	[ ]	[ ]	[ ]	[ ]	[ ]
[ ] Ceramic Tile	[ ]	[ ]	[ ]	[ ]	[ ]	[ ]
[ ] Vinyl	[ ]	[ ]	[ ]	[ ]	[ ]	[ ]
[ ] Wood	[ ]	[ ]	[ ]	[ ]	[ ]	[ ]
Species:_____						
[ ] Cork	[ ]	[ ]	[ ]	[ ]	[ ]	[ ]
[ ] Other:_____	[ ]	[ ]	[ ]	[ ]	[ ]	[ ]

LIGHTING/ELECTRICAL: 162-165

	5	4	3	2	1	0	
[ ] Improved lighting	[ ]	[ ]	[ ]	[ ]	[ ]	[ ]	
[ ] General (Fluorescent required)	[ ]	[ ]	[ ]	[ ]	[ ]	[ ]	
[ ] Task	[ ]	[ ]	[ ]	[ ]	[ ]	[ ]	
[ ] "Mood"	[ ]	[ ]	[ ]	[ ]	[ ]	[ ]	
[ ] Multiple outlets	[ ]	[ ]	[ ]	[ ]	[ ]	[ ]	(GFI required)
[ ] Dimmer switches	[ ]	[ ]	[ ]	[ ]	[ ]	[ ]	
[ ] Telephone	[ ]	[ ]	[ ]	[ ]	[ ]	[ ]	
[ ] Cable TV	[ ]	[ ]	[ ]	[ ]	[ ]	[ ]	
[ ] Computer	[ ]	[ ]	[ ]	[ ]	[ ]	[ ]	
[ ] Other:_____	[ ]	[ ]	[ ]	[ ]	[ ]	[ ]	

INITIALS/DATE:_____

```
                              5  4  3  2  1  0  INFO. PG./NOTES
COLOR SCHEME:
    [ ] Updated              [ ] [ ] [ ] [ ] [ ] [ ]
        [ ] Lighter          [ ] [ ] [ ] [ ] [ ] [ ]
        [ ] More dramatic    [ ] [ ] [ ] [ ] [ ] [ ]
        [ ] Special finish   [ ] [ ] [ ] [ ] [ ] [ ]

    Favorite color(s):        _____

    Least favorite color(s):  _____

STYLE PREFERENCE:
    [ ] Traditional:
        [ ] Louis IV [ ] Empire  [ ] French Country  [ ] 18th Century
        [ ] American Federal     [ ] Greek Revival    [ ] Victorian
    [ ] Modern:
        [ ] Art Noveau          [ ] Art Deco          [ ] European
    [ ] Contemporary:
        [ ] Post-Modern         [ ] European          [ ] Japanese

    [ ] Other: _____

                      5   4   3   2   1   0
OTHER:

    [ ]_____  [] [] [] [] [] []

    [ ]_____  [] [] [] [] [] []

    [ ]_____  [] [] [] [] [] []
```

"Once the 'what' is decided, the 'how' always follows. We must not make the 'how' an excuse for not facing and accepting the 'what.'" (Pearl S. Buck)

INITIALS/DATE:_____

CHAPTER 5

THE "GOOD-BETTER-BEST" CONCEPT

"Everything can be improved." (C.W. Barrow)

The philosophy of good-better-best was first used at the turn of the century by Sears-Roebuck & Company. It's a concept that's easily understood. For our purposes:

GOOD: Reliable quality, brand-name manufacturers. Not the cheapest product on the market. "Good" products may have the same life expectancy as the "best" products. The difference is how the individual product functions, its appearance, features, and serviceability.

> EXAMPLE: Chevrolet, Ford or Honda. Fabric seats, air conditioning, 6-cylinder, automatic transmission, power steering, cassette player with 3 speakers.

BETTER: More expensive brand names, with more features than products in the "good" category.

> EXAMPLE: Buick, Chrysler or Acura. Vinyl+leather power seats, air conditioning with climate control, 6-cylinder, automatic transmission, power steering, keyless entry, power windows, cassette player and single cd player with 6 speakers.

BEST: Most expensive, with the most features and stylish appearance. May have similar life expectancy to products in the "good" and "better" categories.

> EXAMPLE: Cadillac, Lincoln, Mercedes or Lexus. Luxury all-leather seats with 8-way power adjustment. 8-cylinder, automatic transmission, power steering, traction control, ABS brakes, keyless entry, power windows, cassette player and cd changer with 6 speakers and subwoofer; custom pearl finish.

"Life is filled with tradeoffs."

Every decision you make -- whether it's about your remodeling project, or purchasing a car, involves tradeoffs of one kind or another. You must weigh the advantages and disadvantages so you can make the right choice. Your remodeling project can be a blending of all three categories. "Good" projects can include a carefully-selected mix of "better" and "best" products.

The following spreadsheets are for a hypothetical remodeling project. Plans and specifications for this project are shown on Pages 110-117. The project includes:

- A large addition for a new master bedroom/bathroom suite;
- A new family room with a fireplace and eating area;
- Total remodel of the existing kitchen, bathrooms, living room, dining room, and hallways;
- New laundry room;
- Eliminate/move interior walls to create a more open feel, and better traffic flow;
- Framing for nine-foot ceilings and a new roof;
- New doors and windows.

The totals shown are estimates, based on suggested retail figures gathered from reliable current estimating resources. The figures may vary 15% more or less, depending on many factors. There is no guarantee that any individual remodeling project will be exactly the same as represented on the estimate forms that follow. Products listed as examples are not an endorsement of a particular manufacturer or model; products not mentioned are not eliminated for any reason other than limited space.

"I'm not makin' this up, folks ..." (Emeril Lagasse)

"GOOD" WHOLE-HOUSE REMODELING PROJECT

Existing Home = 2,200 sq.ft.
Addition = 1,150 sq.ft.

ARCHITECTURAL FEATURES:	ALT. 1	ALT. 2	AVG.
Interior Doors/Trim + Hardware:	7,500		7,500
Exterior Doors/Trim + Hardware:	4,632		4,632
Garage Door/Trim:	2,550		2,550
Windows/Trim:	11,574		11,574
Skylights:	2,450		2,450
Wood Flooring (Entry, Kitchen only):	5,100		5,100
Bathroom Flooring (SEE Bathrooms)			
Carpeting:	4,230		4,230
(Family Room, Hallway, Bedrooms, Living Room, Dining Room)			
Fireplaces:	3,099		3,099
Doorway Arches (Living Room, Dining Room, Kitchen):	3,000		3,000
Light Fixtures:	5,183		5,183
Switches/Outlets:	1,880		1,880
KITCHEN:			
Appliances (Amana, G.E., Maytag):	5,017		5,017
Cabinets (Modular):	13,306		13,306
Countertops (Laminate, Tile):	2,850	4,750	3,800
Backsplash (Tile):	1,250		1,250
Plumbing (Delta, Kohler, Moen (single sink, faucet):	450		450
MASTER BATHROOM:			
Plumbing (toilet, lavatory, faucet, tub, tub/shower set):	1,137	1,750	1.444
(American Standard, Delta, Kohler, Moen,)			
Cabinets (Modular):	1,428		1,428
Countertop:	1,350		1,350
Backsplash:	450		450
Tub/Shower Walls:	1,225		1,225
Flooring:	1,025		1,025
Shower Enclosure (American Standard, Kohler):	849		849
Lighting/Electrical, Ventilation:	575		575
Accessories (Delta, Moen ; TP holder, towel bar, towel ring, grab bar):	350		350
BATHROOM #2:			
Plumbing (toilet, lavatory, faucet, tub, tub/shower set):	1,137	1,750	1,444
(American Standard, Delta, Kohler, Moen)			
Cabinets (Modular):	996		996
Countertop:	775		775
Backsplash:	350		350
Tub/Shower Walls:	864		864
Flooring:	850		850
Shower Enclosure (American Standard, Kohler):	565		565
Lighting/Electrical, Ventilation:	450		450
Accessories (Delta, Moen; TP holder, towel bar, towel ring, grab bar):	350		350

"GOOD" HOUSE REMODELING (Continued)

BATHROOM #3:	ALT. 1	ALT. 2	AVG.
Plumbing (toilet, lavatory, faucet, shower, shower set):	995		995
(Delta, Kohler, Moen, Porcher)			
Cabinets:	648		648
Countertop:	750		750
Backsplash:	350		350
Shower Walls:	756		756
Flooring:	450		450
Shower Enclosure:	565		565
Lighting/Electrical, Ventilation:	400		400
Accessories (Delta, Moen -- tp holder, towel bar, towel ring):	200		200
LAUNDRY ROOM:			
Plumbing (Delta, Kohler, Moen -- single sink, faucet):	398		398
Cabinets:	875		875
Countertop:	575		575
Backsplash:	200		200
Flooring:	560		560
Lighting/Electrical, Ventilation:	200		200
LABOR (Includes overhead and profit):			
Demolition/Grading:			15,000
Foundation:			30,000
Framing:			60,000
Electrical:			15,000
Plumbing:			15,000
HVAC:			8,000
Drywall/Painting:			20,000
Tile:			15,000
Exterior finish/concrete:			22,500
Roof/Gutters/Downspouts:			10,000
Designer:			26,227
Engineers:			19,975
TOTAL INVESTMENT			355,308
INVESTMENT PER SQUARE FOOT (GARAGE) = $100.00*			
INVESTMENT PER SQUARE FOOT (HOUSE) = $107.00			

*Same figure used for all projects

"It's time for reality thinking!"
(Dr. Robert Schuller)

"BETTER" WHOLE-HOUSE REMODELING PROJECT

Existing Home = 2,200 sq.ft.
Addition = 1,150 sq.ft.

	ALT. 1	ALT. 2	AVG.
ARCHITECTURAL FEATURES:			
Interior Doors/Hardware/Trim:	10,000		10,000
Exterior doors/trim:	6,175		6,175
Garage door/trim:	3,000		3,000
Windows/trim:	15,432		15,432
Skylights:	2,450		2,450
Wood Flooring (Entry, Kitchen Only):	6,200		6,200
(Bathroom Flooring -- see Bathrooms)			
Carpeting:	5,640		5,640
(Family room, Hallway, Bedrooms, Living room, Dining room)			
Fireplace:	3,785		3,785
Doorway Arches (Living room, Dining room, Kitchen):	3,000		3,000
Light Fixtures:	10,410		10,410
Switches/Outlets:	3,047		3,047
KITCHEN:			
Appliances (Amana, G.E., Maytag):	14,353		14,353
Cabinets (Custom Modular):	23,760		23,760
Countertops (Solid surface):	8,550		8,550
Backsplash (Tile):	3,500		3,500
Plumbing (American Standard, Elkay, Grohe, Insinkerator, Kohler):	1,364	2,743	2,054
Lighting (Decorative drop lights):	300		300
MASTER BATHROOM:			
Plumbing (toilet, lavatory, faucet, tub, tub/shower set):	3,853	6,150	5,002
(American Standard, Andre, Grohe, Hansgrohe, Kohler,			
St. Thomas, Toto)			
Cabinets (Custom modular):	2,304		2,304
Countertop:	2,000		2,000
Backsplash:	650		650
Tub/Shower Walls:	1,995		1,995
Flooring:	1,216		1,216
Shower Enclosure (Custom):	1,760	2,650	2,200
Lighting/Electrical, Ventilation:	675		675
Accessories (American Standard, Ginger, Grohe, Kohler, Robern):	1,287	2,218	1,753
(TP holder, towel bar, towel ring, grab bar)			

"BETTER" HOME REMODELING (Continued)

BATHROOM #2:	ALT. 1	ALT. 2	AVG.
Plumbing (toilet, lavatory, faucet, tub, tub/shower set):	3,212	4,966	4,089
(American Standard, Andre, Grohe, Hansgrohe, Kohler,			
St. Thomas, Toto)			
Cabinets (Custom modular):	1,728		1,728
Countertop:	1,350		1,350
Backsplash:	400		400
Tub/Shower Walls:	1,365		1,365
Flooring:	1,035		1,035
Shower Enclosure (American Standard, Kohler):	925	1,100	1,013
Lighting/Electrical, Ventilation:	500		500
Accessories (American Standard, Ginger, Grohe, Kohler, PL):	780	875	828
BATHROOM #3:			
Plumbing (toilet, lavatory, faucet, shower set):	2,712	4,466	3,589
(American Standard, Andre, Grohe, Hansgrohe, Kohler,			
St. Thomas, Toto)			
Cabinets (Custom modular):	848		848
Countertop:	1,050		1,050
Backsplash:	400		400
Tub/Shower Walls:	1,175		1,175
Flooring:	675		675
Shower Enclosure (Custom):	925		925
Lighting/Electrical, Ventilation:	500		500
Accessories (American Standard, Ginger, Grohe, Kohler, PL):	780		780
(TP holder, towel bar, towel ring, grab bar)			
LAUNDRY ROOM:			
Plumbing (American Standard, Kohler, Grohe):	637	1,025	831
Cabinets (Custom modular):	2,250		2,250
Countertop:	750		750
Backsplash:	300		300
Flooring:	775		775
Lighting/Electrical, Ventilation:	300		300
LABOR:			
Demolition/Grading:			15,000
Foundation:			30,000
Framing:			60,000
Electrical:			17,500
Plumbing:			18,750
HVAC:			9,000
Drywall/Painting:			25,000
Tile:			16,885
Exterior finish, Concrete:			30,000
Roof/Gutters/Downspouts:			16,500
Designer:			34,042
Engineers:			19,975
TOTAL INVESTMENT			459,559
INVESTMENT PER SQUARE FOOT (HOUSE) = $143.00			

"BEST" WHOLE-HOUSE REMODELING PROJECT

Existing Home = 2,200 sq.ft.
Addition = 1,150 sq.ft.

ARCHITECTURAL FEATURES:	ALT. 1	ALT. 2	AVG.
Interior doors/trim + hardware:	13,500		13,500
Exterior doors/trim + hardware:	8,337		8,337
Garage door/trim:	4,500		4,500
Windows/trim:	22,198		22,198
Skylights:	4,100		4,100
Wood Flooring:	21,273		21,273
(Entry, Kitchen, Family room, Dining room, Hallway)			
(Bathroom Flooring -- see Bathrooms)			
Carpeting (Bedrooms, Living room):	12,500		12,500
Fireplace:	8,000		8,000
Doorway Arches (Living room, Dining room, Kitchen):	3,000		3,000
Light Fixtures:	32,573		32,573
Switches/Outlets:	27,200		27,200
KITCHEN:			
Appliances (Abbaca, Dacor, Miele, Sub-Zero, Thermador, Viking, Wolf):	30,601		30,601
Cabinets (Custom):	49,600		49,600
Countertops (Stone, concrete):	16,330		16,330
Backsplash (Stone):	7,100		7,100
Plumbing (Dornbracht, Franke, Grohe, Jado, Kallista):	5,394	7,918	6,656
Lighting:	2,795		2,795
MASTER BATHROOM:			
Plumbing (toilet, lavatory, faucet, tub, tub/shower set):	9,788	36,242	23,015
(Aquatic Industries, Bates & Bates, Dornbracht, Jacuzzi, Jado, Kallista,)			
Cabinets (Custom):	10,675		10,675
Countertop (Stone):	17,500		17,500
Backsplash:	3,200		3,200
Tub and Shower Walls:	16,625		16,625
Flooring:	5,935		5,935
Shower Enclosure (Custom, Kallista):	4,400	9,780	7,090
Lighting/Electrical, Ventilation:	3,650		3,650
Accessories (Bacci, Bates & Bates, Dornbracht, Jado, Kallista, Robern):	5,365	8,590	6,978

"BEST" HOME REMODELING PROJECT (Continued)

BATHROOM #2:	ALT. 1	ALT. 2	AVG.
Plumbing (toilet, lavatory, faucet, tub, tub/shower set):	9,788	16,242	13,015
(Aquatic Industries, Bates & Bates, Dornbracht, Jacuzzi, Jado, Kallista, Toto)			
Cabinets (Custom):	6,500		6,500
Countertop:	5,025		5,025
Backsplash:	1,200		1,200
Tub/Shower Walls:	7,560		7,560
Flooring:	4,300		4,300
Shower Enclosure: Custom	4,073		4,073
Lighting/Electrical, Ventilation:	2,750		2,750
Accessories (Bates & Bates, Dornbracht, Jado, Kallista, Robern):	5,365		5,365
(TP holder, towel bar, towel ring, grab bar)			
BATHROOM #3:			
Plumbing (toilet, lavatory, faucet, shower set):	5,174	10,677	7,296
(Bates & Bates, Dornbracht, Jacuzzi, Jado, Kallista, Toto)			
Cabinets (Custom):	5,200		5,200
Countertop:	5,025		5,025
Backsplash:	1,200		1,200
Tub/Shower Walls:	5,335		5,335
Flooring:	3,150		3,150
Shower Enclosure (Custom):	4,073		4,073
Lighting/Electrical, Ventilation:	2,750		2,750
Accessories (Bates & Bates, Dornbracht, Jado, Kallista, Robern):	3,500		3,500
(TP holder, towel bar, towel ring, grab bar)			
LAUNDRY ROOM:			
Plumbing (Dornbracht, Franke, Jado):	983	1,820	1,402
Cabinets (Custom):	3,250		3,250
Countertop:	2,300		2,300
Backsplash:	800		800
Flooring:	1,500		1,500
Lighting/Electrical, Ventilation:	900		900
LABOR (Includes overhead and profit):			
Demolition/Grading:			15,000
Foundation:			30,000
Framing:			60,000
Electrical:			28,000
Plumbing:			27,000
HVAC:			21,000
Drywall/Painting:			45,000
Tile:			28,675
Exterior Finish, Concrete, Tile, Stone:			65,000
Roof/Gutters/Downspouts:			25,000
Designer:			66,199
Engineers:			19,975
TOTAL INVESTMENT			893,689

INVESTMENT PER SQUARE FOOT (HOUSE) = $293.00

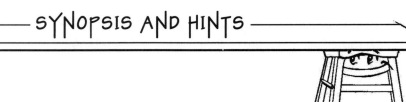

"A little help at the right time is better than a lot of help at the wrong time." (Tevye)

Based on the examples, you can see that two factors affect your investment:

The scope of your project
The products you select

As stated earlier, the same project was used for the "good," "better," and "best" examples. Higher labor figures reflected the homeowners' choice of more unusual products. Let's review a couple of specific areas.

ELECTRICAL/LIGHTING:

	LABOR	PRODUCTS	TOTAL
Good:	$ 15,000	$ 8,488	$ 23,488
Better:	17,500	15,132	32,632
Best:	28,000	86,850	114,850

The difference between the three levels is the number of light fixtures and the complexity of installation required. The "best" budget allowed for low-voltage landscape lighting, as well as a state-of-the-art "smart home" control system.

COUNTERTOPS, BACKSPLASH, TILE:

	LABOR	PRODUCTS	TOTAL
Good:	$ 15,000	$ 15,580	$30,580
Better:	27,186	16,885	44,071
Best:	104,096	28,675	132,771

The budget allowed the homeowners to have an interesting mix of materials, and decorative features, whether the overall project was "good," "better," or "best." A lower budget doesn't mean boring results; it requires more careful selection of the materials, and careful attention to important details as they relate to the overall effect.

Homeowners with a limited budget decided to increase their allowance for countertops and backsplash to get tile+tile instead of laminate+tile. The designer included a coordinating decorative liner for visual accent in the backsplash, with 1/2" contrasting tile strips on top and bottom of the liners to enhance the look. The estimates for EACH of the strips varied from $1.19 to $7.95 -- a difference of $900 for that portion of the products.

Hopefully, the spreadsheet examples will help you as you select the products for your project, and as you work with your designer on the layout and details. No matter what your budget is, it's very important to:

- Weigh all of your decisions as they relate to each other and your budget;

- Keep track of your investment in a spreadsheet, from Day 1 through the end of your project;

- Avoid the "might as well" trap;

- Remember, it's YOUR home and YOUR money.

Young homeowners complained about going over budget, and blamed their architect for the situation. The architect reminded them that he'd strongly recommended spending some up-front money to get the geotechnical report done, which they decided not to do until they were ready to build. Subsequently, the engineer required expensive piers instead of a standard foundation. And, the homeowners didn't follow the architect's warnings about expensive materials (i.e., granite countertops, marble tiles, upgraded appliances and plumbing fixtures, wood flooring, etc.). It was their home and their money, but going over budget had to be somebody else's fault.

"Materialism is buying things we don't need, with money we don't have, to impress people who don't matter."

CHAPTER 6

PRODUCT SELECTION & ESTIMATES

THE "MIGHT AS WELL" FACTOR

"We didn't actually overspend our budget. The allocation simply fell short of our expenditure." (Keith Davis)

It's human nature to want more than we can really afford. The American culture and economy is driven by advertising and trends. It's very easy to justify an investment in luxury items, "We're only going to do this once, so we **might as well** get . . ."

It's okay to splurge on one or two top-priority items, if there's a willingness to make tradeoffs. But if the "might-as-well" argument is applied to everything we <u>think</u> we want, and don't keep track of the investments logically, our target budget is meaningless. How many times have you heard, "Remodeling (building) always takes twice as long and costs twice as much." You CAN be in charge of your investment!

One of your designer's responsibilities is to be the voice of reason -- not to tell you what you can or can't afford, but to offer questions like, "How much value is this (......) really going to add to your home?"

Homeowners had decided not to hire a designer. They were on the fast track for many mistakes (+$$$$$). Friends and family members could give advice, but it wasn't the same as reasonable advice from a professional. One of the many expensive mistakes they made was falling in love with a heated towel bar -- plumbed in line with the tub and shower hot water valve. Heated towels; sounded like a good idea. Problem: Hot water running for 15-20 minutes wasn't sufficient to heat the towels before they were used, and certainly wasn't sufficient to dry the towels after they were used. $700 wasted on the heated towel bar, plus $300 for installation.

You have completed the Surveys, and have read the "Good-Better-Best" product philosophy. Now you're ready to gather preliminary product information for your project, to help you become an informed consumer. By this time, you probably know what you don't like about your home. You have ideas about what you want and why, how you want your home to look and feel. Before you proceed, ask yourself this question: "How long has it been since I/we thought about this project?"

GET THE POINT?

HINTS

Before you select final products and determine your product budget:

Throw away all magazines you've collected since you first started to think about remodeling, unless there's something so unique, you have to have it!

Visit an office supply store and purchase the following items (if you don't already have them):

    "Post-it" notes (large enough to write notes on)
    File folders
    Portable file box
    Accountant's pad (minimum six columns)
        [Not necessary if you have/use "Excel"]
    Small stapler/staples

Visit the best bookstore in your area and purchase no more than six home remodeling magazines.

Use "Post-it" notepaper as bookmarks.

Write notes to yourself, i.e., what appeals to you about the advertised products, or rooms shown in articles.

--OR--

Tear out entire articles, if you want to avoid the clutter of magazines filled with "Post-it" notes. Make sure the name of the magazine and issue date are somewhere on the article. Also, tear out the resource guide (usually in the back of the magazine) and staple it with the article.

Several years ago, a client showed her designer pictures from a magazine with a color scheme and flooring she wanted for her home. There was no information about the magazine or date on the pages -- only the page numbers. The size of the pages were a clue that the article was from "Metropolitan Home". The designer was able to order back issues, but the time and money spent was considerable -- just to get the resource list.

Set up separate files for products, using the survey you've completed. You only need files for major categories: Windows/doors, appliances, plumbing, etc.

Talk with friends, family, acquaintances, and business associates who have built or remodeled their home. Ask questions:

> What did they do?
> When did they do it?
> What products did they use?
>> Cabinets
>> Appliances
>> Plumbing fixtures/fittings
>> Countertops
>> Flooring

Ask more personal questions (if they don't mind) :

> What was their investment?
> Did they do some of the work themselves?
> Did a contractor do the entire job?
> How long did their project take, start to finish?
> Were they happy with the results?
> If they were going to remodel again:
>> What would they do they same?
>> What would they change?

Shop on internet sites, to get basic product information (www.homeportfolio.com is a great site -- check it out!).

Make a list of dealers and showrooms, with phone numbers, addresses (and directions); it's in your best interest to have a system for shopping. You can use the forms at the end of this chapter.

Shop at local showrooms, to get a feeling about product quality and price (more general than specific).

Request specification literature, a written price quote, and the salesperson's business card.

HELPFUL HINTS TO ORGANIZE INFORMATION

➤ Put the date on everything (<u>including</u> the year).

➤ Staple estimates, documents, and related brochures together.

➤ If you get only a business card, write information on the back: The date, the manufacturer and model number, and the price quoted, so you'll have something to refer to when you are ready to order the product.

➤ If a particular salesperson extends especially good service, make a note of it on his or her business card, so you can ask for the same person when you're ready to buy products.

"Doing the best at this moment puts you in the best place for the next moment." (Oprah Winfrey)

HINTS: SHOPPING

PRODUCT SELECTION

You're looking for specific product information in addition to price. Keep in mind -- and ask -- the following questions:

How long has this product been available? (Don't buy the first or last model of any product.)

What are the dimensions?

Are there specific installation requirements or limitations?

What is a realistic delivery schedule for this product?

How does it compare with the closest competitor? What are the advantages or disadvantages of each product?

Is service readily available and reliable?

Are parts available?

What is the base price?

What is the price including extra features (special finish options, touch-pad controls, etc.)?

You can use the Suppliers' Contact form at the end of this chapter to organize and keep valuable information.

Most homeowners want to start shopping for visible finish surface products first -- countertops, tile, and flooring. If you do this, you'll waste valuable shopping time, and you'll probably get overwhelmed with choices. Save shopping for finish surfaces until your designer can help you. If you're installing new doors and windows, put them high on your shopping list, because they will often determine important aspects of the layout.

> The creative homeowner obsessed about tile, flooring, and countertops for many months, when she should have been spending the time working on layout details with her designer. Ultimately, the large remodeling project was delayed for several months when she realized that there were major problems with placement of doors, windows, and the location of the master bathroom.

Don't try to select everything at once.

Don't forget to bring a copy of your Homeowner Survey every time you go shopping, as a reminder.

Select doors and windows first.

KITCHEN: Shop for your appliances next. The dimensions of the appliances _do_ affect the layout. If you want a large range or refrigerator in your kitchen, shop for these items first.

BATHROOM: Shop for the whirlpool tub, steam shower, or sauna, if these are included. Then select your lavatories (bathroom sinks), toilet, and other plumbing fixtures and fittings.

Select cabinetry. How to calculate quantities:

Measure the base cabinets across the front; total everything to the nearest inch (if possible);

Follow the same procedure for the wall cabinets and the tall cabinets (i.e., oven, pantry, broom closet, etc.);

Note how many corners are included that will require special corner cabinets;

Count the number of existing drawers you have (you'll probably want more);

Don't forget to make a note if you want wall or tall cabinets in your bathroom(s). They're an excellent way to add storage, if you have the space.

"The key to your universe is that you can choose!"
(Carl Frederick)

Homeowners didn't listen to the designer's advice. They spent every spare hour shopping for cabinets. When they finally selected the appliances, the homeowners were unhappy to find out that the cabinets weren't compatible with the appliances, so they had to start over.

HINTS: BASIC SPREADSHEET

As soon as you get product prices, enter the figures on spreadsheet pages, or in a spreadsheet program (i.e., Excel). This is not an accounting class! The numbers you get and enter are to help you make the best, most informed decisions.   Page 52 has a sample you can use.

Give yourself several extra lines between products and/or categories, so you can add or change information without rewriting whole pages.

Use the Survey form as a checklist, so you don't overlook something expensive that could cause an over-budget situation later.

After you get reliable price quotes for all of the major categories, add them to get a preliminary products total. Then you will get preliminary labor estimates. The process isn't so overwhelming, if you break it down into logical steps.

"A study of economics usually reveals that the best time to buy anything is last year." (Marty Allen)

PRODUCT SUPPLIERS

DATE	PRODUCT	PERSON	PHONE/ADDRESS	IMPORTANT INFORMATION

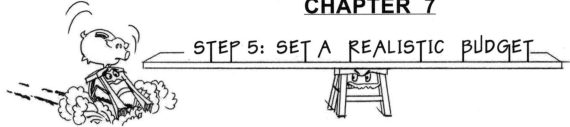

CHAPTER 7

STEP 5: SET A REALISTIC BUDGET

"The way I see it, if you want the rainbow, you gotta put up with the rain." (Dolly Parton)

A couple of things to think about while you're setting your budget, and to keep in mind as you go through Steps 5-9:

    Your home should have integrity with the neighborhood. If you have the nicest, most expensive home, everyone will benefit more than you do, based on real estate comparable lists.

    Avoid trends, especially for large-ticket items like cabinetry, plumbing fixtures, and appliances

    Don't overinvest; don't fall into the "might as well" trap. If you're going to be in your home for five years or less, you should invest less. Why remodel for someone else to enjoy?

In a typical upper-middle-class neighborhood, there's often one house that stands out because it's considerably larger and nicer than the others. Unfortunately, the owners of that home will suffer financially if they try to sell, because the real estate comparables (and the neighborhood appearance) don't justify a buyer paying more than the average square-foot price.

Before you set your budget, you need to know whether your project will comply with local ordinances. Having this information will also help you communicate knowledgeably with your designer and contractor. Visit your local building department (bring the legal description from your deed). You may be able to get lot size information there, or you may have to visit the Recorder's Office (property tax records). The information you need is:

The size of your property;
Setback limitations;
Lot coverage limitations;
Codes that can affect your project;
Plan requirements (to get permits for construction).

SQUARE FOOTAGE METHOD

This estimating method is the quickest, but it's not as reliable as the breakdown method on the next page.

First, you must know the square footage of your existing home. If your mortgage documents include an appraisal, the square footage should be shown there. If you don't have anything, you can use the example on Page 51 and prepare your own square footage calculations. All you need to do is follow these simple steps:

Sketch your house plan (it doesn't have to be to scale);

Take overall dimensions of all exterior walls, starting at a point and working around the perimeter, writing each dimension as you go;

If your house isn't rectangular, break up the areas into rectangles or squares, as large as possible (this may require taking some overall interior dimensions);

Multiply the width times depth of each area to get the square footage of that area;

Add the sums of all areas to get the total square footage.

Second, decide whether your remodeling project fits into the "good," "better," or "best" category explained on Pages 33-43. Each category has a range of investment which varies 25% or more. Multiply the total square footage of your project by the investment per square foot from the "Good-Better-Best" examples to obtain a reasonable budget. Don't forget to add at least 15% contingency for the "might as well's" mentioned earlier.

Homeowners prepared a preliminary spreadsheet in July, to help choose products and select a contractor. Before they finalized the home improvement loan the following January, they prepared a revised spreadsheet. Products had increased a total of $15,000, which was easy to include in the loan. They weren't in a financial position to personally pay the additional $15,000 from their bank account.

"When you change one thing in your life, you will discover it is hitched to everything else in the world." (Dr. Nelson Clements)

BREAKDOWN METHOD

🔨 Make a detailed list in ink (or use your Survey):

All products you need;
All products you <u>want</u> - manufacturer, model, etc.;
Work you <u>want</u> done by others;
Work you <u>need</u> done by others;
Work you can do yourself (to save money, not time);

🔨 Use a simple spreadsheet form (multiple-column), a columnar pad, or spreadsheet program (i.e., "Excel"). Plug in numbers for each item:

Accurate numbers you know;

"Guesstimate" numbers you don't know (you can change the numbers as you get more accurate information).

🔨 Subtotal everything on the spreadsheet(s). Multiply the subtotal by at least 25% (preliminary contingency). Add subtotal and contingency to create the preliminary budget for your products.

🔨 To complete the breakdown method, you (or your designer) will need to get labor estimates, so you can add them to the spreadsheet. This should happen during design, when you have preliminary plans.

 **"There are only two ways of paying for something. Your investment comes from your CHECKBOOK, or your HIDE!!"**

ABOUT YOUR SPREADSHEET . . .

It's important for you to keep the spreadsheet updated with latest product and labor estimates. Don't assume that once you've prepared the spreadsheet, things will remain the same. They won't.

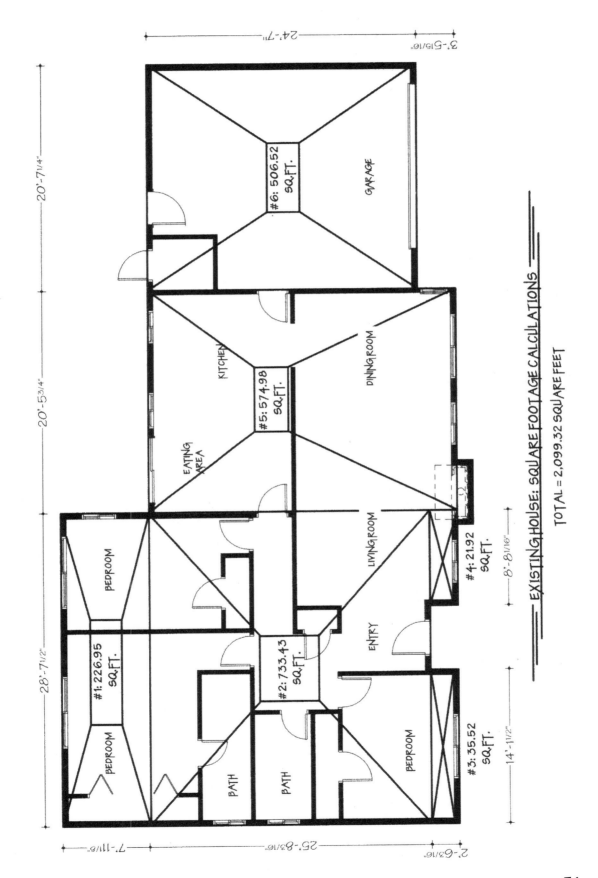

EXISTING HOUSE: SQUARE FOOTAGE CALCULATIONS

TOTAL = 2,099.32 SQUARE FEET

51

SPREADSHEET

DATE	PRODUCT/SUPPLIER	QUOTE	QUOTE	QUOTE

CHAPTER 8

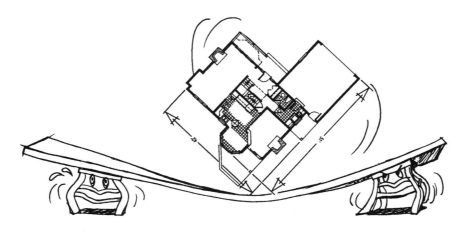

DO YOU REALLY WANT TO BE YOUR OWN DESIGNER?

After you have read the following chapter, and understand everything a design professional can do for you, ask yourself the following question: Am I/are we qualified to perform all of the functions as well as a designer will?

Homeowners who specialized in frugality decided to be their own designer for a small kitchen addition -- less than 50 square feet. Their lovely home was situated on the side of a steep hill. The wife drew floor plans based on a magazine article she'd read -- no elevations, no framing details, no electrical details, or specifications. The couple was upset when the building department kicked back the plans for required information that wasn't included, i.e., floor area ratio, energy calculations, soil test calculations, structural calculations, and mechanical details. The plans were finally approved, but the couple never got accurate labor or product estimates and ended up paying almost double what they'd intended for everything because the "plans" lacked detailed information. The project was finally finished; **NOT** on time, **NOT** on budget and **NOT** as special as they'd visualized.

If you're thinking about being your own designer and preparing your own plans, wait until you read Chapter 13, about Detailed Plans. That should "nail down the point!"

DESIGN PROFESSIONALS -- CLASSIFICATION

"Vision is the art of seeing things invisible." (Jonathan Swift)

Based on the size and scope of your project, you will need someone to prepare plans for you. But it goes beyond just drawing plans -- unless that's all you want. Here are some professional categories of people who can help you, depending on what you want:

Architect
Engineer
Design-Build Firm
Building Designer
Bath/Kitchen Designer
Draftsperson
Interior Designer
Interior Decorator

ARCHITECT: This person has been through many years of schooling and apprenticeship. Architects are licensed by each state, after they pass a rigorous test. They are required to take Continuing Education classes and seminars, to have the latest building and code information that can affect their clients' projects.

"A doctor can always bury his mistakes. An architect can only advise his clients to plant ivy." (Frank Lloyd Wright)

ENGINEER: There are several types of engineer that could be involved with your project, i.e., Energy, Geotechnical, Electrical, Mechanical, and Structural. An architect can also be a structural engineer, but most often, architects rely on engineers for specific knowledge and expertise. Many states require a soil test to be done if an addition is proposed, and they require structural calculations to accompany final plans, showing the type of material, equations for stable building load, wind shear, earthquake, etc. They may also require calculations for energy conservation. You can find out by calling your local Building Department and asking what they will require for your project.

> "Engineers hate risk. They try to eliminate it whenever they can. This is understandable, given that when an engineer makes one little mistake, the media will treat it like it's a big deal or something." (Anonymous)

DESIGN-BUILD FIRM: Companies that exemplify one-stop shopping for your remodeling project. If you retain a design-build firm, you will be working with several people who represent that company, from initial design through construction.

> "A common mistake that people make when trying to design something completely foolproof is to underestimate the ingenuity of complete fools." (Douglas Adams)

BUILDING DESIGNER: This person may have all of the qualifications of an architect, excluding the license. Your state may have laws governing a building designer's scope of work and responsibilities.

> "Building Designer, n. One who drafts a plan of your house, and plans a draft of your money." (Ambrose Bierce)

BATH/KITCHEN DESIGNER: This person has specialized knowledge and experience about every aspect of kitchens and bathrooms, that architects or other designers may not have. Many architects prefer to work with a bath-kitchen specialist after the space has been defined architecturally (i.e., walls, doorways, windows).

> "My kids always perceived the bathroom as a place where you wait it out until all the groceries are unloaded from the car." (Erma Bombeck)

DRAFTSPERSON: This person has training and experience to draw what you tell him or her to. Most (but not all) draftspersons avoid the design process, especially product recommendation and construction coordination, so homeowners may need to hire someone to provide these services.

> "An draftsman's most useful tools are an eraser and the drafting board, and a wrecking bar at the site." (Frank Lloyd Wright)

INTERIOR DESIGNER: This person may have education, training, and experience to handle a whole-house remodeling project, but there is ongoing discussion about the actual scope of work -- whether an interior designer can sufficiently prepare drawings for a complex project. Many states have begun certifying interior designers and defining the specific role they play in building and remodeling.

> **"Take care of the luxuries and the necessities will take care of themselves." (Frank Lloyd Wright)**

INTERIOR DECORATOR: This person is not required to have any specific education or training to be an interior decorator in most states. An individual person may have as much education as a building designer, bath-kitchen designer, or interior designer, but the scope of his or her responsibilities should only be for furniture, furnishings, and decorative accessories.

> **"You can't use up creativity. The more you use, the more you have." (Maya Angelou)**

The term "designer" is used generically to cover all of the categories above, unless a specific discussion focuses on one professional category.

DESIGNERS' FEE STRUCTURE

> **"The pain of poor-quality workmanship lasts longer than the pleasure of a cheap fee."**

There are four basic methods that Designers use for compensation:

A. Flat fee
B. Percentage of project value
C. Hourly
D. Markup on products sold plus fee (A, B, or C)

FLAT FEE: To arrive at a flat fee, the designer has to have many years of experience with similar projects, to estimate how much time s/he will devote to your project; this equation should be explained to you fully. There should be progress payments, a willingness by the designer to justify his/her time spent for each payment, and a written "maximum not to exceed" total.

PERCENTAGE OF PROJECT VALUE: The normal fee structure is based on 8%-10% of the project value. There should be a clear understanding and agreement (in writing) that if the project investment increases, the fee will be re-negotiated for the additional investment.

56

HOURLY: The designer should verify what their hourly fee is, and give you a "maximum not to exceed" estimate -- which should be stated in the agreement. With progress invoices, the designer should notify you how much time is remaining before s/he reaches the maximum.

MARKUP ON PRODUCTS SOLD, PLUS FEE: Most decorators, and many designers, use this form of fee structure. This compensation method is not applicable to larger projects, unless it is in conjunction with one of the other fee structures for plan preparation and construction coordination.

"The highest reward for a person's work is not what they get for it, but what they become by it" (John Ruskin)

Many design professionals charge for the first in-person meeting. The fee can be nominal, or it can be a significant amount -- several hundred dollars, which may or may not apply to the design fee.

Designers may require a retainer to begin work. Part of the retainer may apply towards the final payment. You should get a complete explanation verbally, and in writing, how the designer calculates his/her fee and payments. There should be progress payments, which can be:

A percentage of the fee based on progress;
A total of hours spent multiplied by the hourly rate.

Designers also submit invoices for reimbursable out-of-pocket expenses, i.e.:

Original plots;
Blueline copies;
Regular and special photocopies;
Photographs;
Fax transmissions;
Long-distance and mobile phone calls;
Assistants' specific services (measuring, document preparation, drafting, procuring estimates, etc.);
Postage and other delivery services.

If you know how each design professional calculates and invoices for services and expenses, you will ultimately make the best decision about the value of the services s/he provides. This information must be included in written proposals and agreements (including how partial hours are calculated and invoiced).

STEP 6: HOW and WHERE TO FIND A QUALIFIED DESIGN PROFESSIONAL

Ask for referrals from business associates, family members, neighbors, and acquaintances. Let everyone know you're planning to remodel as soon as you make the decision. If you have the opportunity, ask them some questions about their designer:

> Did s/he understand what they wanted?
> Did s/he offer creative solutions and interesting ideas that were
> budget-sensitive?
> Did s/he recommend products that fit the project and the budget?
> Were the plans detailed, complete and on time?
> Did s/he provide construction coordination?
> How much did s/he charge for professional services?
> (If it was more than six months ago, don't expect to pay the
> same fee for similar services.)
> If they were doing another project, would they hire the same designer?
> Why, or why not?

Call your local chamber of commerce, or get a referral from professional organizations:

> American Institute of Architects [AIA]
> American Society of Interior Designers [ASID]
> National Association of Home Builders [NAHB]
> National Association of the Remodeling Industry [NARI]
> National Kitchen and Bath Association [NKBA]

All of these associations have websites with links to local affiliations in your city and/or state. It may take several weeks for them to process your request. Be patient and persistent.

"Luck is a matter of preparation meeting opportunity."
(Oprah Winfrey)

58

INITIAL DISCUSSION WITH DESIGN PROFESSIONAL!

Talk with three or four designers initially. The first screening process can be a telephone conversation. During that discussion with the prospective designer, after you've described your project, you can ask qualifying questions:

"How long have you been in business?"

"How do you work with your clients?"

"Why did you get into the business?"

"What is it that you like most about your business?" What continues to motivate you?"

"How do you recommend design solutions? Do you do quick sketches during meetings?"

"How many projects can you take care of at the same time? How many projects do you have now?"

"Do you recommend products? Do you sell products?"

"Do you recommend contractors and suppliers? What's your criteria for recommendations? Do you accept and give referral fees?"

"How do you charge for your services?"

"Do you prepare all your own plans? Are they hand-drawn, or do you use CAD?"

"Are you certified and/or licensed?"

"What professional organizations do you belong to?"

FOLLOW-UP MEETING
AND HIRING A DESIGNER

The first in-person meeting with the designer should be with **the major decision maker(s), head(s) of the household**. It should be during the day, so s/he can see your home, get a feeling for your personal style, and see the existing lighting conditions. S/he will want to walk around the perimeter of your house, to see the roofline and where your house is in relationship to neighbors' property, trees, etc. Be prepared to offer a tour of the interior, too.

During your first meeting, show the designer your survey and magazine pictures. Talk about your project from a *wish list* standpoint. It will be helpful if you get input about your possible investment, how long the design process will take, and how long construction will take. You may get different answers from each designer.

There should be a short discussion about ergonomics, function, and safety:

Who's right-handed and who's left-handed;

Physical limitations;

Products for safety and function (grab bars, lever handles, shower seats, etc.);

Physical height in relationship to countertops, toilets, etc.

The designer should have a portfolio of projects to show you. Look carefully at the pictures, to see if there's a particular style or theme shown. If it's different from what you want, ask questions about the designer's preferred style. If the dream home you visualize is French country and the designer's portfolio shows mostly contemporary projects, there may be a potential problem -- but not necessarily. Best to find out early.

If there's a high percentage of portfolio projects in an obviously different investment category from your target budget, clarify that, too. A designer who is accustomed to working with large-budget projects may have difficulty relating to (and sticking to) a smaller target budget. The ability to buy large four-color ads represents only one (small) aspect of a designer's qualifications.   A great reputation is desirable, too, but you must consider everything. You need/want someone who's going to understand and work within your reasonable budget, and design for your unique lifestyle.

At the end of the first meeting, tell the designer that you are interviewing other designers, and agree to discuss the progress of your decision. Two weeks is a reasonable time. Next, check all references. Ask the questions listed on Page 58, plus:

> "Did s/he meet most deadlines?"
>
> "Were the plans finished on time?
>
> "How would you rate (his/her) product knowledge?" Did s/he help you
>   make good choices?"
>
> "Did s/he help you with your budget?"
>
> "Did s/he make recommendations to help you stay in your budget?"
>
> "How would you rate (his/her) communication skills?"
>
> "How would you rate (his/her) construction knowledge?"
>
> "Were there any problems with the design?"
>   (If "Yes," then "What were they?" And, "How were they resolved?")

When you have made your decision who to hire, a courtesy call to the other designers, thanking them for their time and interest in your project, is the appropriate thing to do.

Next, you'll set an appointment with the design professional you've selected to work with you. S/he may take measurements of your home during that appointment, or set another appointment to take measurements.

Review the agreement/contract. Read everything carefully, and don't be shy about asking questions or asking for written insertions to clarify the terms. Don't sign anything unless you fully understand and approve it before the designer does <u>any</u> work for you. You may pay the deposit or retainer requested, in good faith; that's your judgment call. Don't let unanswered questions pass by, and don't assume that everything will work out like you want it to.

 "The unanswered question will turn into a challenge. The unresolved challenge will turn into a problem. The unresolved problem will turn into conflict."

On every document you receive -- whether it's from the designer, contractor, suppliers, or others -- check everything, even the spelling of your name, your address, and phone number. For each agreement, or proposal, it's crucial that information is clearly stated about **what's included** and **what's not included** is clearly stated. Everyone understands the pitfalls of assumptions!

 In the first meeting with the designer, the homeowners talked about what they wanted in their new kitchen. They also talked about the adjoining laundry ("mud") room, thinking that they'd made it clear they wanted it remodeled, too. The designer didn't understand, and didn't include the laundry room in her proposal or agreement. Fortunately, the oversight was discovered during the design process, not during construction!

Your designer should give you a general timeline for production of preliminary and final plans, but the actual amount of time will depend largely on two factors:

How quickly you make product and layout decisions;
How frequently you can meet with the designer.

You have an advantage, because you've taken the time to define what you want, you've done some preliminary shopping, and you've gotten preliminary product estimates. But as the design evolves, you will have the opportunity to re-think and discuss alternatives that may be better.

Whether it's concerning the layout or products, advice that your designer (or contractor, or supplier) gives should be backed by solid reasons -- not just, "This is the way I/we always do it." If reasons aren't offered to back up suggestions, ask for the reasons. After all, every recommendation has the potential for financial impact!

"When <u>anyone</u> tells you something is 'marginally better,' you should ask if it's his profit margin he's talking about."

This book is to help you understand the design process, not to tell your designer how to do his/her job. Your designer should explain in detail -- it should be in a written proposal or agreement -- exactly what s/he will provide for the fee s/he will charge.

Congratulations! You have gotten to the next step: The Design Process.

NOTES

_____
_____
_____
_____
_____
_____
_____
_____
_____
_____
_____
_____
_____
_____
_____
_____
_____
_____
_____
_____
_____

DESIGNER REFERENCE FEEDBACK FORM

NAME	PUNCTUALITY	BUDGET ASSISTANCE	DEADLINES	COMMUNICATION	PROBLEM RESOLUTION	PRODUCT KNOWLEDGE	CONSTRUCTION KNOWLEDGE	HIRE AGAIN?	COMMENTS

CHAPTER 9

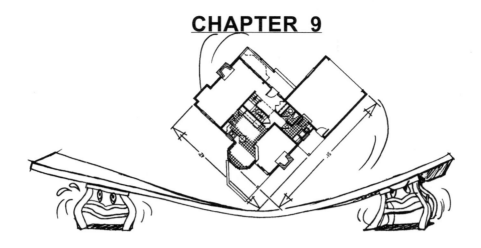

STEP 7: THE DESIGN PROCESS

"The greatest accomplishments have resulted from the transmission of ideas and enthusiasm." (Thomas Watson, Jr.)

The following list is a guideline, a tool to help you achieve good results. You and your designer should agree, as soon as possible, how long each step will take.

1. Review Homeowner Survey and Design Agreement, and discuss ergonomics.

2. Take as-built measurements of house and property.

3. Prepare "as-built" plans of the house and property.

4. Double-check local requirements about setback limitations and lot coverage (floor area ratio).

5. Prepare preliminary plans, using the Homeowner Survey.

6. Submit preliminary plans to engineers so they can begin to work on their portion of the project.

7. Get technical information about doors and windows (i.e., sizes available, framing requirements, optional features, etc.).

8. Get technical specifications for appliances, plumbing fixtures, lighting and switching.

9. Prepare preliminary product specifications.

10. Talk with homeowners about product and contractor alternatives. Refer homeowners to appropriate products and service providers.

11. Get feedback from homeowners about preliminary design; revise preliminary plans as needed.

12*. Talk with engineers and submit revised plans. If the scope of the project is changed considerably, talk with contractors to get input about the financial impact of changes.

13*. Send copies of preliminary plans to contractors, cabinet manufacturers, and product suppliers for written estimates.

14*. Give homeowners estimate information, or take over responsibility of data entry into the spreadsheet.

15*. Talk with homeowners about estimates, and help them make informed decisions about the project and products. Revise plans and specifications as needed to reflect homeowner decisions.

*NOTE: See next section, "Preliminary Labor Estimates."

16. Talk with contractors and engineers if homeowner decisions affect the scope of work and submit revised plans.

17. Double-check homeowner product decisions, and spreadsheet information.

18. Prepare final plans, specifications, and details for final labor estimates, product orders, and permits.

19. Review all documents with homeowners and get their approval signature on every page of plans, specifications, and final spreadsheet.

20. Provide construction coordination.

There are 20 logical steps included in the design process. If each step takes only a week, you've got 20 weeks to finalize your product and project decisions. Your designer has 20 weeks to coordinate preparation of final plans with the engineers; it could take 40 weeks (or more) to complete all 20 steps.

> "Learn the art of patience. Apply discipline to your thoughts when you become anxious over the outcome of a goal. Impatience breeds anxiety, fear, discouragement and failure. Patience creates confidence, decisiveness, and a rational outlook, which eventually leads to success." (Brian Adams)

If your designer has given several general contractors the same information, the preliminary estimates should be within a range of 5%. Be suspicious of estimates that are out of this range, higher or lower.

"Few things are harder to put up with than the annoyance of a good example." (Mark Twain)

Several years ago, a couple got three estimates from contractors for their kitchen remodeling project. Two of the contractors' estimates were within $1,000, a 3% range. The third contractor's estimate was $5,000 below the lowest of the other two estimates. The homeowner said, "I can't afford <u>not</u> to hire John." John was given an opportunity to review (and change) his estimate, but held fast to his numbers. A $36,000 project that should have taken 6 to 8 weeks stretched beyond 12 weeks. The homeowners were furious and stressed beyond their limits. When the project was finally finished, the investment difference didn't ease the frustration and anger the homeowners had felt. Ultimately, the contractor lost his license for abandoning other clients, as he had done with this couple. His fees weren't sufficient to pay his trade contractors, the materials bills, and afford him operating capital.

It's time to test reality. At this point, you're checking to see if the "real" numbers are within your budget. Add the product estimates and the averaged labor estimates. Don't forget to calculate/add 15-20% for contingencies. The total should be an accurate estimate for your total investment.

If the estimated total investment is outside of your budget, it's time to think about alternatives. You (or your designer) should call the contractors to get their input about what you can do to lower your investment (without sacrificing the scope of your project or your highest priority items).

"As a child my family's menu consisted of two choices: take it, or leave it." (Buddy Hackett)

You have more than two choices: You can change the scope of the project to fit your budget, select alternative products, increase your budget (if possible), or combine the choices to fit your priorities and budget.   You've paid the designer for preliminary plans; you're not so far into the design process that necessary tradeoffs should discourage you. As you become an informed consumer, you are making better decisions. You are protecting your most valuable asset.

After working for months with their designer and engineers, paying a fair amount of money for final plans, and getting all excited about their project, homeowners finally obtained estimates. It was a bitter pill for them, because the estimates were so far beyond their budget, they had to go back to square one. They were angry about the time they felt had been wasted, and resented paying the designer another fee.

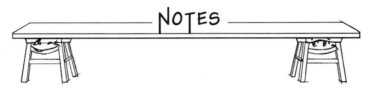

NOTES

"Do it right, and do it with style." (Fred Astaire)

MEETINGS

Meetings should be structured, with an agenda, and last no more than 3 hours. Everyone should be prepared for the meeting; you should have a written list of questions.

Meetings should be weekly or every other week. If more time passes between meetings, it may affect your construction deadline. Everyone should feel good about the progress. If not, there should be open discussion about the progress and how to improve it. Also see Chapter 16, Remodeling Etiquette, for more meeting hints.

Homeowners had a very demanding schedule, and traveled frequently. Meetings with their designer happened once a month, at best; often, several months passed between meetings. Time was spent trying to remember the previous meeting, rather than making important decisions. This ultimately slowed the progress, which was frustrating for the homeowners, the designer, and the contractor. After an honest discussion, the homeowners decided to make their project #1 priority. All decisions were made and the plans were completed by the end of the following month.

At the end of each meeting, an appointment should be set for the next appointment, based on an agreed "to do" list for you and your designer. "To do" items for you may include:

- Research products and shopping.
- Make decisions that will affect the layout.

"To do" items for your designer may include:

- Research products from a technical or financial standpoint, to help you make informed decisions.
- Prepare plans for your review.
- Work with engineers on technical details.
- Work with contractors to achieve the best estimates and results.
- Submit preliminary plans to contractors, cabinet manufacturers and suppliers for written estimates.

CHAPTER 10

"To Be Or Not To Be..."

Your Own General Contractor

Many homeowners believe that they can be their own general contractor. Usually, the motivation behind this belief is to save the 15 to 30 percent that a general contractor would charge to run the job.

Qualified (i.e. licensed, experienced) general contractors must know the logical job progression, how long each step takes, what the labor investment will be, what the building materials will total, and how much to figure for his or her overhead and profit. They are familiar with building codes. General contractors have experienced trade contractors in each category, and know who to hire for each project.

The general contractor takes responsibility for his or her employees, for scheduling each tradesman so there aren't delays or serious overlaps. S/he schedules deliveries, and communicates regularly with homeowners, engineers and the design professionals. Contractors have to know everything about construction and products that are used in today's homes, so they can solve problems that pop up unexpectedly. Most of them have spent many years as an apprentice before becoming a general contractor.

Contractors are usually at the lumber yard by 7:00 a.m., when they need to purchase building materials. They work a full day, making sure that everything goes smoothly. Evenings are usually spent doing paper work, meeting with clients and prospective clients, and returning phone calls. They really do earn their income!

You may have an extensive general knowledge of home construction. You may have tackled several smaller projects. You may have participated in a larger remodeling project, or you may have built your home. Only you know the extent of your knowledge and experience. Before you get into deep, hot water, take the following test. If you pass, it's possible that you may, in fact, be able to take charge of your remodeling project. Passing this five-page test won't get you a contractor's license in any state. Passing a "guaranteed" contractor test will get you a license in the state of confusion, if you don't have practical experience..

HOMEOWNER-CONTRACTOR QUALIFYING TEST

1. Have you ever been an active participant in a large-size remodeling project, in a capacity other than homeowner?

    Y [ ]   N [ ]

2. Have you ever been an active participant in a medium-size remodeling project, in a capacity other than homeowner?

    Y [ ]   N [ ]

3. Have you ever been an active participant in a small remodeling project, in a capacity other than homeowner?

    Y [ ]   N [ ]

4. Have you ever helped build or remodel a home, in a capacity other than the homeowner?

    Y [ ]   N [ ]

5. Do you know how to read design plans?

    Y [ ]   N [ ]

6. If your answer to #5 above is "Yes," are you proficient enough to answer any question that may arise during construction?

    Y [ ]   N [ ]

7. If your answer to #5 above is "No," are you willing to spend hours studying the plans, asking questions of the design professional, and reading books in preparation for your remodeling project?

    Y [ ]   N [ ]

8. How much time do you have on a daily basis, Monday through Friday, to devote to your remodeling project?

    [ ] 8-10 hours   [ ] 5-8 hours   [ ] 3-5 hours
    [ ] 1-3 hours   [ ] Less than 1 hour

9. Have you read/studied the Uniform Building Code, the Uniform Mechanical Code, the Uniform Plumbing Code, and current energy codes?

    Y [ ]   N [ ]

10. How many of the following trade contractors do you know well enough to hire for your project?

	YES	NO
Framing carpenter	[ ]	[ ]
Finish carpenter	[ ]	[ ]
Concrete	[ ]	[ ]
Electrician	[ ]	[ ]
Insulation	[ ]	[ ]
Plumber	[ ]	[ ]
Drywall/plaster	[ ]	[ ]
Tile setter	[ ]	[ ]
Stone mason	[ ]	[ ]
Marble/granite manufacturer	[ ]	[ ]
Stucco	[ ]	[ ]
Hardwood floor installer	[ ]	[ ]
Roofer	[ ]	[ ]
Vinyl floor installer	[ ]	[ ]
Cabinet maker	[ ]	[ ]
Carpet installer	[ ]	[ ]
Painter	[ ]	[ ]
Wallpaper hanger	[ ]	[ ]

11. If you become the general contractor for your project, are you willing to spend hours getting comparative labor estimates, checking status of license and bonding, to assure the best price and service from trade contractors?

Y [ ]   N [ ]

12. Hypothetical scenario: You are remodeling your kitchen, which includes an addition, and a dispute arises between the framing contractor and the plumber, who has just drilled through the center of 8 joists to run a drain line, which caused the inspector to fail an inspection for you. How do you resolve the situation?

[ ] A   Bang the framing contractor's and the plumber's heads together in front of the inspector, to show them who's boss.

[ ] B   Fire the plumber and get a new plumber to correct the situation.

[ ] C   Try to bribe the inspector to change his mind.

[ ] D   Have the framing contractor add appropriate blocking and additional support framing, as suggested by a licensed structural engineer. Pay for the additional labor and negotiate to deduct the additional fee from the plumber's fee.

"Continued on next page!"

13. Hypothetical scenario: You, as the homeowner and general contractor, supplied a downdraft cooktop, and instructed the finish carpenter to install it. He threw away the packaging material and the installation instructions after he finished. Now the downdraft unit isn't working properly. Your carpenter claims the unit is defective, and the supplier won't accept its return without all of the packing material and installation instructions. What do you do?

[ ] A   Demand that the finish carpenter un-install and re-install the unit; it has to be his fault that the cooktop doesn't work.

[ ] B   Donate the defective unit to Goodwill for a full tax credit; they can fix anything.

[ ] C   Picket the appliance dealer for selling you a lemon; if they don't respond to your negative advertising, file a small-claims lawsuit.

[ ] D   Call the manufacturer and explain the situation. Ask a manufacturer's representative to verify that the unit needs warranty repair. If the manufacturer offers no support, be prepared to write letters and eventually file a small claims lawsuit. In the meantime, you'll have to live without a cooktop, or pay for a new one until the matter is settled.

"So I ask myself, 'SELF! How do I kick this up another notch?'" (Emeril Lagasse)

BAM! We've kicked this test up another notch!

14. What is the progression of a complete kitchen remodeling that includes an addition?
(Fill in the blanks with only one letter; don't look ahead -- don't cheat!)

A	_____	14.	Inspection (___ days)
B	_____	15.	Insulation (___ days)
C	_____	16.	Demolition (___ days)
D	_____	17.	Walk-through/Punch List
E	_____	18.	Debris box
F	_____	19.	Plan Check (___ days)
G	_____	20.	Rough Electrical (___ days)
H	_____	21.	Appliances Delivered
I	_____	22.	Inspection (___ days)
J	_____	23.	Double-check Measurements (overall)
K	_____	24.	Rough Plumbing (___ days)
L	_____	25.	Framing (___ days)
M	_____	26.	Grading (___ days)
N	_____	27.	Inspection (___ days)
O	_____	28.	Flooring Installed (___ days)
P	_____	29.	Drywall/Plaster (___ days)
Q	_____	30.	Foundation (allow ___ days)
R	_____	31.	Doors/Windows Installed (___ days)
S	_____	32.	Inspection (___ days)
T	_____	33.	Countertops Installed (___ days)
U	_____	34.	Workers' Comp., Proof of Insurance
V	_____	35.	Appliances Installed (___ days)
W	_____	36.	All Products Ordered
X	_____	37.	Doors/Windows Delivered _____
Y	_____	38.	Exterior Siding/Stucco (___ days)
Z	_____	39.	Inspection (___ days)
AA	_____	40.	Exterior/Interior Painting (___ days)
BB	_____	41.	Cabinets Delivered
CC	_____	42.	Permits Issued
DD	_____	43.	Double-check Measurements (cabinets)
EE	_____	44.	Cabinets Installed (___ days)
FF	_____	45.	Plumbing/Lighting Installed (___ days)
GG	_____	46.	Countertops Measured

47. For the kitchen remodeling project above, what is your estimate of how long it should take from start to completion of construction?

Answer: _____ working days, or _____ weeks.

Hopefully, you have a renewed appreciation for what contractors do. If you are still leaning towards being your own general contractor, keep in mind that you will have to pay Workmens' Compensation for everyone who works on your home, if the value of their work exceeds $300 (check with your state to verify the exact maximum; it does vary). You'll discover that contractors pay a very high rate for on-the-job injury insurance. If someone is injured while working on your home, and you're the contractor, it could jeopardize your major asset. What have you REALLY saved?

"Paying more for labor doesn't guarantee a better quality workmanship. Paying less for labor doesn't guarantee that you'll get good value for your investment."

NOTES

_____
_____
_____
_____
_____
_____
_____
_____
_____
_____
_____
_____
_____

ANSWERS:
12. D;
13. D;
14. N (1); 15. Q (1); 16. G (5); 17. QQ; 18. F; 19. C(25); 20. L (5); 21. DD; 22. R (1); 23. P; 24. K (5); 25. J (5); 26. H (2); 27. FF (1); 28. CC (5); 29. S (10); 30. I (10); 31. P (2); 32. T (1); 33. AA (5); 34. D; 35. EE (2); 36. A; 37. O; 38. U (7); 39. V (1); 40. X (10); 41. W; 42. E; 43. M; 44. Y (5); 45. BB (4); 46. Z
47. 84 = 16.8

75

CHAPTER 11

 STEP 8: HOW TO FIND A GENERAL CONTRACTOR

The best way to find a contractor is referrals -- from neighbors, friends, family, or business associates. These are your best resources -- especially neighbors who have remodeled recently. You can also get referrals from the showrooms you've visited. Don't rely too heavily on advertisements. They can be misleading. You'll be better off to contact your local Chamber of Commerce or professional remodeling organizations (NAHB, NARI, or NKBA) for several names and phone numbers. Most local building departments will not refer contractors -- conflict of interest.

Two warnings about referrals:

Don't hire a one-person contractor who says s/he does everything. An unforeseen family emergency, illness or injury can ruin time projections. There aren't enough hours in the day for a general contractor to draw plans, manufacture cabinets, **and** work on your project. Overall quality will suffer.

Don't hire family members or friends. If something goes wrong, it will ruin a good relationship. (There's a great example about this later.)

"Always do right. This will gratify some people and astonish the rest." (Mark Twain)

76

INITIAL DISCUSSION WITH CONTRACTORS

Most homeowners believe the first thing to do when they've decided to remodel is to have a contractor come to their home. This is a waste of time and effort, unless they're calling a design-build firm. Unfortunately, most homeowners also expect a detailed preliminary estimate, in writing, after a two-hour evening appointment with the contractor (and no plans). If you're testing the water to see if your proposed project is feasible, you can do it by telephone.

The contractor will have questions for you about your project. The first question a general contractor will ask when you call is, "Do you have plans?" Without plans, your project is just a verbal wish for the future. After you give information about your project, ask "What is the normal range of investment for a similar project?"

Call at least 3 contractors. If you are interviewing more than 5 contractors, it will be very hard to remember each one's qualifications, even if you take notes. You don't have to make appointments with every contractor you call. If you pre-screen the contractors on the telephone and "weed out" ones you're not interested in hiring. The ones you meet should be ones you'd seriously consider hiring. Begin by asking, "If you have a few minutes, may I ask some questions about your experience?" Get general information, such as:

"How long have you been in business? Do you have employees, or do you use the same subcontractors for every project?"

"Are you licensed in this state?"

"What type of construction projects do you prefer?"

"Have you worked in our area?"
    (If "yes," ask what type of project and when);

"Are you familiar with our neighborhood?"

"Do you normally provide products, or do you allow homeowners to provide their own products?"

"How do you feel generally about architects and designers?"

"Are you familiar with [name of your designer]? Have you worked with him/her before?"

Don't be surprised if the contractor is surprised that you have specific information about your project, although you don't have plans; most homeowners don't have a clue! The time you took to fill out the Survey and do preliminary shopping will help you communicate more knowledgeably (and honestly) with the contractor about:

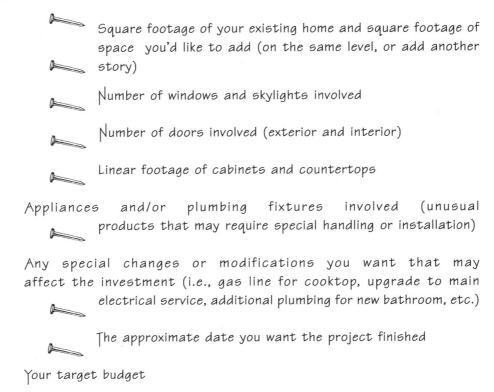

- Square footage of your existing home and square footage of space you'd like to add (on the same level, or add another story)

- Number of windows and skylights involved

- Number of doors involved (exterior and interior)

- Linear footage of cabinets and countertops

- Appliances and/or plumbing fixtures involved (unusual products that may require special handling or installation)

- Any special changes or modifications you want that may affect the investment (i.e., gas line for cooktop, upgrade to main electrical service, additional plumbing for new bathroom, etc.)

- The approximate date you want the project finished

- Your target budget

Based on the preliminary information, ask if the contractor can (and will) give you a budget <u>range</u> during your phone conversation, based on his/her experience. Your chances of getting a thumbnail estimate are about 50-50.

"We ought to be very grateful that we have tools. Millions of years ago, people did not have them, and home projects were extremely difficult." (Dave Barry)

INITIAL MEETING WITH CONTRACTORS

The major decision-maker(s)/head(s) of the household should be available to meet all of the contractors. When contractors come to your home for the first time, it should be during daylight hours, so they can see details inside and out that may affect your project. You may have to accommodate a very early morning appointment, or you may have to take time away from work for the meeting. They will want to see your electrical panel and other utility connections, in addition to seeing all areas adjacent to the areas you're planning to remodel. They may want to quickly inspect the attic and crawl space (or basement); these things could also affect your ultimate investment.

Ask what the contractor uses for communication, i.e., cell phone, pager, e-mail, and/or voicemail. Ask the contractor if s/he works with the crew, or personally supervises the work. If the contractor is mainly a supervisor, ask how frequently s/he is at the jobsite.

> A well-known contractor sent his crew to the jobsite every day, but rarely visited the jobsite himself. The first month went well, but gradually, the crew began showing up later, taking longer coffee and lunch breaks, and leaving earlier. Frustrated, the homeowner called the designer, who advised the homeowner to call the contractor directly. Work improved for a period of weeks, but again, the bad pattern was repeated, until the homeowner got mad and demanded the contractor to drive by immediately -- to see his crew washing their trucks at 3:30, using the homeowners' garden hose when they should have been working!

At the end of your discussion with each contractor, let him or her know that you're interviewing other contractors. Set a date for a telephone update about the status of your project -- getting preliminary estimates, updating the progress of your design and preliminary plans.

Soon after your meeting, call your local building department to check the contractor's status regarding licenses and insurance. Call your Contractor's License Board and check the status of licensing, bonding, and complaints. Contact the local Consumer Protection Agency if you have any suspicions. Also call **all** of the references given -- former clients, trade contractors, suppliers. Ask questions:

> Did s/he meet most deadlines? Were there construction delays?
>   (If "Yes," then "Why?" and "How long?")
>
> Was the contractor punctual? Was the crew punctual?
>
> How would you rate (his/her) product knowledge? Did s/he follow installation instructions?

Did s/he make recommendations to help you stay within your budget?

Were there many change orders for extra work? (If "Yes," then "Why?")

How would you rate (his/her) communication skills?

How would you rate (his/her) construction knowledge and managerial skills?

Was the contractor responsive to questions about problems or scheduling? Were problems resolved quickly?

Was the crew large enough to handle your project?

How would you rate the contractor's communication skills?

How would you rate the contractor's communication skills with the project designer, crew, trade contractors and suppliers?

If you were doing your project over, would you hire the same contractor? Why, or why not?

Your decision to hire a contractor should be based on four equal factors:

The contractor's knowledge/experience;

The contractor's reputation;

The estimate;

The personality "chemistry" between you and the contractor.

The contractor (and his or her employees or trade contractors) will be showing up between 7:30 and 8:00 every weekday morning for the next six months or longer. In addition to your drastically-changed lifestyle, remodeling is going to test your patience. Your relationship with the contractor has to be great at the beginning, based on honest communication, so you can survive the process.

When you've made your decision about a general contractor, call the other contractors as a courtesy, thanking them for their time and interest in your project.

Homeowners had a hard time deciding between two contractors who had been referred to them. They called Contractor #1 to let him know he had been chosen, and they called Contractor #2 as a courtesy. Two weeks later, Contractor #1 had a family emergency and decided not to take on the project. The homeowners had no guilt about calling Contractor #2 and explaining the circumstances. Their courtesy paid off, and the project started on time.

Two comments about trade contractors:

➤ The general contractor is only as good as his weakest trade contractor. The contractor has control, and can fire an irresponsible trade contractor, UNLESS the trade contractor has been hired directly by the homeowners. This is a potentially bad situation. When a general contractor loses control of the project scheduling and financial authority, everyone ends up unhappy -- especially the homeowners.

➤ There shouldn't be direct communication between trade contractors and homeowners about the project or their fee. Nothing should reduce the general contractor's control over the project.

The plumber didn't know reasons for the homeowners' plumbing selection -- which was based on a tight budget. All he knew is that he'd had previous problems with the same lavatory faucets. Instead of telling the contractor and designer about his experience, he told the homeowners they'd made a bad choice and he wouldn't be responsible for callbacks if there were problems. Of course, this angered the homeowners. They called the contractor and designer immediately to verify the plumber's information. After talking with the plumber, the contractor and designer resolved the situation by supplying extra cartridges at no charge to the homeowners.

CONTRACTOR REFERENCE FEEDBACK FORM

NAME	PUNCTUALITY	BUDGET	CHANGE ORDERS	DEADLINES	COMMUNICATION	CONSTRUCTION KNOWLEDGE	PRODUCTS	PROBLEM RESOLUTION	CREW & TRADES	HIRE AGAIN?	COMMENTS

CONTRACTS, CHANGE ORDERS and LIENS

When you hire a contractor, carefully read the contract. It should contain not only what the contractor is going to do and provide and how much you're going to pay him or her, but it should also contain what work and products are **not** included in the scope of your project.

Your contractor should know about everything related to your project. S/he should have studied the design plans, gotten estimates from trade contractors, building material suppliers, and product suppliers. S/he needs to use this information to prepare a detailed proposal and contract, to achieve the best results for you.

 "Education is what you get when you read the fine print. Experience is what you get when you don't read the fine print."

Warranty information should be included in the contract -- what the contractor will repair for what length of time. The contract should also state who's responsible for final cleanup, which should be done by a professional crew. If you have asked for special terms, they should be included, i.e., installing cabinets from the kitchen in the garage, saving old lumber for firewood (although it is dangerous to store and burn if it has nails).

"A verbal contract isn't worth the paper it's written on."
(Samuel Goldwyn)

Most, if not all, states protect homeowners with a three-day cancellation clause for contracts signed in the purchaser's home; this should be included in the contractor's agreement. Everything should be clearly defined and detailed, to protect you and the contractor. Talk about contract discrepancies openly, and ask for explanations to clarify information.

The contract should contain information about the deposit (usually, the maximum is $1,000 or 10% of the value of the work, whichever is less), progress payments, and other fees such as permits, dumpster charges, etc. It's normal and reasonable to withhold approximately 10% at the end of the project, until everything is completed to your satisfaction, within reason.

One question that most homeowners ask: "Can we have a penalty clause if the contractor doesn't meet our deadline?" You can ask for one, but it's doubtful that residential contractors will agree to a penalty clause. Residential construction and remodeling isn't in the same league, financially, as commercial construction and remodeling. A one-week delay of residential construction can cost a couple hundred dollars in interest, whereas a one-week delay of commercial construction can cost several hundred thousand dollars in interest. How about this alternative answer/solution: Offer to pay the contractor a **bonus** if s/he finishes on time and on budget!

"The path of least resistance is what makes rivers run crooked." (William James)

If your contractor works on a time-and-materials basis, s/he must give you a "maximum not to exceed" total, based on experience with similar projects.

During construction, situations may arise that require a change order -- unforeseen problems (i.e., termites or hidden dry rot), or additional work you want done ("While you're here..."). There shouldn't be a lot of change orders, if the plans are fully detailed, and followed. Change orders should always be in writing, NEVER VERBAL, submitted by the contractor to you, with total(s), before the additional work is done. Don't sign anything without a full written description, date, and total amount; if you do, you might as well give the contractor a blank check!

The plans clearly showed the toilet off-center, closer to the lavatory [sink] than the adjacent wall (within code limitations), for a good reason: the bifold doors hiding the laundry equipment wouldn't open if the toilet was centered on the 3' space. The plumber got a verbal "OK" from the wife to install the toilet centered, because <u>he</u> felt it looked better -- without consideration of the bifold doors. He presented a change order for $350 to move the toilet drain. When the designer saw what had happened, she insisted that the toilet installation comply with the plans. The plumber tried to assess another change order, but the homeowners appealed to the contractor, who made the plumber credit his final bill to the homeowners by $700 for moving the toilet unnecessarily.

Laws in most states allow general contractors, trade contractors, and suppliers to place a lien on a property for uncollected payments. There are three steps to this process:

1. Preliminary Lien Notice. This document notifies the homeowners that someone has reserved the right to place a lien on their house. Receiving this notice is traumatic, especially if the invoice has been paid. Most homeowners jump to the conclusion that it is a lien on their property, which it's not.

2. Mechanics' Lien. This is the official lien on the property. Money owed to the contractor or supplier must be paid for the lien to be cleared, otherwise it places a cloud on the title, which prevents the property from being sold until the lien is cleared.

3. Release of Lien. This document is filed to clear the lien, when the financial obligation is paid.

When you receive a Preliminary Lien Notice, call your contractor immediately to verify that s/he has paid the supplier or trade contractor. Ask for a written release from the contractor, trade contractor, or supplier; you will receive a copy in the mail when this has been done. Put this document in a safe place with your mortgage and deed; it could be your only evidence to remove a cloud on your title if the information didn't get entered by the local government agency.

If you're paying the trade contractors and suppliers directly, and you receive a Preliminary Lien Notice, you should call the person immediately. Don't call your contractor, because s/he isn't involved in the transaction. If you have paid the balance and you don't receive the release form within two or three weeks, talk to the person again. There could be a problem. Don't just let it go. This is a great reason for letting the contractor have control/responsibility for the entire project.

Here's the example referred to earlier in this chapter. It applies equally to taking financial responsibility for your project, and not hiring a friend.

> Homeowners hired a friend who was a general contractor -- first mistake! When they started getting Preliminary Lien Notices from trade contractors and suppliers, they asked the general, "What gives?" He replied, "Oh, don't worry, it's a normal thing." So the homeowners let it go, until they received Mechanics' Liens. Again, they called the contractor. This time, they were really upset. As it turned out, the general contractor had been audited for mistakenly claiming employees as independent contractors, and a US Marshall was sitting in his office, collecting every cent that came in, to pay withholding taxes. Subcontractors and suppliers hadn't been paid. To get release of the liens, the homeowners ended up paying twice for products and services, then suing their ex-friend for breach of contract.

A final comment about contracts. The written proposal and the contract you receive from the contractor are not the only legal documents between you. By agreeing to work with you, your contractor also agrees to the terms and conditions of the plans. The plans for your project are as binding as the written contract, and it's your contractor's responsibility to follow the plans (unless there are oversights or mistakes -- which will be addressed in Chapter 14).

> "Money talks,
> I'll not deny.
> I heard it once,
> It said 'Good-bye.'"
> (Anonymous)

CHAPTER 12

STEP 9: THE CONSTRUCTION PROCESS

"I do not believe in failure. It is not failure if you enjoyed the process." (Oprah Winfrey)

During the design process, and definitely before construction begins, rent or buy "Mr. Blandings Builds His Dream House." It's a hilarious movie from the '40's starring Cary Grant and Myrna Loy. The original book written by Eric Hodgins is a fun read. Both are available at amazon.com.

"Advice for the whole family (based on personal experience): <u>Always</u> wear shoes in the construction area until you see the contractors' tail lights for the last time!"

It's a puzzlement how optimistic Americans are, and how hooked we've become on immediate gratification. Homeowners can be thinking and talking about their remodeling process for years, but when they finally make the decision to do it, they want it NOW -- not next month, or six months from now -- NOW!

You've read in the previous chapter that the design process for your project could take 20 weeks (or more). Your expectations are more realistic than 99% of most other homeowners, because you have reliable information -- not empty promises. Now you're going to be armed with more real information, that will increase your realistic expectations quotient.

"Achieving your goal is rarely produced by a superhuman effort. Instead it is the result of faithfully executing many small but essential tasks." (Woodrow Wilson)

Construction technically begins when your plans are approved by the local Building Department. For more details about the plan-check and permit process, see Chapters 14 and 15. The contractor should give you a critical path calendar, with each step of the construction blocked out. As construction progresses, though, the schedule may change. You should get a revised critical path calendar whenever there are changes.

There should be a pre-construction meeting with you, your contractor and designer, and all of the trade contractors (if possible). During the meeting, there should be open, honest discussion about the plans, details, and anything that's particularly important to you:

> "Don't let the cats out!"
> "Avoid walking through the flower beds, if you can."
> "Don't block the neighbors' driveway."

A Project Master Binder should be set up with pocket dividers. One person should be in charge of collecting and filing the installation instructions, warranty cards, homeowner operation manuals, etc., but it's everyone's responsibility to give the literature to that person. At the end of your project, you'll have everything you need in one place -- not scattered, or inadvertently thrown away.

This advice can't be stressed too strongly:

ORDER PRODUCTS AS SOON AS POSSIBLE!

Virtually every contractor will agree that most problems occurring during (and after) construction are associated with products -- delays, cost overruns, and bad feelings. Unfortunately, most homeowners don't make product decisions soon enough. If your project is delayed by two weeks, you may lose the contractor for several months, because of his/her commitment to another project. The following example illustrates the importance of listening to and following professional advice, and getting your products before construction.

An architect had two kitchen projects simultaneously. Homeowners #1 listened and followed the expert advice of the architect and the appliance dealer, and made their decision about a built-in refrigerator before the plans were finalized. All information was included in the plan specifications: location of the water supply and electrical outlet, and all dimensions. The contractor, cabinet maker, plumber, electrician, and carpenter knew exactly what to do.

On the other hand, Homeowners #2 didn't follow any advice. They changed their minds three times. The refrigerator was ordered AFTER the cabinets were ordered. The architect had to make "overnight" revisions for everyone. Cabinets adjacent to the refrigerator had to be re-ordered. No work happened for over two weeks, after the plumber and electrician changed location of the outlet and water supply. And there were change orders from the contractor, cabinetmaker, plumber, and electrician -- totaling about $1,000.

"Everything is funny as long as it is happening to somebody else." (Will Rogers)

THE CONSTRUCTION PROCESS DEFINED

1. Get your home ready for construction as soon as you have a definite starting date from your contractor. Most homeowners don't realize how much stuff they've accumulated until they start to pack it up.

2. If your project includes most of your home, move to an apartment or rented home. This may sound like a waste of money, but it's really an investment in your sanity, and the well-being of your relationships. Clients who balked at this recommendation initially were grateful as they saw their home evolve from solid walls and roof to see-through sticks.

"A clay pot sitting in the sun will always be a clay pot. It has to go through the white heat of the furnace to become porcelain." (Mildred Straveh)

3. Immediately before demolition begins, the dumpster arrives. You're on the Rollercoaster!

4. Demolition starts. Most homeowners are amazed how quickly a crew of workmen armed with crowbars, screwguns and hammers can tear their house apart. The full dumpster will be replaced after a couple of days with an empty dumpster.

5. After demolition, the contractor will pour new foundations required, or reinforce your existing foundation (depending on the scope of your project). This may take two weeks or more, and will include one or two inspections by a building official.

6. The framers begin installing new mud sills, studs, joists, beams, and rafters; this may take two to four weeks. There may be a separate inspection of the framing, or it may be combined with the application of sheathing.

7. If roof work is required, it will be done next, it will include framing and plywood sheathing. Plywood or oriented strand board (OSB) may be applied to exterior walls at the same time. Often, there is another inspection after this step. This step will take about three weeks.

8. Next, new windows and exterior doors will be installed. This could take only 2-3 days, if you have less than 6 new windows and exterior doors. It could take 2-3 weeks if you're having new windows and exterior doors installed for the entire house.

9. Electrical wires and plumbing pipes are installed in the walls, and the subfloor will be installed. The building official will come to inspect this work before insulation is installed.

10. Insulation is installed in ceiling, floors, and walls. There may be another inspection of the insulation installation, depending on local building codes. Steps 8 - 10 will take a month or more.

For about two or three months (or more), there have been strangers invading your home daily. It's exciting, and unnerving for everyone in your family. You may reach an emotional low during the next step, drywall installation; don't worry, it's not uncommon. It may be a year since you decided to remodel, and you're tired of the emotional rollercoaster. Warning: It may also be a low point for your contractor and his/her crew, too -- a time when tempers can flare up.

**"Chaos, panic and disorder -- my work here is done."
(Anonymous Contractor)**

11. Drywall installation for an entire house can take two weeks, but the mud application can take twice or three times as long, especially if the mud is applied by hand (not machine). After that, there's the application of drywall sealer, one or two coats of primer plus two (or three) coats of paint. It will take four to six weeks (or more) to complete this part of your project. Many homeowners decide to do their own priming and painting; there's a big tradeoff, though.

To save money, homeowners decided to do all their own painting. It took four weeks to finish, which used up all available vacation time for the couple. They had to finish quickly, so the contractor could finish the job. This added unbelievable stress to their relationship. When the contractor asked how things went, the couple admitted that the money saved wasn't worth the effort, time, and heartache.

12. At the same time, exterior wall finish, trim, and paint (or stain) may be applied, to maximize the progress. It's beginning to look like a real home.

13. You'll be excited when new cabinets are installed and interior rooms come to life. Cabinet installation can be tricky, especially if there are compound trim mouldings and angles. It can take three weeks or longer to install the cabinets.

14. Tile countertops and backsplashes can be installed immediately after the cabinets are installed. For laminate, solid-surface, or stone slab countertops, the manufacturer will come and make a template based on the cabinet layout. Lead time for the finished countertop can be one week at best, but more likely, the lead time will be approximately three weeks.

15. If the project includes a bathroom, it is during this time that tubs, shower bases, tile floors and finish wall surfaces will be installed. You can now understand contractors' reluctance to have a wood floor installed before tile setters walk on it, carrying buckets of wet concrete. There will be an inspection of a new shower pan, if it's included in your project.

16. Floor installation and finishing will take two or three weeks, depending on the number of finish applications (should be two, minimum), and weather conditions which can delay curing time at least 50%.

17. While waiting for countertops (and flooring), the contractor's crew can be installing interior doors and locksets, interior trim, light fixtures and switches. This should nicely fill the void between cabinet installation and countertop installation.

A couple had decided to live in their home during construction. Everything was put into storage, except the basics (bed, wardrobe box, microwave, coffee pot, TV, and cats' litter box). For 8 months, they lived in the 10x10 den, which was the only room not affected by construction. During the floor refinishing, when no one could walk on the floors for a week, the husband and wife crawled out of the window -- to get takeout breakfast, lunch, and dinner, and to change the litter box. It was like camping out, in jail. Not recommended for people who don't have a strong relationship, and a great sense of humor!

18. After countertops and floors are installed, appliances and finish plumbing will be installed and hooked up, and painting touch-up will be completed. If your project includes a cooktop or range which requires a new gas line, there will be a pressure test and inspection of the gas line (takeout dinner just one more night!).

19. There will be a final inspection, after everything is installed and tested. You should also inspect everything yourself, and make a written punch list with copies for everyone. You should do a walk-through with your designer and contractor to review every item on the punch list, and agree on a reasonable date for resolution of each item.

The following is quoted from the humor section of a well-known contractors' website:

PHASES OF A REMODELING PROJECT:

1. ENTHUSIASM
2. DISILLUSIONMENT
3. PANIC
4. SEARCH FOR THE GUILTY
5. PUNISHMENT OF THE INNOCENT
6. PRAISE & HONORS FOR THE NON-PARTICIPANTS

When the contractor and designer arrived for the punchlist walk-through, both of them had to control their urge to laugh out loud. The new quarter-sawn, tongue-and-groove oak floor in the entry, kitchen, and family room had over 200 "post-it" notes to designate what the homeowners thought were flaws in the wood -- natural grain patterns that were obvious only to someone crawling on the floor. Now, that's a "fine-tooth" inspection!

Construction may take about 26 weeks, but it could take a year (or more); there are so many variables involved. During that time, your project will be inspected at least eight times. Most building departments set inspections 24-48 hours in advance, and will commit to morning or afternoon inspections only (not specific times).

The contractor should be at the project to meet with the inspector, to answer questions or review what's been done. If the building department sets a morning inspection, the contractor should be there from 7:30 in the morning until the inspector arrives, which could be 11:45. The contractor has sat, waiting (patiently?) for over four hours.

94

When all of the punch list items are completed, you will sign final approval. Pay the contractor and designer the full amount owed. It's not an appropriate time to complain about poor workmanship, or delays that happened early in the process, as an excuse to withhold money. There's more about this in Chapter 16.

A SPARKLING CLEAN, HEALTHY NEW HOME

Before you move back into your "new" home, a professional cleaning crew should be hired. You should open all of the windows to completely air your home for at least a week before you move in, to allow the new materials to finish outgassing. Because new homes are built so much tighter than ever, to be energy efficient, fumes and particulate matter have no way of escaping. This can lead to the "sick building syndrome," a very serious matter.

Also, all furnace ducts should be thoroughly vacuumed, even if the contractor covered them with plastic during construction. It's amazing how much construction dust and debris can collect in the ducts -- to blow around/settle/blow around for months after you're done.

More is being written about "green" building -- using renewable resources, and resources that don't take a lot of energy to produce. As more people use environmentally-friendly products, the availability becomes better, and the price goes down. Also, keep in mind there are "green" (aka financial) incentives for thinking and building "green," in addition to the money you'll save on energy expenses.

THE CONSTRUCTION/REMODELING SEASONS

"Have realistic priorities: Never let the urgent crowd out the important." (Kelly Catlin Walker)

Most remodeling occurs during spring and summer months, when the weather is warmer and more predictable. Many projects can be partially or totally accomplished during other times of the year. It's a judgment call, and should be discussed with your designer and contractor.

Many homeowners have imposed artificial deadlines on their projects, which caused serious problems. The worst time of year to remodel is immediately before Thanksgiving and during the winter holiday season. It's better to wait until after the new year to begin a project, than add the stress of remodeling on top of an already-stressful period. Remodeling should be an enjoyable experience. It can even be fun, if kept in context with everything else.

But people continue to disregard sound, logical advice. Why? Eternal optimism. "Challenges happen to everyone else -- not us!"

> Homeowners were motivated to remodel their master and guest bathrooms before Christmas, because it was their year to entertain the family. They hired a designer in early September. The design process went smoothly, until the designer discovered that the plumbing selected wouldn't be available until mid-December at the earliest, so alternate products were selected. The homeowners hired the contractor who'd remodeled their kitchen two years previously -- but his best tile setter was fully booked until February. All things considered, the project went smoothly, EXCEPT the homeowners hadn't factored the amount of time it would take to decorate the house. Several boxes of ornaments got mixed up with product boxes, and almost thrown in the dumpster. Last-minute decorating, baking, cleaning AND remodeling erased the enjoyment of the season and the remodeling process. By the time the family members arrived, the homeowners just wanted to pack up and go to Hawaii for a quiet vacation!

Another bad time to target completion of a remodeling project is for a major event, i.e., birthday, anniversary, wedding, or family reunion. If you're planning one of these events in less than a year, and want your home remodeling completed before, stop and ask yourself some questions. "What if ..."

"...there's a fire at the cabinet plant, or the cabinet manufacturer quits before our order is complete?"

"...there's a transportation strike?"

"...our order gets sent to 'never-never land,' lost in transit?"

"...the contractor (or designer) has a family emergency and has to be out of town for over a month?"

"...our new (#1 priority item) is discontinued without warning?"

"...the manufacturer delivers the wrong item?"

"...there's a major downturn in the economy and we lose most of the money we're counting on to fund our remodeling?"

Okay. You've got the picture. All of these are true examples that have happened to other homeowners. The point is, you should be in control of your project, and enjoy it. Remodeling is a PART of your life -- NOT your life. If you demand to finish your remodeling project for an imposed deadline, plan ahead for alternatives, if your project doesn't get completed when you want.

CHAPTER 13

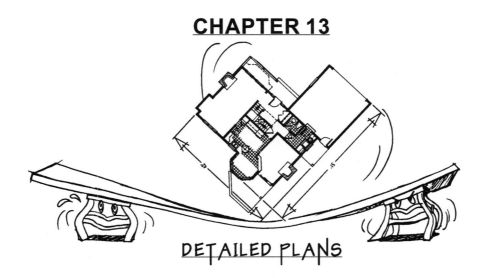

DETAILED PLANS

In Chapters 4 and 5, detailed plans were mentioned. In this chapter, plans will be discussed and defined, so you have an understanding why they're so important to the success of your project.

If you were traveling to a new area, how would you find your destination? You'd refer to a map, or get on-line directions. Detailed plans are the map that everyone uses to define your destination and the exact route. Everyone should be traveling on the same road, even when there are tight curves and unmarked intersections.

> **"Striving for excellence motivates you; striving for perfection is demoralizing." (Harriet Braiker)**

Plans are always drafted to scale. Most whole-house projects are drafted in quarter-inch scale (1/4" = 1'-0"). Bathrooms and kitchens, which have minute details, are drafted in half-inch scale (1/2" = 1'-0"). Structural framing details and other details are drafted in three-quarter-inch scale (3/4" = 1'-0") to one-and-one-half-inch scale (1-1/2" = 1'-0").

It's very important for you to learn how to read and understand basic plans. It's not difficult -- just takes some practice. Knowing how to read plans will make you capable of talking with your designer and contractor about the details that will create your new home. It will protect you from nasty surprises during construction.

Designers aren't mind-readers. If you make an effort to study your plans, you will have a better chance to achieve what you want. Don't be shy about asking questions about your plans, and giving feedback to your designer; s/he NEEDS this input!

Homeowners were adding a family room onto their three-story house. The kitchen and proposed family room were located on the middle level. To achieve the large opening required between the kitchen and family room, the structural engineer designated a beam to carry the load of the third floor. The wife was very upset when she discovered that the beam created a shelf she didn't like. She hadn't taken the time to familiarize herself with plans, or ask questions ("What's this line?" "What's this above my peninsula?").

Today, technology can help communicate and translate plans and details into 3-D. Many CAD programs allow designers to show the proposed area in perspective, like a photograph, from any angle. Your designer should be able to sketch quick perspectives, also, to help you visualize areas and/or details that aren't clear to you. It's really okay to admit you don't understand; that's why you're paying a designer.

Detailed plans should contain the following information:

>
> Your name, address and phone number on every sheet
> Your designer's name, address and phone number on every sheet
> Page index
> List of abbreviations and terms
> Energy calculations
> Area map
> Existing plot plan
> Proposed plot plan (showing grading, if it's included)
> Existing house plan
> Proposed house plan
> Exterior elevations
> Proposed kitchen plan and elevations
> Proposed bathroom plan(s) and elevations
> Proposed electrical/lighting plan
> Miscellaneous details (i.e., cabinetry, moulding, etc.
> Structural details
> Product schedules/specifications

Appliances	Cabinets
Doors/Windows	Electrical
Lighting	Plumbing

The schedules/specifications will also include valuable information about surface finishes: Ceiling, walls, trim and moulding, countertops and backsplash, and flooring.

"There is nothing in a caterpillar that tells you it's going to be a butterfly." (Buckminster Fuller)

HINTS

Whenever you get a revised set of plans, mark through the title block of the old plans with a bold red pen.

Don't leave old sets of plans in a place where a trade contractor could use them accidentally.

Homeowners who didn't follow this advice got into a dispute with their electrician, who used the wrong plans to place the junction box for the pendant fixture over the table. It was supposed to be centered, but ended up one foot off-center. The homeowners paid for a change order to have the electrician move the junction box and fixture, because of their neglect.

Plans are **NOT** meant as guidelines. They are legal documents, meant to be followed by everyone working on your project. If there's a problem with the plans, your contractor should resolve it directly with the design professional, to get the best results for you with no hassles.

Problems often arise when cabinet manufacturers and contractors don't read and study the plans, elevations, details, and specifications to understand the scope of your project. This is why it was strongly recommended in Chapters 5 and 6 to have at least one in-depth pre-construction meeting between the designer, general contractor, lead carpenter, project supevisor, cabinet supplier, electrician, and plumber.

The designer worked with the homeowners for weeks, helping them select field tile and decorative tile for their kitchen backsplash, then she spent days preparing detailed elevations, showing the tile in relationship to cabinets, windows, and electrical junction boxes. Centerline of the junction boxes was shown as 40-1/4" A.F.F. (above finish floor), and off-center from the cabinets, which allowed room for the decorative inserts to be midway in the backsplash, centered on the cabinets. Everything was dimensioned. If the plans lacked this detail, and if there hadn't been a pre-construction meeting, chances are the junction boxes would have been installed at the typical 48" height and random 24" distance. The contractor knew to call the designer to approve the framing and rough electrical before he called for an inspection. There were no surprises for anyone, and the homeowners were delighted with the results.

CODES

Soon, building departments will begin applying the new International Codes to projects. Until then, the accepted standards are the Uniform Building Code, the Uniform Plumbing Code, the Uniform Mechanical Code, and the Uniform Electrical Code. It's **VERY** important for whoever draws your plans to be familiar with the codes, so the appropriate information can be included in your plans. It's **VERY** important for whoever works on your home to know and follow the codes, so you have a safe home. Building Codes should not be taken lightly. They are laws, enforced by the building officials. They are every bit as important to home building and remodeling as speed laws are to safe driving.

"When I entered the design profession, codes were overwhelming; now there are three times as many codes! They're getting more complex and comprehensive as time passes."

NKBA RECOMMENDED GUIDELINES FOR KITCHEN PLANNING

You know that the most important room in your home is your kitchen. It is the center of daily activities, and the logical gathering place, especially at parties (when many people just want to be left alone in the kitchen!). The following guidelines are included to help you understand what certified kitchen designers use as a basis for the best function and safety in the kitchens they create.

Guideline K1:
A. Doorways should be at least 32" wide and not more than 24" deep in the direction of travel.
B. Walkways (passages between vertical objects greater than 24" deep in the direction of travel, where not more than one is a work counter or appliance) should be at least 36" wide.
C. Work aisles (passages between vertical objects, both of which are work counters or appliances) should be at least 42" wide in one-cook kitchens, at least 48" wide in multiple-cook kitchens.

Guideline K2:
The work triangle should total 26' or less, with no single leg of the triangle shorter than 4' nor longer than 9'. The work triangle should not intersect an island or peninsula by more than 12". (The triangle is the shortest walking distance between the refrigerator, primary cooking surface and primary food preparation sink, measured from the center front of each appliance.)

Guideline K3:
No major traffic patterns should cross through the work triangle.

Guideline K4:
No entry, appliance or cabinet doors should interfere with one another.

Guideline K5:
In a seating area, 36" of clearance should be allowed from the counter/table edge to any wall/ obstruction behind it if no traffic will pass behind a seated diner. If there is a walkway behind the seating area, 65" of clearance, total, including the walkway, should be allowed between the seating area and any wall or obstruction.

Guideline K6:
Wall Cabinet Frontage:
Small Kitchens - under 150 sq. ft. -- allow at least 144" of wall cabinet frontage, with cabinets at least 12" deep, and a minimum of 30" high (or equivalent) which feature adjustable shelving. Difficult to reach cabinets above the hood, oven, or refrigerator do not count unless devices are installed within the case to improve accessibility.

Large Kitchens - over 150 sq. ft. - allow at least 186" of wall cabinet frontage, with cabinets at least 12" deep, and a minimum of 30" high (or equivalent) which feature adjustable shelving. Difficult to reach cabinets above the hood, oven, or refrigerator do not count unless devices are installed within the case to improve accessibility.

Guideline K7:
At least 60" of wall cabinet frontage, with cabinets at least 12" deep, a minimum of 30" high (or equivalent), should be included within 72" of the primary sink centerline.

Guideline K8:
Base Cabinet Frontage:
Small Kitchens -under 150 sq ft. - allow at least 156" of base cabinet frontage, with cabinets at least 21" deep (or equivalent). The blind portion of a blind corner box does not count.

Large Kitchens - over 150 sq ft. require at least 192" of base cabinet frontage with cabinets at last 21" deep (or equivalent). The blind portion of a blind corner box does not count.

Guideline K9:
Drawer/Roll-out Shelf Frontage
Small Kitchens -under 150 sq. ft. - allow at least 120" of drawer or roll-out shelf frontage.

Large Kitchens - over 150 sq. ft. - allow at least 165" of drawer or roll-out shelf frontage.

Multiply cabinet width by number of drawers/roll-outs to determine frontage. Drawer/roll-out cabinets must be at least 15" wide and 21" deep to be counted.

Guideline K10:
At least five storage/organizing items, located between 15"-48" above the finished floor (or extending into that area), should be included in the kitchen to improve functionality and accessibility. These items may include, but are not limited to: lowered wall cabinets, raised base cabinets, tall cabinets, appliance garages, bins/racks, swing-out pantries, interior vertical dividers, specialize drawers/ shelves, etc. Full-extension drawers/roll-out shelves greater than 120" minimum for small kitchens or 165" for larger kitchens, may also be included.

Guideline K11:
For a kitchen with usable corner areas in the plan, at least one functional corner storage unit should be included.

Guideline K12:

The top edge of a waste receptacle should be no higher than 36". The receptacle should be easily accessible and should be removable without raising the receptacle bottom higher than the unit's physical height. Lateral removal of receptacle which does not require lifting is most desirable.

Guideline K13:

Knee space (which may be open or adaptable) should be planned below or adjacent to sinks, cooktops, ranges, and ovens whenever possible. Knee space should be a minimum of 27" high by 30" wide by 19" deep under the counter. The 27" height may decrease progressively as depth increases.

Guideline K14:

A clear floor space of 30" x 48" should be provided at the sink, dishwasher, cooktop, oven, and refrigerator. (Measure from face of cabinet or appliance, if toe kick is less than 9" high.)

Guideline K15:

A minimum of 21" clear floor space should be allowed between the edge of the dishwasher and counters, appliances and/or cabinets which are placed at a right angle to the dishwasher.

Guideline K16:

The edge of the primary dishwasher should be within 36" of the edge of one sink.

Guideline K17:

If the kitchen has only one sink, it should be located between or across from the cooking surface, preparation area, or refrigerator.

Guideline K18:

There should be at least 24" of clearance between the cooking surface and a protected surface above, or at least 30" of clearance between the cooking surface and an unprotected surface above. (If the protected surface is a microwave-hood combination, manufacturer's specifications may dictate a smaller clearance.)

Guideline K19:

All major appliances used for surface cooking should have a ventilation system, with a fan rated at 150 cfm minimum.

Guideline K20:

The cooking surface should not be placed below an operable window unless the window is 3" or more behind the appliance and more than 24" above it. Windows, operable or inoperable, above a cooking surface should not be dressed with flammable window treatments.

Guideline K21:

Microwave ovens should be placed so that the bottom of the appliance is 24" to 48" above the floor.

Guideline K22:

At least two work-counter heights should be offered in the kitchen, with one 28"-36" above the finish floor and the other 36"-45" above the finish floor.

Guideline K23:

Countertop Frontage:
Small Kitchens - under 150 sq. ft. - allow at least 132" of usable countertop frontage.

102

Large Kitchens - over 150 sq. ft. - allow at least 198" of usable countertop frontage.

Counters must be a minimum of 16" deep, and wall cabinets must be at least 15" above their surface for counter to be included in total frontage measurement. (Measure only countertop frontage, do not count corner space.)

Guideline K24:
There should be at least 24" of countertop frontage to one side of the primary sink, and 18" on the other side (including corner sink applications), with the 24" counter frontage at the same counter height as the sink. The countertop frontage may be a continuous surface, or the total of two angled countertop sections. (Measure only countertop frontage, do not count corner space.) For further instruction on these requirements, see Guideline 31.

Guideline K25:
At least 3" of countertop frontage should be provided on one side of secondary sinks, and 18" on the other side (including corner sink applications), with the 18" counter frontage at the same counter height as the sink. The countertop frontage may be a continuous surface, or the total of two angled countertop sections. (Measure only countertop frontage, do not count corner space.) For further instruction on these requirements, see Guideline 31.

Guideline K26:
At least 15" of landing space, a minimum of 16" deep, should be planned above, below, or adjacent to a microwave oven. For further instruction on these requirements, see Guideline 31.

Guideline K27:
In an open-ended kitchen configuration, at least 9" of counter space should be allowed on one side of the cooking surface and 15" on the other, at the same counter height as the appliance. For an enclosed configuration, at least 3" of clearance space should be planned at an end wall protected by flame retardant surfacing material and 15" should be allowed on the other side of the appliance, at the same counter height as the appliance. For further instruction on these requirements see Guideline 31.

Guideline K28:
The plan should allow at least 15" of counter space on the latch side of the refrigerator or on either side of a side-by-side refrigerator, at least 16" of landing space which is no more than 48" across from the refrigerator. (Measure the 48" distance from the center front of the refrigerator to the countertop opposite it.) For further instruction on these requirements see Guideline 31.

Guideline K29:
There should be at least 15" of landing space which is at least 16" deep next to or above the oven if the appliance door opens into a primary traffic pattern. At least 15" x 16" of landing space which is no more than 48" across from the oven is acceptable if the appliance does not open into a traffic area. (Measure the 48" distance from the center front of the oven to the countertop opposite it.) For further instruction on these requirements, see Guideline 31.

Guideline K30:
At least 36" of continuous countertop which is at least 16" deep should be planned for preparation center. The preparation center should be immediately adjacent to a water source. For further instruction on these requirements, see Guideline 31.

Guideline K31:

If two work centers are adjacent to one another, determine a new minimum counter frontage requirement for the two adjoining spaces by taking the longest of the two required counter lengths and adding 12".

Guideline K32:

No two primary work centers (the primary sink, refrigerator, preparation or cooktop/range center) should be separated by a full-height, full-depth tall tower, such as an oven cabinet, pantry cabinet or refrigerator.

Guideline K33:

Kitchen seating areas require the following minimum clearances:

30" high tables/counters--allow a 30" wide by 19" counter/table space for each seated diner, and at least 19" of clear knee space.

36" high counters--allow a 24" wide by 15" deep counter space for each seated diner, and at least 15" of clear knee space.

42" high counters--allow a 24" wide by 12" deep counter space for each seated diner, and 12" of clear knee space.

Guideline K34:

(Open) countertop corners should be clipped or radiused; counter edges should be eased to eliminate sharp corners.

Guideline K35:

Controls, handles and door/drawer pulls should be operable with one hand, require only a minimal amount of strength for operation, and should not require tight grasping, pinching or twisting of the wrist. (Includes handles/knobs/pulls on entry and exit doors, appliances, cabinets, drawers and plumbing fixtures, as well as light and thermostat controls/switches, intercoms and other room controls.)

Guideline K36:

Wall-mounted room controls (i.e.: wall receptacles, switches, thermostats, telephones, intercoms, etc.) should be 15" to 48" above the finish floor. The switch plate can extend beyond that dimension, but the control itself should be within it.

Guideline K37:

Ground fault circuit interrupters should be specified on all receptacles within the kitchen.

Guideline K38:

A fire extinguisher should be visibly located in the kitchen, away from cooking equipment and 15" - 48" above the floor. Smoke alarms should be included near the kitchen.

Guideline K39:

Window/skylight area should equal at least 10 percent of the total square footage of the separate kitchen, or a total living space which includes a kitchen.

Guideline K40:

Every work surface in the kitchen should be well-illuminated by appropriate task and/or general lighting.

NKBA RECOMMENDED GUIDELINES
FOR
BATHROOM PLANNING

Bathrooms are also important rooms -- especially an updated master bathroom. The return on investment for a bathroom addition can exceed 75%. Following are the 41 guidelines that certified bathroom designers use:

Guideline B1
A. The clear space at doorways should be at least 32" (81 cm) wide and not more than 24" (81 cm) deep in the direction of travel.

B. The clear space at a doorway must be measured at the narrowest point.

C. Walkways (passages between vertical objects greater than 24" (61 cm) deep in the direction of travel), should be a minimum of 36" (91cm) wide.

Guideline B2
A clear floor space at least the width of the door on the push side and a larger clear floor space on the pull side should be planned at doors for maneuvering to open, close, and pass through the doorway. The exact amount needed will depend on the type of door and the approach.

Guideline B3
A minimum clear floor space of 30" x 48" (76 cm x 122 cm) either parallel or perpendicular should be provided at the lavatory [bathroom sink].

Guideline B4
A. A minimum clear floor space of 48" x 48" (122 cm x 122cm) should be provided in front of the toilet. A minimum of 16" (41cm) of that clear floor space must extend to each side of the centerline of the fixture.

B. Up to 12" (30 cm) of the 48" x 48" (122 cm x 122 cm) clear floor space can extend under the lavatory when total access to a knee space is provided.

Guideline B5
A minimum clear floor space of 48" x 48" (122 cm x 122 cm) from the front of the bidet should be provided.

Guideline B6
A. The minimum clear floor space at a bathtub is 60" (152 cm) wide by 30" (76 cm) deep for a parallel approach, even with the length of the tub.

B. The minimum clear floor space at a bath tub is 60" (152 cm) wide x 48" (122 cm) deep for a perpendicular approach.

Guideline B7
The minimum clear floor space at showers less than 60" (152 cm) wide should be 36" (91cm) deep by the width of the shower plus 12 (30 cm). The 12" (30 cm) should extend beyond the seat wall. At a shower that is 60" (152 cm) wide or greater, clear floor space should be 36" (91 cm) deep by the width of the shower.

Guideline B8
Clear floor spaces required at each fixture may overlap.

Guideline B9
Space for turning (mobility aids) 180° should be planned in the bathroom. A minimum diameter of 60" (152 cm) for 360° turns and/or a minimum turn space of 36" (91 cm) x 36" (91 cm) x 60" (152 cm).

Guideline B10
A minimum clear floor space of 30" x 48" (76 cm-122 cm) is required beyond the door swing in a bathroom.

Guideline B11
When more than one vanity is included, one may be 30"-34" (76 cm-86 cm) high and another at 34"-42" (86 cm-107 cm) high. Vanity height should fit the user(s).

Guideline B12
Knee space (which may be open or adaptable) should be provided at a lavatory. The knee space should be a minimum of 27" (69 cm) above the floor at the front edge, decreasing progressively as the depth increases, and the recommended width is a minimum of 30" (76 cm) wide.

Guideline B13
The bottom edge of the mirror over the lavatory should be a maximum of 40" (102 cm) above the floor or a maximum of 48" (122 cm) above the floor if it is tilted.

Guideline B14
The minimum clearance from the centerline of the lavatory to any side wall is 15" (38 cm).

Guideline B15
The minimum clearance between two bowls in the lavatory center is 30" (76 cm), centerline to centerline.

Guideline B16
In an enclosed shower, the minimum usable interior dimensions are 34" (86 cm) x 34" (86 cm). These dimensions are measured from wall to wall. Grab bars, controls, movable and folding seats do not diminish the measurement.

Guideline B17
Showers should include a bench or seat that is 17"-19" (43 cm-48 cm) above the floor and a minimum of 15" (38 cm) deep.

Guideline B18
The width of the door opening must take into consideration the interior space in the shower for entry and maneuvering. When the shower is 60" (152 cm) deep, a person can enter straight into the shower and turn after entry, therefore 32" (81 cm) is adequate. If the shower is 42" (107 cm) deep, the entry must be increased to 36" (91 cm) in order to allow for turning space.

Guideline B19
Shower doors must open into the bathroom.

Guideline B20
Steps should not be planned at the tub or shower area. Safety rails should be installed to facilitate transfer to and from the fixture.

Guideline B21
All showerheads should be equipped with pressure balance/temperature regulator or temperature limiting device.

Guideline B22
A. Shower controls should be accessible from inside and outside the fixture. Shower controls should be located between 38" - 48" (96 cm - 122 cm) above the floor (placed above the grab bar) and offset toward the room.

B. Tub controls should be accessible from inside and outside the fixture. Controls should be located between the rim of the tub and 33" (84 cm) above the floor, placed below the grab bar and offset toward the room.

Guideline B23
A. A minimum 16" (41 cm) clearance should be allowed from the centerline of the toilet or bidet to any obstruction, fixture or equipment (except grab bars) on either side.

B. When the toilet and bidet are planned adjacent to one another, the 16" minimum (41 cm) centerline clearance to all obstructions should be maintained.

Guideline B24
The toilet paper holder should be installed within reach of a person seated on the toilet. Ideal location is slightly in front of the edge of the toilet bowl, centered at 26" (66 cm) above the floor.

Guideline B25
Compartmental toilet areas should be a minimum 36" (91 cm) x 66" (168 cm) with a swing-out door or a pocket door.

Guideline B26
A. Walls should be prepared (reinforced) to receive grab bars at the time of construction. Grab bars should also be installed in the bath tub, shower and toilet areas at the time of construction.

B. Alternatives for grab bars in the toilet area include, but are not limited to, side grab bars attached below the toilet seat, a rail system mounted to the back wall with perpendicular support arms at sides of the toilet seat, an electronic seat elevator or hand rails suspended from the ceiling.

Guideline B27
Storage for toiletries, linens, grooming and general bathroom supplies should be provided within 15" - 48" (38 cm-122 cm) above the floor.

Guideline B28
Storage for soap, towels and other personal hygiene items should be installed within reach of a person seated on the bidet or toilet and within 15" - 48" (38 cm-122 cm) above the floor. Storage areas should not interfere with the use of the fixture.

Guideline B29
In the tub/shower area, storage for soap and other personal hygiene items should be provided within the 15"- 48" (38 cm-122 cm) above the floor within the universal reach range.

Guideline B30
All flooring should be slip resistant.

Guideline B31
Exposed pipes and mechanicals should be covered by a protective panel or shroud. When using a console table, care must be given to keep plumbing attractive and out of contact with a seated user.

Guideline B32
Controls, dispensers, outlets and operating mechanisms should be 15" - 48" (38 cm-122 cm) above the floor and should be operable with a closed fist.

Guideline B33
All mechanical, electrical and plumbing systems should have access panels.

Guideline B34
Mechanical ventilation systems to the outside should be included in the plan to vent the entire room. The minimum size of the system can be calculated as follows:

$$\frac{\text{Cubic Space (LxWxH) x 8*}}{60 \text{ minutes}} = \text{minimum cubic feet per minute (CFM)}$$

(*changes of air per hour)

Guideline B35
Ground fault circuit interrupters must be specified on all receptacles, lights and switches in the bathroom. All light fixtures above the bathtub / shower units must be moisture-proof special-purpose fixtures.

Guideline B36
In addition to a primary heat source, auxiliary heating may be planned in the bathroom.

Guideline B37
Every functional area in the bathroom should be well illuminated by appropriate task lighting, night lights and/or general lighting. No lighting fixture, including hanging fixtures, should be within reach of a person seated or standing in the tub/shower area.

Guideline B38
When possible, bathroom lighting should include a window / skylight area equal to a minimum of 10 percent of the square footage of the bathroom.

Guideline B39
Controls, handles and door/drawer pulls should be operable with one hand, require only a minimal amount of strength for operation, and should not require tight grasping, pinching or twisting of the wrist. (Includes handles knobs/pulls on entry and exit doors, cabinets, drawers and plumbing fixtures, as well as light and thermostat controls/switches, intercoms, and other room controls.)

Guideline B40

Use clipped or radius corners for open countertops; countertop edges should be eased to eliminate sharp edges.

Guideline B41

Any glass used as a tub / shower enclosure, partition, or other glass application within 18" (46 cm) of the floor should be one of three kinds of safety glazing; laminated glass with a plastic interlayer, tempered glass or approved plastics such as those found in the model safety glazing code.

On the following pages, you will see reduced samples of a set of plans, with full-scale details.

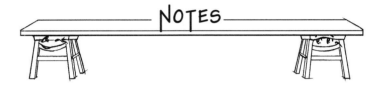
NOTES

"Form Follows Function -- that has been misunderstood. Form and Function should be one, joined in a spiritual union." (Frank Lloyd Wright)

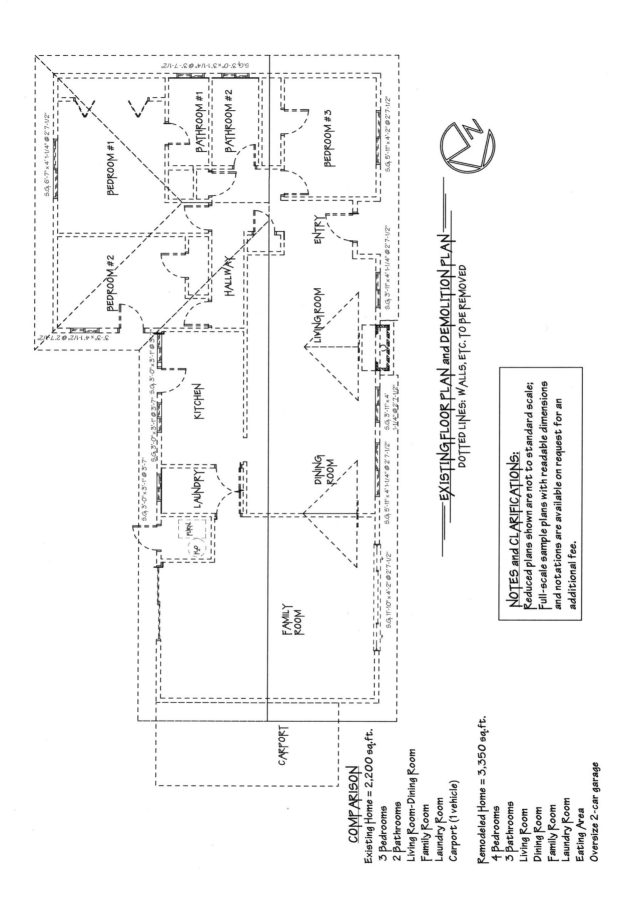

EXISTING FLOOR PLAN and DEMOLITION PLAN
DOTTED LINES: WALLS, ETC. TO BE REMOVED

BEDROOM #1

BEDROOM #2

BATHROOM #1

BATHROOM #2

BEDROOM #3

HALLWAY

ENTRY

LIVING ROOM

KITCHEN

LAUNDRY

FURN.

H2

DINING ROOM

FAMILY ROOM

CARPORT

S.G. 6'-7" x 4'-1-1/4" @ 2'-7-1/2"

S.G. 3'-0" x 3'-1/4" @ 3'-7-1/2"

3'-3" x 4'-1-1/2" @ 2'-7-1/2"

S.G. 3'-0" x 3'-1" @ 3'-7"

S.G. 3'-0" x 3'-1" @ 3'-7"

S.G. 5'-11" x 4'-2" @ 2'-7-1/2"

S.G. 3'-11" x 4'-1-1/4" @ 2'-7-1/2"

S.G. 5'-11" x 4'-1-1/4" @ 2'-7-1/2"

S.G. 3'-11" x 4'-1-1/4" @ 2'-7-1/2"

S.G. 11'-10" x 4'-2" @ 2'-7-1/2"

NOTES and CLARIFICATIONS:
Reduced plans shown are not to standard scale;
Full-scale sample plans with readable dimensions
and notations are available on request for an
additional fee.

COMPARISON
Existing Home = 2,200 sq.ft.
3 Bedrooms
2 Bathrooms
Living Room-Dining Room
Family Room
Laundry Room
Carport (1 vehicle)

Remodeled Home = 3,350 sq.ft.
4 Bedrooms
3 Bathrooms
Living Room
Dining Room
Family Room
Laundry Room
Eating Area
Oversize 2-car garage

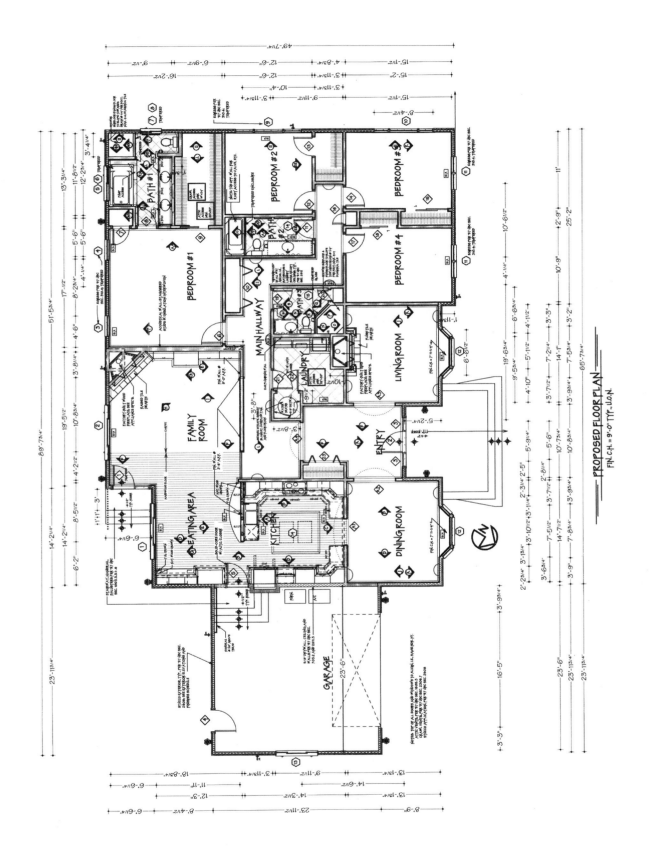

PROPOSED FLOOR PLAN
FIN. C.H. = 9'-0" TYP. U.O.N.

GARAGE

KITCHEN

DINING ROOM

ENTRY

LIVING ROOM

LAUNDRY

MAIN HALLWAY

FAMILY ROOM

EATING AREA

BEDROOM #1

BATH #1

BATH #2

BATH #3

BEDROOM #2

BEDROOM #3

BEDROOM #4

111

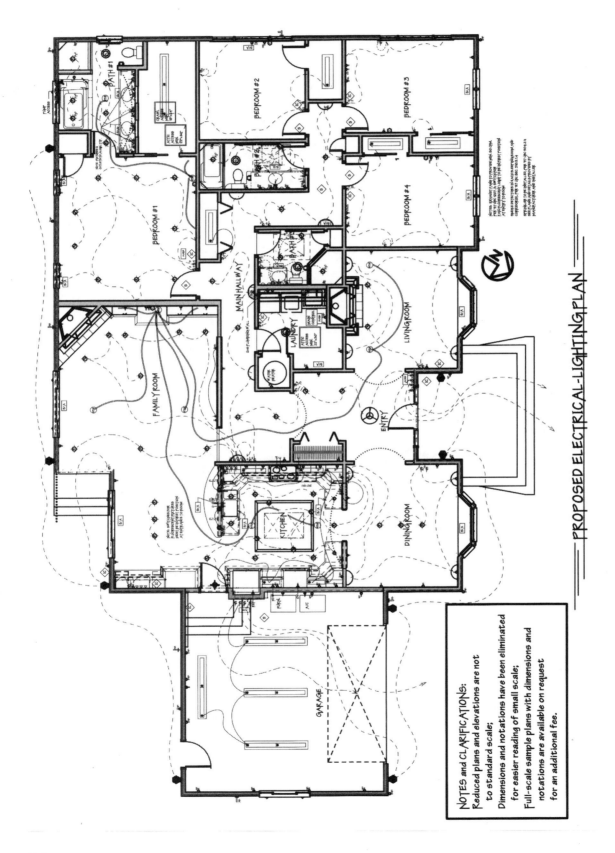

— PROPOSED ELECTRICAL-LIGHTING PLAN —

NOTES and CLARIFICATIONS:
Reduced plans and elevations are not
to standard scale;
Dimensions and notations have been eliminated
for easier reading of small scale;
Full-scale sample plans with dimensions and
notations are available on request
for an additional fee.

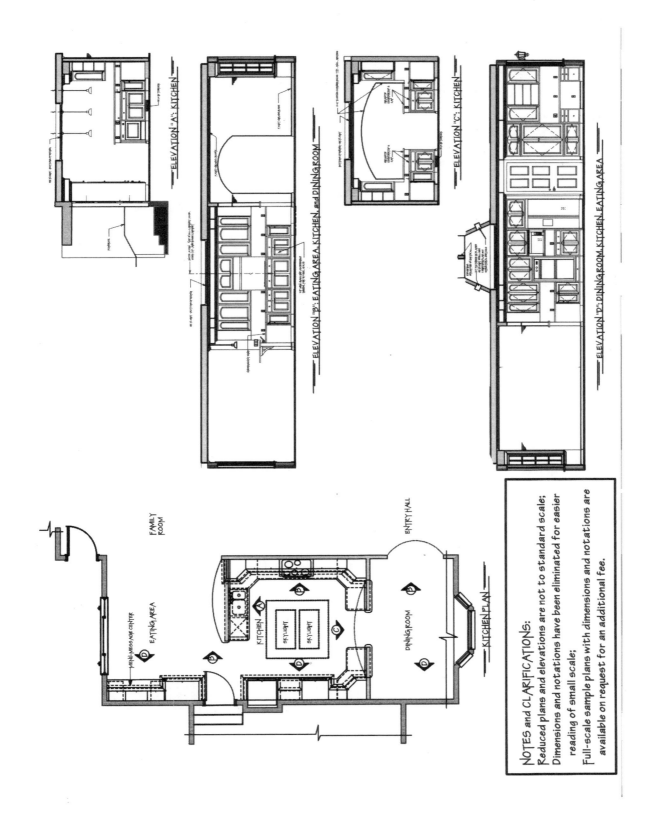

ELEVATION "A": KITCHEN

ELEVATION "B": EATING AREA, KITCHEN, and DINING ROOM

ELEVATION "C": KITCHEN

ELEVATION "D": DINING ROOM, KITCHEN, EATING AREA

FAMILY ROOM

EATING AREA

MENU-MESSAGE CENTER

KITCHEN

SKYLIGHT

SKYLIGHT

DINING ROOM

ENTRY HALL

KITCHEN PLAN

NOTES and CLARIFICATIONS:
Reduced plans and elevations are not to standard scale;
Dimensions and notations have been eliminated for easier
reading of small scale;
Full-scale sample plans with dimensions and notations are
available on request for an additional fee.

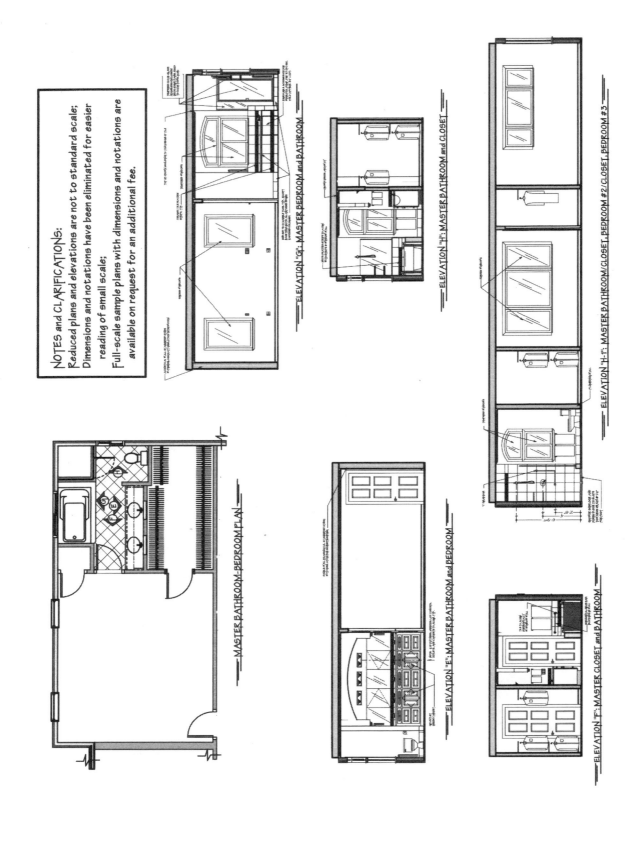

NOTES and CLARIFICATIONS:
Reduced plans and elevations are not to standard scale;
Dimensions and notations have been eliminated for easier
reading of small scale;
Full-scale sample plans with dimensions and notations are
available on request for an additional fee.

MASTER BATHROOM-BEDROOM PLAN

ELEVATION "G": MASTER BEDROOM and BATHROOM

ELEVATION "H": MASTER BATHROOM and CLOSET

ELEVATION "I-I": MASTER BATHROOM/CLOSET, BEDROOM #2/CLOSET, BEDROOM #3

ELEVATION "E": MASTER BATHROOM and BEDROOM

ELEVATION "F": MASTER CLOSET and BATHROOM

114

SAMPLE SPECIFICATIONS

LIGHTING SPECIFICATIONS

SYMBOL	DESCRIPTION	PROP.	INSTALL.
[under-cabinet]	UNDER-CABINET FLUORESCENT FIXTURES, GENERAL AND TASK LIGHTING. ( ) ALKCO 12" ( ) ALKCO 21" ( ) ALKCO 24"	H	C
[R]	RECESSED INCANDESCENT FIXTURES, MOOD AND TASK LIGHTING - KITCHEN: ( ) HALO H7-ICT/429 PAR30-75W BATHROOMS: ( ) HALO H7-ICT/429 PAR30-75W OTHER ROOMS: ( ) HALO ____	H	C
[R]	RECESSED INCANDESCENT "EYEBALL" FIXT.- ( ) HALO ____	H	C
[R H₂O]	RECESSED INCANDESCENT FIXTURES, APPROVED FOR WET LOCATIONS - BATHROOMS: ( ) HALO H7-ICT/ 60W A19	H	C
[FL]	( ) PANASONIC, BROAN, OR NUTONE FAN-FLUORESCENT LIGHT, MIN. 150 CFM. MAX 1.5 SONES. NOTE: MEETS REQUIREMENTS FOR GENERAL LIGHTING IN BATHROOMS & LAUNDRY ROOMS	H	C
[+]	( ) SURFACE-MOUNT BATHROOM FIXTURES, T.P.S. NOTE: USE STANDARD RECTANGULAR J-BOX, NOT ROUND OR OCTAGON J-BOX - MAX. 2.5"W x 4.5"H	H	C
[D]	( ) SURFACE-MOUNT WALL SCONCE, T.P.S. @ 5'-9" A.F.F.	H	C
[sconce]	( ) SURFACE-MOUNT EXTERIOR SCONCE, T.P.S., HT, T.P.S.- ON TIMER AND/OR MOTION SENSOR, IF POSS.	H	C
[safety light]	( ) SURFACE-MOUNT EXTERIOR MOTION-SENSOR SAFETY LIGHT, AT SIDES OF HOUSE. T.P.S., HT, T.P.S.	H	C

ELECTRICAL SPECIFICATIONS

SYMBOL	DESCRIPTION	PROP.	INSTALL.
[S diamond]	Smoke detectors in every bedroom, and hallways, per '97 UPC Sec. 310.9 (Make/Model T.P.S.)	C	C
[GFI]	GFI convenience outlets - Kitchen: ( ) Lutron "Lumea" or equiv. in backsplash; color T.P.S. NOTE: If standard splash = 4", outlets so to be higher than full-height splash	C	C
[GFI]	GFI convenience outlets - Bathrooms: ( ) Lutron "Lumea" or equiv. in backsplash, aligned with fixtures, color T.P.S. ( ) "Standard" GFI outlets @ 15" A.F.F., inside cabinets	H	C
[outlet]	Dedicated 110V outlets for built-in appliances: Dishwashers (D/W); Disposals (D); CookTop igniter (C); Hood (H);Refrigerator (Ref) -- "standard" (Not Lutron)	C	C
[DED]	( ) Dedicated 110V outlets for computers; Lutron "Lumea" or equiv.	H	C
[outlet]	( ) Dedicated 220V outlets for built-in appliances	C	C
[outlet]	( ) Half-hot outlets controlled by switches; Lutron "Lumea" or equiv.	H	C
[triangle]	( ) Lutron "Lumea" or equiv. telephone jacks; color T.P.S.	H	C
[diamond]	( ) Cable TV and/or Internet J-box/trim; Lutron "Lumea" or equiv., color T.P.S.	H	C
(SPKR)	WIRING FOR SPEAKERS IN FAMILY ROOM, KITCHEN, LIVING ROOM, AND MASTER BEDROOM/BATHROOM; SPEAKERS TO BE FREE-STANDING (PROVIDED BY HOMEOWNERS), OR BUILT INTO CEILING. T.P.S.	C	C
ALARM	ALARM SYSTEM. T.P.S. SWITCHING PANEL TO BE IN NON-OBVIOUS LOCATION. CONTROL PANELS TO BE AT BACK DOOR INSIDE GARAGE, BY FRONT DOOR, AND IN MASTER BEDROOM. SYSTEM TO BE CONNECTED TO SMOKE DETECTORS	C	C

SWITCHING SPECIFICATIONS

SYMBOL	DESCRIPTION	PROP.	INSTALL.
S	( ) Single-pole switch: Lutron "Lumea", or equiv., color T.P.S.;	H	C
S	( ) Single-pole triple switch to control fan-light fixture in bathrooms; first/top position	H	C
S_3	( ) Two-way switch: Lutron "Lumea", or equiv., color(s) T.P.S.	H	C
S_D	( ) Single-pole dimmer switch - Kitchen: Lutron "Lumea", or equiv., color(s) T.P.S.	H	C
S_D	( ) Single-pole dimmer switch - Bathrooms: Lutron "Lumea", or equiv., color(s) T.P.S.	H	C
S_{D3}	( ) Two-way dimmer switch: Lutron "Lumea", or equiv., color(s) T.P.S.	H	C
S	( ) Single-pole switch: Lutron "Lumea", or equiv., color T.P.S.	H	C
S_3	( ) Two-way switch: Lutron "Lumea", or equiv., color(s) T.P.S.	H	C
S_D	( ) Single-pole dimmer switch: Lutron "Lumea", or equiv., color(s) T.P.S.	H	C
S_{D3}	( ) Two-way dimmer switch: Lutron "Lumea", or equiv., color(s) T.P.S.	H	C

CABINET SPECIFICATIONS

ROOM: Kitchen/Family Room

NOTE: Cabinet maker/distributor is responsible for notifying project designer if there are any special limitations or requirements, or if particular cabinets/accessories are not available. Cabinet maker/distributor is responsible for taking double-check/verification measurements before the cabinets are ordered/manufactured. If estimate accepted/approved by Homeowners, written order must be supplied, containing all appropriate codes and pricing. NO DEVIATIONS FROM DESIGN PLANS ALLOWED, UNLESS VERBAL DISCUSSION FOLLOWED BY WRITTEN CONFIRMATION WITH/BY DESIGNER.

GENERAL DETAILS:

CONSTRUCTION: Face Frame; extended bottom rail (2-1/2") to hide fluorescent fixtures

WOOD SPECIES, ETC.: Maple (finish T.B.S.)
EXTERIOR FINISH: Stain T.B.S.
INTERIOR FINISH: Alt A: Melamine
Alt B: Plywood with maple veneer

UPPER DOOR STYLE: Raised-panel "ROMAN ARCH"; outside edges routed for fingerpulls
LOWER DOOR STYLE: Raised-panel square; outside edges routed for fingerpulls
DRAWER STYLE: Slab; outside edges routed for fingerpulls
HINGES: Fully-concealed "EUROPEAN", minimum 110°
GLIDES: Side-undermount, typ.; heavy-duty ballbearing glides on wide drawers and/or rollouts
PULLS: T.B.S., supplied by homeowner and installed by contractor
TOEKICK: 1/8" plywood to match cabinets
CROWN MOULDING: 3" crown for top of soffit, top of cabinets, perimeter of skylight, and walls between cabinets
OTHER: All tall cabinets shipped loose toe-kick, typ.
All shelves fully adjustable; no fixed shelves.

SPECIFIC DETAILS - WALL CABINETS:
Elevation "A":
W-1: WAC2442 Right-hinged door, finished left, back, and bottom
Elevation "B":
W-1: WAC2442
W-2: W2142 Right-hinged door, finished bottom
W-3: W1842 Left-hinged door, finished right and bottom
W-4: W4218 Butt doors
W-5: W1842 Right-hinged door, finished left and bottom
W-6: W2142 Left-hinged door, finished bottom
W-7: WAC2442 Right-hinged door, finished right and bottom
Elevation "C":
W-7: WAC2442
W-8: WAC2442 Left-hinged door, finished left side and bottom
Elevation "D":
W-8: WAC2442 Left-hinged door, finished left and bottom
W-9: W2742 Butt doors, extended right style 1-1/2" to be trimmed at jobsite by contractor, finished bottom

W-10: W3324 Butt doors at top, microwave shelf and styles 15"deep
+WMS3321 (see appliance specifications for microwave and trim kit dimensions)
W-11: W3924-24 Butt doors, extended left and right styles (1-1/2" each side), to be trimmed at jobsite by contractor; finished bottom
W-12: W2442 Left-hinged door, extended left style (2" inches), to be trimmed at jobsite by contractor finished right side
W-13: WOS2742 Adjustable shelves, finished bottom
W-14: W2442 Right-hinged door, extended right style (2" inches), to be trimmed at jobsite by contractor finished bottom.

SPECIFIC DETAILS - BASE CABINETS:
Elevation "A":
B-1: BFR-L Base filler with left return, 1-1/2" wide
B-2: DWP NOTES: SEE APPLIANCE SPECIFICATIONS
B-3: SB39 Butt doors, tilt-out tray at top, extended left and right styles, to be trimmed at jobsite by contractor; (NOTE: SINK CUTOUT EQUALS 36" +/-); see plumbing specifications
B-4: BAC36 Right-hinged door, recycling bins inside
Elevation "B":
B-5: B33 Butt doors, side-by-side drawers at top, two rollouts below, extended left style (1-1/2"), to be trimmed at jobsite by contractor
B-6: BCP39 Butt doors, two "scoop" drawers at top, two rollouts
B-7: B30 Butt doors, single drawer at top, two rollouts below, extended right style (2"), to be trimmed at jobsite by contractor
NOTE: ONE OR BOTH ROLLOUTS TO BE REDUCED DEPTH TO ALLOW FOR GAS LINE VALVE; CONTRACTOR TO VERIFY LOCATION AND MAKE NECESSARY MODIFICATIONS
B-8: BAC36 Right-hinged door, two full lazy susan units (DOOR NOT ATTACHED TO LAZY SUSAN)
Elevation "C":
B-8: BAC36
B-9: B27 Butt doors, single drawer at top, two rollouts below, finished right side
B-10: B27 Butt doors, single drawer at top, two rollouts below, finished left side
B-11: BAC36 Left-hinged door, two full lazy susan units (DOOR NOT ATTACHED TO LAZY SUSAN)
Elevation "D":
B-11: BAC36
B-12: BFH15 Full-height right-hinged door, extended right style (1"), to be trimmed at jobsite by contractor
B-13: B33 Side-by-side drawers at top, butt doors, two rollouts
B-14: BDD18 Desk-height three drawers (equal drawers at top, file drawer below), finished right side
B-15: BDD21 Desk-height three drawers (equal drawers at top, file drawer below), extended right style (1"), trimmed by contractor at jobsite, finished left side
Elevation "E":
B-16: BCOR Three each corbels to support extended cap

SPECIFIC DETAILS - TALL CABINETS:
Elevation "D":
T-1: TOV33 Butt doors at top with tray dividers at 4" cc, single drawer at bottom (NOTE: SEE APPLIANCE SPECIFICATIONS FOR CUTOUT DIMENSIONS), finished left and right sides
T-2: TRP1-1/2 Left refrigerator panel, finished left side
T-3: TRP4 Right refrigerator panel, finished right side (NOTE: SWITCHES TO BE LOCATED ON FACE OF RETURN)
T-4: TP42 Butt doors at top, pull out pantry units in middle - OR - five adjustable rollouts. Two adjustable rollouts at bottom

---

DOOR SPECIFICATIONS

EXTERIOR DOORS:

Note: All exterior doors to be weatherstripped and caulked, per '97 UBC

ROOM	NUMBER	DESCRIPTION
Family Room	1	3'-0" x 8'-0" inswing single french door with 2'-0" x 8'-0" sidelite on strike side. DEADBOLT LOCKSET T.B.S.
Entry Hall	2/3	3'-0" x 8'-0" right-hinge exterior, T.B.S. with 2'-0" x 8'-0" sidelites ea. side, T.B.S. LOCKSET; Baldwin "Vancover" #6924 or "Stanford" #6951 or equiv, brushed chrome
Garage	4	3'-0" x 8'-0" 6-panel solid core left-hinge door DEADBOLT LOCKSET T.B.S.
Kitchen	5	3'-0" x 8'-0" 6-panel 1-hr. solid-core right-hinge with automatic closer; DEADBOLT LOCKSET, T.B.S.
Garage	N/A	T.B.S., raised-panel garage door, max. height and width possible

INTERIOR DOORS:
Six-panel paint-grade pre-hung smooth masonite hollow-core, typ. u.o.n.
LOCKSETS: Baldwin #5103, polished chrome, or equivalent
HINGES: Polished chrome, typ. U.O.N.

ROOM	NUMBER	DESCRIPTION
Bedroom #1	6	3'-0" x 8'-0" right-hinge; privacy lockset, lever both sides
Bedroom #1	7	2'-4" x 8'-0" left-hinge; passage closet, lever one side only
Bathroom #1	8	2'-8" x 8'-0" right-hinge; privacy lockset, lever both sides
Closet #1	9	2'-8" x 8'-0" left-hange; passage lockset, lever both sides
Linen Closet	10	6'-0" x 8'-0" 3-panel double bifold; polished chrome bifold door pulls
Bathroom #2	11	2'-8" x 8'-0" left-hinge; privacy lockset, lever both sides

116

APPLIANCE SPECIFICATIONS

TYPE	MANUFACTURER/MODEL #	DESCRIPTION
REFRIGERATOR: (T.B.S.)	GE	TFX30PPDWW White 5x5 OA Width: with doors closed 35-3/4" OA Height: with hinge 69-3/4" without hinge 68-3/4" OA Depth: plus handles 34-1/2"
-OR-	GE	TFX30PPDWW White 5x5 OA Width: 35-3/4" OA Height: 69-3/4" height: to top of case 68-3/4" OA Depth: 34-1/2" Air Clearances: each side 1/8" top 1", back 1/2"
DOUBLE OVEN: (T.B.S.)	KitchenAid	KEBS277DWH White OA: 26-3/4" x 51" x 23-7/8" Cutout: 25-1/2" x 49-3/4" x 23-1/4" Minimum cabinet width: 27"
	-OR- Thermador	SC272W White, convection upper oven OA: 26-3/4" x 51-1/2" x 23-7/8" CO: 25-1/2" x 51-1/8" x 24"
COOKTOP:	Amana	AK3050WW White Exterior: 29-1/2" x 21-1/2" Height: 3" C.O.: 28-1/2" x 19-3/16" Minimum to sidewall: 6-3/8"
EXHAUST/HOOD:	Zephyr	AK2036W 36" White OA: 35-3/4" (net width) x 7-5/8" x 22-1/4" Duct: vertical ducting 6" RD to 3-1/4" x 10" 695 CFM, 115 v, 60 hz
DISHWASHER:	Maytag	MDB4100AWW White OA: 24" x 34-35" x 24"
MICROWAVE:	GE	JEM31WA White OA: 23-25/32" x 11-3/16" x 12-9/32" JX827WN Trim kit
	GE	OA: 26-1/8" x 16-1/4" CO: 24-13/16" - 24-15/16" x 14-15/16"
DISPOSAL:	Maytag	DFC5000A 8-5/8" x 13-1/4" x 8-5/8"
FIREPLACE: (Family Room)	Majestic	BR/BC42 Wood-burning Rough opening: 47" x 40-3/4" x 20-1/2" Underwriter's Laboratory: MH6018R ICBO: NER219
(Living Room)	Majestic	36BDVRJT Gas, black Rough opening: 36-1/2" x 34-3/4" x 16-1/2" Logs T.B.S. HGA Certified: 10000471 Tested by Warnock Hersey Test Labs ICBO: NER219

PLUMBING SPECIFICATIONS

ROOM: MASTER BATHROOM

TOILET	Toto "Carlyle" MS874114S
LAVATORY	Porcher, American Standard, Prescott 11050, 17" x 14", white
FAUCET	American Standard, "Iris", 3841-542-002
TUB	Aquatic, "Clearwater", biscuit, 72" x 36", jetted
TILE FLANGE	Aquatic, factory installed
IN-LINE HEATER	1.5 HP, 3 speed pump, factory installed
WASTE OVERFLOW	Geberit
FILLER (TUB SPOUT)	American Standard, "Amarillie", deck mount
TUB VALVE/TRIM	A.S., Lexington spout, 8971-542-002
DIVERTER	Grohe, chrome, 29.735.000
PERSONAL SHOWER	Grohe, 28.179.000
SHOWERHEAD	Grohe, 28.275.000
SHOWER ARM	Grohe, 27.412.000
SLIDE BAR/HOOK	Grohe, 28.621
HOSE	Grohe, 28.151
UNION	Grohe, 28.627.000
SHOWER VALVE/TRIM	Grohe, 19.628.000, 34.901.000
TUB GRAB BAR	Ginger, Chelsea, 1168R/26
SHOWER GRAB BAR	Ginger, Chelsea, 1168L/26
SHELF/TOWEL BAR	Ginger, Chelsea, 1143/24/26, chrome
TP HOLDER	Ginger, Chelsea, 1109/26
32" TOWEL BAR(S)	Ginger, Chelsea, 1104/26
SHOWER ENCLOSURE	Custom, "L" handle, both sides door, clear glass, frameless
SHOWER PAN	Custom, Hot mop
SHOWER DRAIN	E/Z Test Drain, chrome
MEDICINE CABINETS	(2)Robern, PLM2450W (L) and (R), frameless

ROOM: KITCHEN

SINK	Elkay LCGR-3822-LS2 or RS2, T.B.S, to be undermounted OA: 38" x 22" LS2 Inside each bowl: Left: 13-1/4"w x 11-3/4"l x 6-7/16"d Right: 18-5/8"w x 21"l x 8"d RS2 Inside each bowl: Left: 18-5/8"w x 21"l x 8"d Right: 13-1/4"w x 11-3/4"l x 6-7/16"d
FAUCET	Moen 7560c Pull-out chrome with water filter 1/2" IPS connections Integral vacuum breaker

INTERIOR DOORS (Continued):

ROOM	NUMBER	DESCRIPTION
Bedroom #2	12	2'-8" x 8'-0" right-hinge; privacy lockset, lever both sides
Laundry Room	13	(2 ea.) 3'-0" x 7'-8" Left-hinge SOLID-CORE; Privacy lockset, levers both sides
Bath #3	14	(5 ea.) 2'-8" x 7'-8" Right-hinge; Privacy lockset, levers both sides
Bedroom #4		
Bedroom #2		
Bedroom #3	15	(2 ea.)2'-8" x 7'-8" Left-hinge; privacy lockset, levers both sides
Bathroom #2		

WINDOW SPECIFICATIONS

ROOM	NUMBER	DESCRIPTION
Dining Room+	1	(4 ea.) 1'-6" x 5'-0" @ 2'-8" a.f.f.; DG w/removable grides; double-hung
Living Room	2	(2 ea.) 4'-0" x 5'-0" DG fixed picture window @ 2'-8" a.f.f.
Bedroom #3+4	3	(2 ea.)3'-0" x 5'-0" DG left-hinge casement @ 2'-8" a.f.f. NOTE: MEETS EGRESS REQUIREMENTS
Bedroom #3+4	4	(2 ea.)2'-6" x 5'-0" @ 2'-8" a.f.f.; DG left-hinge casement w/removable grids
Bedroom #3+4	5	(2 ea.)2'-6" x 5'-0" @ 2'-8" a.f.f.; DG right-hinge casement w/removable grids NOTE: WINDOWS 3, 4, AND 5 MULLED TOGETHER
Bedroom #2	6	8'-0" x 5'-0" DG double sliding with 3'-0" fixed picture in center NOTE: MEETS EGRESS REQUIREMENTS
Master Path	7	3'-0" x 3'-0" DG horizontal slider @ 3'-3" a.f.f. NOTE: TEMPERED GLASS
	8	3'-0" x 1'-6" DG half-round, mulled with window #7 NOTE: TEMPERED GLASS
	9	2'-0" x 2'-0" DG fixed picture window w/obscure glass (preferably "glue-chip." If possible) NOTE: TEMPERED GLASS
	10	5'-0" x 3'-0" DG horizontal slider w/semi-obscure glass,same as #9
	11	5'-0" x 1'-6" DG half-round,mulled with window #15 NOTE: TEMPERED GLASS
M.Bedroom	12	(2 ea.) 3'-6" x 5'-0" @ 2'-8" a.f.f.; DG double or single-hung NOTE: MEETS EGRESS REQUIREMENTS
Family Room	13	(2 ea.) 8'-0" x 6'-0" @ 1'-8" a.f.f.; DG slider left and right vents NOTE: TEMPERED GLASS
Garage	14	8'-0" x 3'-0" @ 3'-8" a.f.f.; DG slider left and right vents

CHAPTER 14

PERMITS

Permits are not required for projects which are limited to new cabinets and countertops, or other decorating improvements (window treatments, wall covering, painting, etc.), or minor repairs. Permits **are** required for projects when any of the following are included in a project:

Framing;
Electrical work;
Plumbing work;
A new roof;
A new deck (height may be a factor).

If you are thinking about doing any major work without obtaining the necessary permits, one word of advice: <u>DON'T!</u> It's one of the fastest ways to kill a potential sale in the future, if you can't prove that everything was done according to the building codes, which means getting a permit and having regular required inspections.

A licensed electrician decided to completely remodel his own kitchen. He called favors from other contractors to provide their services in exchange for his labor on their projects. Everyone knew the codes; nothing was done in the kitchen that didn't comply. The project proceeded smoothly, until the cabinet manufacturer's truck was at the house one day when an inspector happened to drive past. He knew the electrician, and didn't remember inspecting the job. Curious about what was going on, he parked his car and went into the house. "Hi, guys. What's happening?" "We're just installing cabinets for Joe's new kitchen." When he got back to his office, the inspector checked the records to discover that permits hadn't been obtained. To teach Joe a lesson, and set an example, he red-flagged the job, required that everything be reopened to the bare studs so the work could be inspected. The permits would have cost Joe only a couple hundred dollars. The lack of permits cost him thousands of dollars, and weeks of work.

It may sound to you like this was an extreme case, that the inspector was being arbitrary. Maybe he was. But he had a legal right to do what he did.

> "Bureaucrats: they are dead at 30 and buried at 60. They are like custard pies; you can't nail them to a wall."
> (Frank Lloyd Wright)

The permit and inspection process is meant to set and uphold <u>minimum</u> standards that create safe environments. Building officials review and upgrade the codes regularly; it's not an easy task. They discuss and debate every aspect of construction, to make the codes better and clearer with each review.

How many homes have you been in that had squeaky floors? The reason most floors squeak is because the joists supporting the subfloor and flooring are flexing as we walk across them, which causes the subfloor joints to rub against each other. There's nothing in the code that talks about squeaky floors, because that's not a safety issue. If your contractor exceeds the minimum requirements, i.e., larger joists spanning a smaller area, spaced closer together, with a thicker tongue-and-groove subfloor which is glued and screwed to the joists, the floor won't flex and squeak. You'll pay more for it than you would if he met the minimum standards -- but cost isn't a code issue, either.

Codes are reviewed and updated every four years by building officials. It is the responsibility for everyone in the building/remodeling industry to be familiar with the codes that affect their clients. When plans are drafted, code information must be included to insure that the project will comply. The permit process works this way:

Your designer drafts plans that include not only what you want, but also what's safe. There may be notes on your plans that say, "Egress window, per UBC Section 0000.000.000."

Final plans are submitted to the building department for plan check by the building officials and the fire marshall. Depending on the size of your project, your plans may be checked by three or more departments.

A letter requesting a list of modifications and additional notes may be submitted to your designer, structural engineer, soils engineer, energy engineer, mechanical engineer. They are given a specific amount of time to reply in writing, with a corresponding list of corrections that have been made. New sets of plans will be submitted with the response letter.

The revised/corrected plans are checked again. If all of the corrections are satisfactory, the building department will issue permits. Permits are valid for a specified period, but if the time runs out before you begin, they can usually be renewed -- unless there have been major changes to the code.

California homeowners didn't realize how long it would take to select products for their new home (located within 10 miles of the major fault line). They obtained permits, then started looking for windows, doors, cabinets, etc., and finalized their financing. October, 1989, the Bay Area had a 7.0 earthquake. All building came to a halt for several months. Building officials reviewed and upgraded seismic codes, which ultimately cost the homeowners thousands of dollars. Their new home was eventually built, and it complied with the new codes. No one can answer this question: Did the seismic upgrades make it **that** much safer, for each additional dollar?

Permit cards and an approved set of plans will be given to whoever gets the permit. The approved plans should be the only documents that everyone uses, except for minor modifications or clarifications drawn during construction. The plans and permit cards should be kept in a safe place inside, out of the weather. By the end of your project, the approved plans will be faded, stained, and torn. Don't throw them away! Also, keep the permit cards in a safe place. Both of them qualify as legal documents!

As mentioned in Chapter 9, your project will be inspected several times during construction. Your contractor will call the building department to schedule an inspection 24 hours before the inspector arrives. It's the inspector's duty to look at what's been accomplished since the last inspection, to verify that the contractor and his/her crew have performed work and used materials as prescribed by code and detailed in the plans. Again, it's a minimum standard that the inspector is grading, unless there are tougher local codes to be met.

When the inspector comes to your home for the final inspection, s/he's not inspecting the quality of your cabinets, the color of your walls, the plushness of your carpeting, or the magnificence of your new chandelier. S/he sees a lot of homes every year, and probably doesn't notice the details that are important to you.

"If you can laugh at it, you can live with it." (Erma Bombeck)

CHAPTER 15

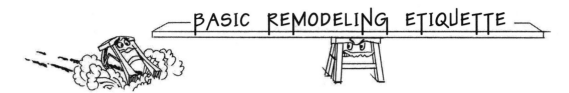

BASIC REMODELING ETIQUETTE

"Please don't accuse me of sitting on a throne, dictating that you must follow these recommendations. I often forget them myself -- my family and clients remind me how human I am!"

What is etiquette? It's anything that makes a relationship better, that ultimately benefits everyone in the relationship. We are, after all, merely human. We do make mistakes, and often do things without thinking about the effect our words and actions have on others. It's how we respond to our mistakes that make a big difference.

The following recommendations are made only to help your project proceed more smoothly, with fewer misunderstandings. These suggestions generally apply to Homeowners, Contractors, Designers, and Suppliers:

Don't make promises unless you really mean them and intend to follow through. For example: "I'll call you back." Or, "I'll have this done by . . ."

If you've underestimated the time needed to meet a deadline, admit it. No excuses. And apologize.

Return phone and e-mail messages as promptly as possible.

Preface every phone call with, "Is this a convenient time for you?"

Treat others as you would like to be treated, aka the Golden Rule. Many people follow the alternate Golden Rule: "Whoever has the gold, rules." Which one would you prefer?

Avoid the blame game. Try to get past "It's your fault," "It's her fault," or "It's his fault." It's difficult, but try to see a challenge in proportion to everything that's going on -- the bigger picture. And, if you can see some humor in the situation, that's great!

"Humor is a social lubricant that helps us get over some of the bad spots." (Steve Allen)

The homeowners had been through one difficult remodeling experience. Although many months had passed, they still had a chip on their shoulders when they started another project. To make matters worse, they were both pessimists, and had no sense of humor. Unfortunately, problems did arise during the second project; they immediately started pointing fingers and sending accusatory e-mails. It was a difficult situation for everyone involved.

"Good breeding consists of concealing how much we think of ourselves and how little we think of the other person."
(Mark Twain)

MEETING ETIQUETTE

➤ Be on time for meetings. Allow for sufficient travel time, and add at least 15 minutes if you're traveling during rush hour. 15 minutes +/- is acceptable in today's hectic world. It's very easy to overbook our time, or get stuck in very heavy traffic. If you're going to be more than 15 minutes early or late, take the extra minute or two and call to let the other people know your revised arrival time. Chronic tardiness sends the message to other people that they're not important enough for you to make the effort to be on time.

➤ Be prepared to start the meeting on time.

➤ Try not to waste time chatting. Chatting is important, because it allows you to get to know the other person(s), their likes and dislikes, and other information that can help during the process. Agree very early in the relationship how much time you're willing to allow for "non-project" chatting.

ETIQUETTE FOR HOMEOWNERS

"Don't expect perfection. Expect good work."

⬛ Offer water or other beverage at meetings. If it's a hot day, the construction crew will appreciate something cool to drink -- non-alcoholic!

⬛ Make a list of questions. Instead of several phone calls, it's easier to combine questions and answers into one phone call (or meeting). If you write your questions (or key words) down and leave space for the answer, you'll save time and avoid future misunderstandings.

⬛ Make an appointment to talk with your contractor, either before work begins, or after the trade contractors have left, so you can talk openly.

⬛ Value service. Don't switch loyalties because someone came in with a lower bid or estimate after a supplier, contractor, or designer has spent valuable time to help you, or worked on multiple estimates.

> The wife was an excellent price shopper, and placed higher value on low price than service. She had no reservations about spending hours at an appliance store known for excellent service, to make her appliance decisions. She bought her appliances at a discount store -- saved a total of $300 -- about 2%. When there were problems with the cooktop, the discount store wouldn't help. The woman (with more moxy than manners) called the first store, who gave her the name and phone number of the manufacturer's representative.

⬛ Notify neighbors about your project as soon as possible. Apologize in advance for traffic/parking problems, noise or construction dust. Ask them to call you directly with complaints, not bother the contractor or trade contractors.

⬛ Criticize in private; praise in public (this includes EVERYONE: your designer, contractor, and family members -- especially spouses!).

"If you want to get the best out of people, you must look for the best that is in them." (Bernard Haldane)

⬛ Don't disturb contractors' tools.

⬛ Don't borrow contractors' tools.

Don't leave your tools in a "convenient" place where they can get confused with contractors' tools.

Don't be the cause of a delay. Make all decisions in a timely manner. If you're doing some of the work yourself, finish on time (just as you'd expect a trade contractor to do).

Discuss and resolve any problems before your project is completed. If you make changes that vary from the plans, or add work to the scope of the project, be prepared to pay for the changes.

"One ounce of Good Attitude is worth more than a pound of Good Aptitude."

Make progress payments promptly, especially if work is progressing on schedule.

Don't expect contractors and designers to reduce their fees, just so you can have "Rolls Royce" appliances, light fixtures, and plumbing.

> A young couple told their contractor and designer that they had a very limited budget, and negotiated the fees to be as low as possible. Halfway through the project, the homeowners upgraded all products to "better" and "best" categories, but still claimed they barely had enough money to do the project. The contractor and designer felt like fools, resentful, and distanced themselves from the homeowners. Communication and trust suffered.

Don't expect your designer or contractor to be available to you 24/7. Don't use guilt as a way of getting what you want; in most cases, it won't work.

> Often, emergencies were created by the homeowner's procrastination. She would call the designer and expect immediate solutions. Of course, the homeowner would get upset when the designer had other commitments, but she never accepted personal responsibility for situations. Ultimately, the designer had to impose scheduled telephone meetings, restrict the number of emergency phone calls, and inform the homeowner (in writing) that last-minute solutions would be charged at a higher rate. Pretty drastic regulations, but sometimes they're needed, to preserve the working relationship.

124

Don't expect the contractor to do minor repairs (i.e., touch-up painting) at no charge after you've lived in your remodeled home more than three months. Up to one year after remodeling, reasonable "no-charge" repairs include:

Appliances not working properly;

Plumbing leaks or malfunctions;

Light fixtures that make noise or malfunction when dimmed;

Electrical outlets and switches that don't work;

Cabinet adjustments (i.e., door/drawer alignment);

Grout or caulk touch-ups.

Pay promptly for chargeable repairs or work, which include:

Malfunction of appliances due to improper use;

Replacement of lamps (light bulbs);

Changes/modifications requested by you.

Don't ask the general contractor or trade contractors to do work that's not in the scope of the project.

Don't expect the contractor to watch your children and pets. Keep kids and "fur-persons" out of trouble, and out of harm's way.

The contractor was within a week of finishing a big, expensive job. He had asked the homeowners repeatedly to keep their four-year-old son away from the project area. One morning, the contractor was installing new solid-wood raised-panel stain grade doors ($$$!) in the main hallway, using a sharp chisel to fine-tune the lock and strike plate. He put the chisel in his tool box before he went to the truck to get another tool. When he returned, he heard two things: the mother talking on the phone, and the little boy carving the new doors.

"When a thing is funny, search it carefully for a hidden truth."
(George Bernard Shaw)

ETIQUETTE FOR CONTRACTORS

"Life is like a game of tennis. The person who serves well seldom loses." (Bill Tilden)

- Notify all of the neighbors about the project before it begins (this is a great way to market your services!).

- Be respectful to the homeowners by taking care of their home and objects.

- Notify homeowners at least 24 hours in advance (if possible), when power and water will be off for significant periods.

- Confirm toilet facilities before you start the project (if one of the bathrooms is designated, make sure the lid is down and "overspray" is cleaned up).

- Keep everyone in the communications loop about project scheduling, etc.

- Avoid finger pointing; if there's a problem that can be resolved directly with the designer, it's best not to upset the homeowners.

Halfway through construction, the contractor realized that one of the specified cabinets was the wrong size. Instead of calling the designer, he went to the homeowners and complained that the designer had ordered the wrong cabinet, which greatly upset the homeowners, and created bad feelings for everyone. The problem could have (and should have) been resolved quickly and painlessly if the team spirit had prevailed. The project was finished, but the process wasn't as enjoyable as it might have been for everyone involved in the relationship.

- Pick up tools.

- Throw away debris and garbage (including food containers).

- Cover ducts and wall openings (to prevent children and pets getting into dangerous areas.

- Don't let pets (or children) get out accidentally.

- Talk with homeowners about potential problems, who's responsible for what (contractors aren't baby sitters or pet sitters!).

- Avoid saying, "I always do it this way." There are always exceptions and always reasons for other methods.

ETIQUETTE FOR DESIGNERS

"Real success is finding your lifework in the work that you love."
(David McCullough)

Keep everyone in the communications loop, especially if products are substituted or other changes are made that can affect a deadline, the project, or the homeowners' investment.

Avoid finger pointing, even if you're working with people who point fingers and don't accept responsibility when they should.

Be honest about deadlines. It's better to admit a missed deadline than build up unrealistic expectations.

Never say, "I'll try to....." People only hear, "I'll do," or "I'll have this by....."

Even if the homeowners are younger than you are, refer to them with respect. Wait until they invite you to use their first name before you automatically refer to them as "Tom" or "Mary," etc.

Avoid pre-judging people. Make an effort to get to know and appreciate the people who will turn your plans into reality.

> The designer stopped by a jobsite during the lunch break. The crew had gone to lunch, except one of the roofers, who was sitting on the lawn, reading a book and listening to music while he ate his sandwich. From a distance, he looked like any other trade contractor, but as the designer approached, she heard he was listening to classical music and saw that he was reading "Gaijin," which was one of her favorite books. "Mind if I join you?" she asked as she approached. "Sure, I don't mind," he said as he put down the book. Until the rest of the crew arrived, they had a delightful conversation about the "Shogun" series. She also discovered that the roofer was actually a classical violinist, making extra money as a roofer's assistant.

Never comment negatively about another designer or their work. You may have designed the object, room, or house differently, possibly better. Bringing other designers down doesn't raise you to a higher level. All it accomplishes, ultimately, is a bad reputation for being "bitchy."

CHAPTER 16

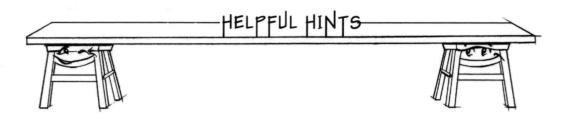

HELPFUL HINTS

"The best advice you'll get is from someone who made the same mistake himself." (Judith Martin)

The following hints will also help your project proceed smoothly. So, what's a helpful hint? It's anything that achieves the best results. It may also help a relationship, but it's more goal-oriented than etiquette.

HINTS FOR EVERYONE

➤ Be honest about the remodeling time frame and investment parameters.

➤ Be honest about the budget.

➤ Write things down and keep all of your notes in one place (preferably an expandable file folder or dedicated notebook).

➤ If a delay (or problem) occurs, try to take things in stride. Resolve the challenge, then move on (to the next challenge!).

➤ Be prepared for meetings.

Homeowners: Have a list of written questions, magazine or newspaper clippings, your remodeling notebook, and calendar.

Designer: Have copies of all drawings, sketches, and product literature for everyone who's going to attend the meeting; also have all samples ready to show, the clients' file, and notebook, and calendar.

Contractor: Have the clients' file, estimates, other documents pertinent to the project, notebook, and calendar.

➤ Have an agenda and try to follow the agenda.

HINTS FOR HOMEOWNERS

When the design professional or contractor is taking measurements, avoid chatting or asking questions. Your thoughts, questions, and comments are important, but wait until there's a logical break, so the designer or contractor will be able to pay full attention to you. It could easily cause serious mistakes when their thoughts are broken.

Keep everyone in the communications loop. If you have a discussion with your contractor, call your designer to inform him or her what was discussed and decided. The same should be true if you have a discussion with your designer -- especially if your discussion affects construction, or your product selection.

Talk about any problems immediately. Don't wait for the "perfect" time, and don't wait until the end of the project. The best results happen in clear air.

Be available to the contractor and design professional. Give them your work phone numbers and emergency phone numbers (available neighbors or family members). Inform the contractor when you will not be available, and try to arrange for someone to be available in case of emergency.

Communicate about your project only with your contractor and designer, not trade contractors. Don't continually question why things are done/not done a certain way.

Keep accurate records. Be the project "secretary." Many contractors dislike business procedures. Get a book of three-part "Extra Work Order" forms at your local office supplier. Fill out the forms accurately, with the date, the extra work required or requested, and the amount estimated by the contractor. Both of you should sign it. Give one copy to the contractor, put one copy in your file, and keep the third copy in the book.

One project several years ago involved such a situation. The contractor discovered a structural beam during demolition, which needed to be changed in order to maintain the project goals. He told the homeowners how much the extra work would be, and the homeowner typed the change order. At the end of the project, the contractor had forgotten how much they'd agreed was reasonable, and requested twice as much as he'd quoted several months before. The homeowner produced the signed Change Order form; the contractor was obligated to honor the amount he'd quoted, and apologized for forgetting.

Make an effort to read plans, and understand the remodeling lingo.

Don't use oversights, a change of mind, or unforeseen problems as an excuse not to make the final payment. A "walk-through" with the contractor upon completion is normal. At this time, you should make a detailed "punch" list that everyone signs. When the items on the "punch" list have been taken care of, your final payment should be given immediately.

HINTS FOR CONTRACTORS

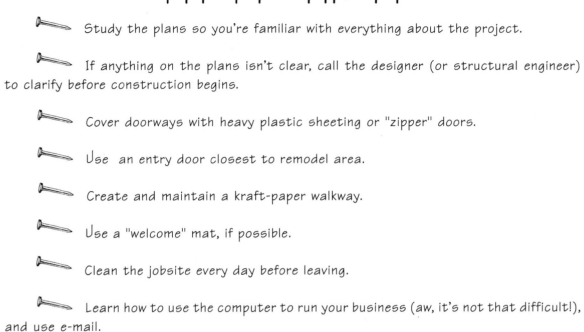

☛ Study the plans so you're familiar with everything about the project.

☛ If anything on the plans isn't clear, call the designer (or structural engineer) to clarify before construction begins.

☛ Cover doorways with heavy plastic sheeting or "zipper" doors.

☛ Use an entry door closest to remodel area.

☛ Create and maintain a kraft-paper walkway.

☛ Use a "welcome" mat, if possible.

☛ Clean the jobsite every day before leaving.

☛ Learn how to use the computer to run your business (aw, it's not that difficult!), and use e-mail.

HINTS FOR DESIGNERS

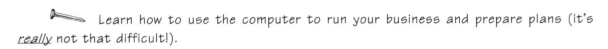

☛ Learn how to use the computer to run your business and prepare plans (it's _really_ not that difficult!).

☛ Have homeowners initial and date your copy of all working documents reviewed during meetings.

☛ If you send documents by fax or e-mail, always include a transmittal cover letter. With most e-mail and many fax machines, you can request a return receipt showing the person received what you've sent.

☛ Have homeowners and contractors sign and date a receipt for documents and samples that you give them. If an approval sample must be signed and returned, ask homeowners to write very large, then cut through the signature so that you can retain part of the sample for your records.

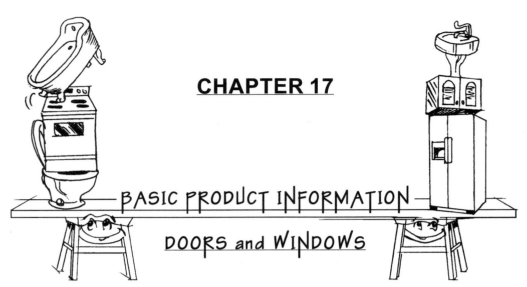

CHAPTER 17

BASIC PRODUCT INFORMATION

DOORS and WINDOWS

This chapter is written to give basic information so you can talk more knowledgeably about doors and windows. There are hundreds of door and window manufacturers in North America. There are large companies whose products are distributed through lumber yards, specialty resellers, and home products chain stores, as well as local custom manufacturers. You may do an online search, through Yahoo, Google, Alta Vista, or other search engines, to get specific information about a manufacturer and the products offered. One of the very good sites is arcat.com.

EXTERIOR DOORS:

Any door that is a portal between the interior and exterior is an exterior door, including the door between your home and garage. These doors may be manufactured of solid wood, steel, or a combination of materials (wood with vinyl or aluminum exterior cladding). French doors and patio doors may be manufactured of wood, aluminum, steel, vinyl, or a combination of materials (wood with vinyl or aluminum exterior cladding). Hundreds of styles and colors are available which will enhance the architectural style of your home.

The range of your investment in front entry doors is $300 for standard raised-panel, paint-grade to over $25,000 for custom-manufactured doors. Of course, the more you're willing to pay, the greater your selection. Door hardware is sold separately and can vary in price, too -- from $150 to over $3,000.

With so much emphasis today on energy-efficient homes, all exterior doors should have weatherstripping. There should be insulation in the walls, and all openings should be caulked. The Building Code requires solid-core fire doors between your home and garage, and separating any space that has mechanical equipment such as furnaces and water heaters. Local codes may require that french doors and patio doors have dual glazing (two layers of glass with a pocket of air or gas between them), which will keep your home warmer in the winter and cooler in the summer. French doors, patio doors, doors with glass inserts, and sidelites should have certified safety glass. The Building Code requires safety glazing in the following conditions:

1. The exposed area of an individual pane is greater than 9 square feet;

2. The exposed bottom edge is less than 18 inches above the floor;

3. The exposed top edge is greater than 36 inches above the floor;

4. One or more walking surfaces is within 36 inches horizontally from the glass.

A word of caution about exterior doors: Before you or anyone orders your doors, verify whether the doors are viewed from the interior or exterior. You don't want your doors swinging or sliding in the wrong direction! See the example below.

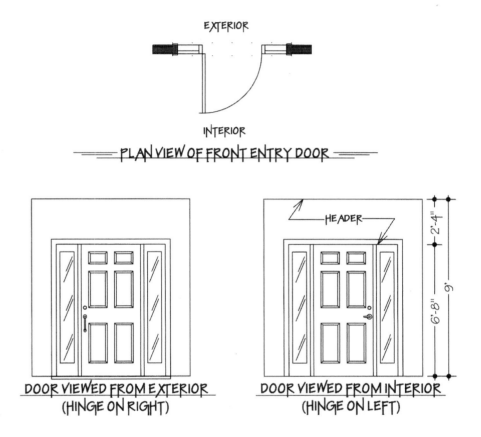

EXTERIOR

INTERIOR

PLAN VIEW OF FRONT ENTRY DOOR

DOOR VIEWED FROM EXTERIOR
(HINGE ON RIGHT)

DOOR VIEWED FROM INTERIOR
(HINGE ON LEFT)

Exterior doors are available in a range of standard (and custom) widths and heights, with or without sidelites or transoms. A single-swing door should be a minimum of 3'-0" wide by 6'-8" high. With the popularity of higher ceilings, keep in mind the relative proportion of your door and window heights, and the impact that will have on your budget. With standard eight-foot ceilings, there is a 1'-4" header between the top of the door (or window) and the ceiling. If you maintain the standard 6'-8" height in nine- or ten-foot high rooms, the header can look strange.

INTERIOR DOORS:

Interior doors may be solid wood, hollow-core, or composite material. They are classified as raised-panel, recessed-panel, or louvered; stain-grade or paint-grade. Your investment in a standard interior door can range from $75 to $400 each, not including handles and locks.

The standard size for most interior doors is 2'-8" wide by 6'-8" high. I recommend, if possible, that interior doors to bedrooms and bathrooms be a minimum of 3'-0" wide, to accommodate the passage of a person on crutches or in a wheelchair. Planning for the future should include consideration for people with physical or mental limitations. (Remember injuries can happen to anyone, at any age.)

Interior doors are usually ordered as they are viewed from the hinge side, with the door swinging toward you. It's best to verify this, to avoid a bad investment.

A word about closet doors. For years, the standard has been bypass mirrored doors on single closets. The only problem is that one-third to one-half of the closet contents are hidden by the door(s). If there's room for doors to swing into the room, I suggest thinking about bifold doors, which allow full access to the entire width of your closet. The tradeoff is, your designer has to consider the floor space covered by the door swing; it shouldn't be more than 1/4 of the available walking area, to maintain safe passage.

WINDOWS:

Windows, too, are available in a wide range of finishes and sizes. They are classified by type: casement (swinging out vertically), awning (swinging out horizontally), double-hung (both top and bottom slide up and down), single-hung (only the bottom portion slides up), and fixed. There are also specialty windows: bay (standard 45-degree and 30-degree angled sides), bow (bands of casement, fixed, and/or double-hung windows that form a graceful curve), and garden windows. In addition, many manufacturers also make windows in special shapes: arch-top, trapezoid, triangular, etc.

It has been popular for several years to have grids in windows, which can be selected from a variety of styles: fixed grids (between the two layers of glass), removable grids (usually on the inside only), and true divided lites (fixed grids with glass installed between them). The first category is often associated with the lowest investment, and the last category is definitely associated with the highest investment.

If your project includes a bedroom, that room must have emergency egress, which is usually a window. The current Uniform Building Code defines emergency egress as:

> "Escape or rescue windows shall have a minimum net clear openable area of 5.7 square feet. The minimum net clear openable height dimension shall be 24 inches. The minimum net clear openable width dimension shall be 20 inches. When windows are provided as a means of escape or rescue, they shall have a finished sill height not more than 44 inches above the floor."

If your project includes a bathroom, the Uniform Building Code requires safety glass:

> "...in doors and enclosures for hot tubs, whirlpools, saunas, steam rooms, bathtubs and showers. Glazing in any portion of a building wall enclosing these compartments where the bottom exposed edge of the glazing is less than 60 inches above a standing surface and drain inlet."

Safety glass should also be used for casement and awning windows that project into (or close to) a walkway or patio.

If you have different-sized windows (or a patio door with a window) in the same room, with grids, verify that the grid pattern will be the same. See the example (below) of an undesirable situation, where the right window grids are almost square. The left window and patio door grids are rectangular, but none of the windows (lites) are the same size. The only way to prevent this mistake is to ask questions of your design professional, your contractor, and the door-window supplier.

=== "GRIDLOCK" NIGHTMARE ===

Energy efficiency is very important. Most local governments require windows to be double-glazed (two panes of glass with air or gas between them), and they may require proof that the windows meet certain efficiency requirements. Large manufacturers usually provide this information in their brochures and technical specifications; it may be more difficult to obtain this information from smaller manufacturers.

DOOR AND WINDOW HARDWARE:

The hardware for your new doors and windows should be consistent with the finish you've chosen for plumbing and light fixtures. Door hardware includes: locks, levers, handles, and <u>hinges</u>. Window hardware includes: hinges, locks, and control devices (such as window cranks, etc.). Standard finishes include polished brass, antique brass, bronze, polished chrome, and powder-coat (white or almond). Some manufacturers also have brushed chrome. There is often an upcharge for special finishes, between $50 and $100 per window.

Every minute you spend researching doors and windows will help you make good decisions, and save money!

"Hey! Wake up out there!" (Emeril Lagasse)

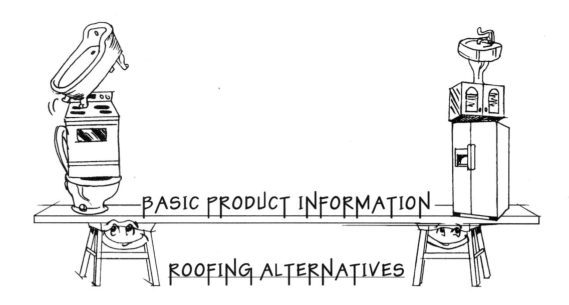

BASIC PRODUCT INFORMATION

ROOFING ALTERNATIVES

This is not a glamorous subject, but it's very important that you know your alternatives, so you can talk with your contractor and design professional about your preferences. Three things are important to think about when you're considering a new roof: How long it will last, how much you'll invest, and what it will look like.

Roofing materials are an important architectural feature, especially if your roof pitch is steeper (which is the popular trend). The diagram below shows the relative roof pitches used for new construction and remodeling projects and simple perspectives showing how prominent the roof becomes when the pitch is steeper.

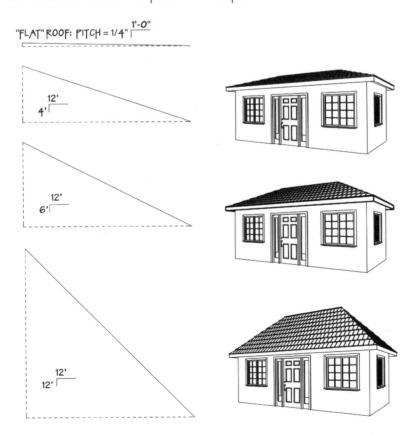

"FLAT" ROOF: PITCH = 1/4" 1'-0"

12'
4'

12'
6'

12'
12'

ROOFING MATERIALS

Your design professional and contractor will have recommendations about specific types and manufacturers, based on their experience. Your roof pitch will also be a consideration for their recommendations, as well as the physical weight of the roof ("live load" on the walls and foundation).

Cedar Shakes: This material has a warm, "country" look, but the shakes must be penetrated with a fire retardant to comply with most local building codes. Shakes require more maintenance than other types of roofing, which should be considered in your budget spreadsheet. Search the internet for specific information under the key words "cedar shake roofing."

Composition: As the name suggests, this material is a composite of fiberglass reinforcing mat at the center which is coated with asphalt and mineral fillers. The fillers adhere to the fiberglass and the asphalt surrounds the structure, making it waterproof. Its top surface is embedded with a layer of ceramic granules. Composition roofing falls into three major categories: three-tab, standard laminate, and premium.

Three-tab shingles are the least expensive option. This type of roofing has been refined over the years, and is available with 20- to 30-year warranties.

Standard laminates (also known as dimensionals) have become the most common choice in composition roofing. Because they have a second layer fused to the base shingle, the thickness is doubled. They have a strong resemblance to wood shake and are available in a wide range of colors. This type of roofing is available with 25- to 40-year warranties.

Premium shingles are a heavier laminate and represent the absolute top of the line in composition. They are thicker, heavier and physically larger than standard laminates and often incorporate extra features like moss retardants. This type of roofing is available with warranties of 50 years to lifetime.

For more information, search the internet with the key words "composition roofing."

Concrete Tiles: Available in lightweight to heavyweight interlocking tiles for specific applications. Concrete tiles are available in a wide range of colors and styles, including slate, wood shake, and conventional tile to blend with every architectural style: American contemporary, ranch, European, Mediterranean, Spanish, Oriental, etc. Search the internet for specific information under the key words "concrete roofing." If you want technical information, a good site (among others) is eagleroofing.com (Adobe Acrobat format).

One word of caution: Even the lightweight concrete tiles can be heavier than composition or shake roofing. A structural engineer must calculate the relative load factor before your plans are finalized, or your local building department may reject the plans for insufficient information.

Membranes: The materials available have greatly improved since tar and felt roofs, also known as built-up roofing. Some membrane materials can be used for flat roofs, sloped roofs, and decks. Most have a UL Class-A fire rating, and a lifetime warranty similar to other roofing materials. Search the internet for specific information under key words "membrane roofing."

Metal: The typical metal roofing material you see is standing-seam roofs on commercial buildings. There are other types available, that look like tile, slate, or shakes. Metal roofs are available in a wide range of colors. Search the internet for specific information at metalroofing.org.

Tile: Tile is a ceramic/clay- or cement/sand-based product that can last 50 years or more. It is available in several styles and colors, each providing a unique appearance, and the ability to withstand extreme weather conditions. High wind, high heat and severe cold have no real effect on this type of roofing. Search the internet for specific information under the key words "tile roofing," or go directly to an excellent website for information, ntrma.org (The National Tile Roofing Manufacturers' Association).

The same caution applies to tile roofing as well as concrete roofing.

"If advertisers spent the same amount of money on improving their products as they do on advertising then they wouldn't have to advertise them." (Will Rogers)

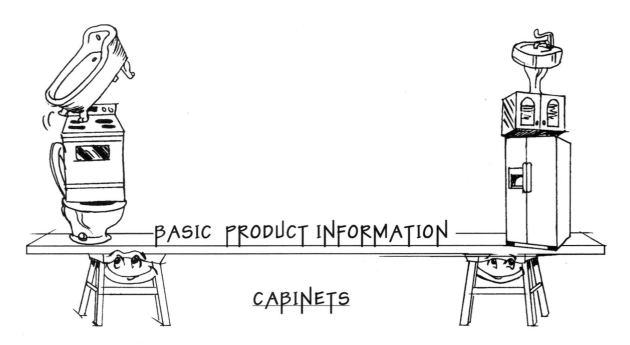

BASIC PRODUCT INFORMATION

CABINETS

After you have read this chapter, you will have knowledge about the types of cabinet construction and how they look. You'll also have an understanding of classifications, styles and finish materials available, as well as the storage accessories you can choose. You'll see line drawings to illustrate the alternatives.

CONSTRUCTION

There are two basic types of cabinet construction: Face-frame or frameless (which is also known as European or 32-millimeter). Both types start with a cabinet box, usually 3/4" thick. A frame is installed on the front of the box for face-frame construction. The frame stabilizes the box, to keep it from twisting ("racking"), but it reduces the opening by at least 1/2". A sub-type of face-frame construction looks similar to frameless, but when you open the doors, you will see the frame inside.

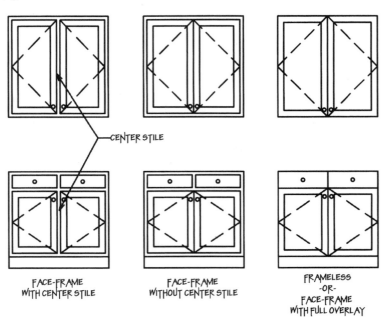

CENTER STILE

FACE-FRAME
WITH CENTER STILE

FACE-FRAME
WITHOUT CENTER STILE

FRAMELESS
-OR-
FACE-FRAME
WITH FULL OVERLAY

CLASSIFICATION

There are three classifications for cabinet manufacturers: Modular, Custom-Modular, and Custom, which easily fall into the "Good-Better-Best" categories explained earlier. Many manufacturers offer all three categories, but most offer one or two categories.

Modular cabinets will have the lowest investment range. These cabinets are manufactured in three-inch width increments only. The cabinet heights may be limited to one or two sizes, and usually there is no choice on the depth available. Examples:

> WALL CABINETS: 9" - 48" wide, in 3" increments; 24", 30" and 36" tall; 12" deep (24" deep may be available for over-refrigerator area).

> BASE CABINETS: 9" - 48" wide, in 3" increments; 29-1/2" and 34-1/2" tall; 24" deep.

> TALL CABINETS: 12", 24", 27", 30", and 36" wide; 84" or 96" tall; 12" or 24" deep, depending on type of cabinet (i.e., pantry or oven, etc.).

In addition to size limitations, there may also be limited availability of storage accessories, styles, woods, and finishes that are determined by each manufacturer. It's best to know what these limitations are as soon as possible, so you don't waste time and effort.

Custom-modular cabinets generally fall into the middle investment range. They're manufactured similar to modular cabinets, but the manufacturer can make modifications requested for an up-charge (which can be significant), often equivalent to 10%-25% of the box being modified. If many boxes are modified, it's best to investigate another manufacturer (custom-modular or custom), or re-think the layout.

There are often more choices available with custom-modular cabinets, for interior storage accessories, styles, woods, and finish alternatives.

Custom cabinets, if they're really custom, have no limitations: any size, any style, any wood, any color. Your investment in custom cabinets may be three or four times as much as modular cabinets, for the same basic layout.

STYLES:

Whether your home is contemporary, traditional, or transitional, your cabinets should have integrity with your home and your lifestyle. Woods, colors, and styles can be carefully mixed for visual pizazz -- determined by your personal preference and your budget.

On the next page are sample styles of wall and base cabinets used in most homes today.

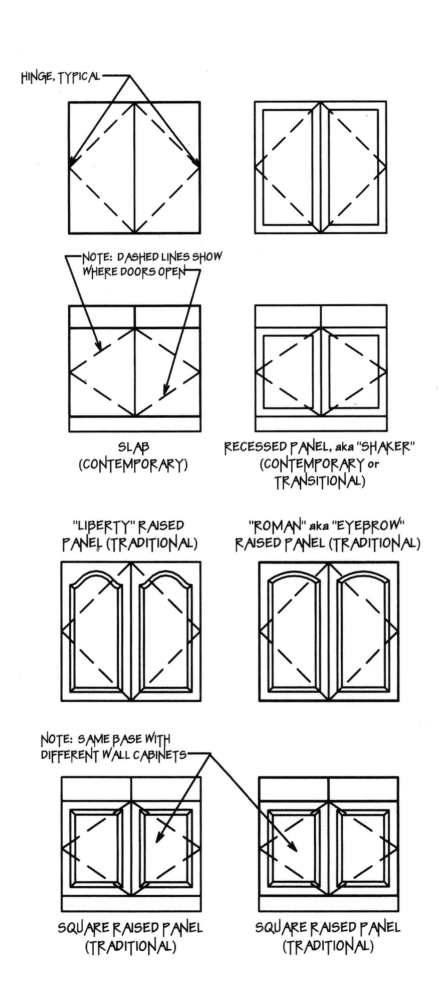

HINGE, TYPICAL

NOTE: DASHED LINES SHOW
WHERE DOORS OPEN

SLAB
(CONTEMPORARY)

RECESSED PANEL, aka "SHAKER"
(CONTEMPORARY or
TRANSITIONAL)

"LIBERTY" RAISED
PANEL (TRADITIONAL)

"ROMAN" aka "EYEBROW"
RAISED PANEL (TRADITIONAL)

NOTE: SAME BASE WITH
DIFFERENT WALL CABINETS

SQUARE RAISED PANEL
(TRADITIONAL)

SQUARE RAISED PANEL
(TRADITIONAL)

142

Hardware was specifically eliminated from the style illustrations. There are hundreds of pulls and knobs available, in addition to finger pulls which can be used only with face-frame cabinets. The technology in the design and manufacture of door hinges and drawer pulls has greatly improved the appearance and function of cabinets since the 1970's. A word of caution about your cabinet hardware selection: Pulls and knobs can be very expensive, a "might as well" investment that pushes you over budget.

> The homeowners knew that the investment in their new kitchen was going to exceed $100,000. It was a large kitchen (over 280 square feet); the ISLAND was 5 feet by 13 feet. Nothing gave them sticker shock until they selected the cabinet hardware -- $23 each. 126 pulls x $23 = $2,898 for cabinet jewelry!

Glass inserts can be added to most cabinet doors (except slab-type doors), with or without grids (which are called muntins or mullions). There is also a wide variety of moulding available, even for less-expensive cabinets, that can accomplish the look you want. These items can be expensive, though -- especially if you want large or complex moulding (popular in traditional homes).

FINISH MATERIALS

Slab doors and drawers can be any material: laminate, metal, or wood veneer over a composite material called MDF (medium-density fiberboard), or particleboard. The doors and drawers can be manufactured from solid wood laminated together, but you will see where the lamination joints are when there's a natural change in the grain and/or color. Slab doors and drawers manufactured from MDF can have wood veneer, laminate, or thermofoil applied, or have lacquer or paint applied. It's possible to achieve a smooth, shiny appearance in virtually any color with this application -- even a pearlized appearance if automobile lacquer is used.

Overglazing has been popular for several years. It's especially effective if your cabinets have beads and grooves to show off the finish. Overglaze can be any color, from the very lightest tint to the very darkest shade. Two cautionary comments:

Not every manufacturer can provide overglazing. If you're interested in the look, ask about available overglazing up front, to eliminate the ones that can't (or won't) do it.

Overglazing will typically add 10% - 20% to your overall cabinet investment.

Some companies also provide "distressing." The cabinets have an old-world, much-used look when they're new.

"A client said, 'Why should I pay them to do distressing? I'll just turn my kids (3 boys) and their friends loose with toys for a couple of hours; that'll do it!'"

Air quality in many states is strictly regulated, which may have an impact on the type of finish applied to your wood cabinets. Large manufacturers are able to comply with air quality regulations, but small custom manufacturers may not have the facility to finish the cabinets before installation. Jobsite-finished cabinets may not be as smooth or as durable as cabinets finished in a professional spray booth.

Recessed-panel and raised-panel doors can be manufactured from MDF, for application of lacquer, paint, laminate, or thermofoil, or they can be manufactured from wood. Recessed-panel doors have a solid-wood frame with a thin plywood panel in the middle. Raised-panel doors have a solid-wood frame and a panel that's carved from laminated strips of solid wood. You will be able to see the strips where the grain and/or color changes for natural or lightly-stained wood, especially if the wood has a more open-grain look.

The two most popular woods continue to be maple and cherry. A wide variety of other woods may be selected, depending on the availability and investment: oak, ash, birch, pecan, fir, pine, mahogany, teak. Wood from deciduous trees is harder, and less prone to damage. Soft woods (pine, fir, etc.) used for kitchen cabinets can develop a sticky surface film, and become very hard to clean where fingers continually touch the wood (around knobs and pulls).

Cabinet interiors are either plywood with a wood veneer (usually finished with clear lacquer), which is more expensive, or particleboard with melamine (available in solid white, solid almond, or maple finishes). Your decision about the interior finish is based on personal preference, and your relative investment.

Another important factor in choosing your cabinets is the location of the manufacturer, and the product lead time. If the manufacturer is 3,000 miles away, and the lead time for your cabinets is 12 weeks, your project could be seriously delayed if there's a problem with the cabinets.

To make a final decision about which cabinets to purchase, you need answers to the following questions:

How are the cabinets constructed?

Are the cabinets modular, custom-modular, or custom?

Is there a door/drawer style that fits into our decor and lifestyle?

Does the manufacturer use the wood we want? Is there a surcharge for the wood we want?

Does the manufacturer apply the color and finish we want? If not, what is the estimate for jobsite-finishing?

Does the manufacturer use the interior material we want? Is there a surcharge for this material?

Does the manufacturer have all of the storage accessories we need and want?

Where is the manufacturer located?

What is the lead time for the initial order?

What is the manufacturer's policy regarding reorder of problem cabinets? Is it the same lead time as the initial order?

What is the investment for these cabinets, compared to the investment for other cabinets?

Below, and on the next two pages, you will see simple line drawings of cabinet storage accessories. Some manufacturers have a long list of accessories, and others have a relatively short list. The most often-requested accessories are: Rollouts, corner lazy susan units, tray dividers, tilt-out sink trays, spice trays and racks, and convenient pantry units. It's easy to load up a kitchen with storage units, but your budget is a major consideration.

WALL CABINET STORAGE ACCESSORIES

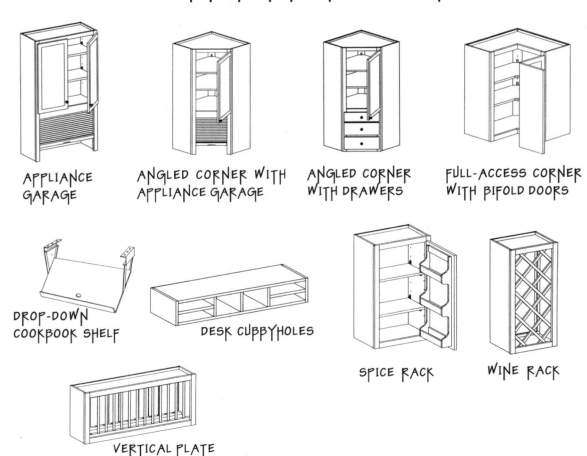

APPLIANCE GARAGE

ANGLED CORNER WITH APPLIANCE GARAGE

ANGLED CORNER WITH DRAWERS

FULL-ACCESS CORNER WITH BIFOLD DOORS

DROP-DOWN COOKBOOK SHELF

DESK CUBBYHOLES

SPICE RACK

WINE RACK

VERTICAL PLATE DIVIDERS

BASE CABINET STORAGE ACCESSORIES

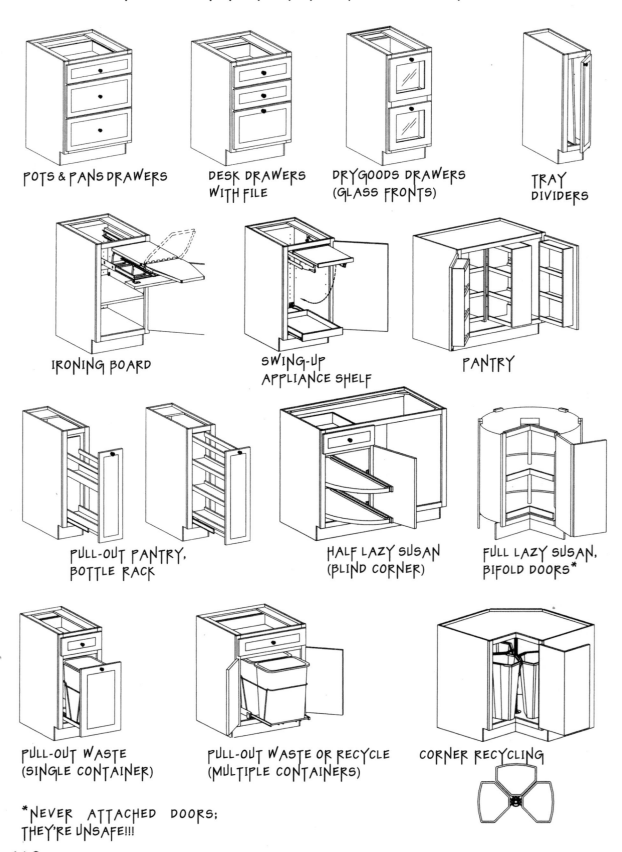

POTS & PANS DRAWERS

DESK DRAWERS WITH FILE

DRYGOODS DRAWERS (GLASS FRONTS)

TRAY DIVIDERS

IRONING BOARD

SWING-UP APPLIANCE SHELF

PANTRY

PULL-OUT PANTRY, BOTTLE RACK

HALF LAZY SUSAN (BLIND CORNER)

FULL LAZY SUSAN, BIFOLD DOORS*

PULL-OUT WASTE (SINGLE CONTAINER)

PULL-OUT WASTE OR RECYCLE (MULTIPLE CONTAINERS)

CORNER RECYCLING

*NEVER ATTACHED DOORS; THEY'RE UNSAFE!!!

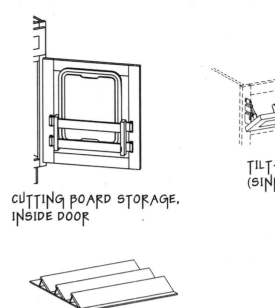

CUTTING BOARD STORAGE,
INSIDE DOOR

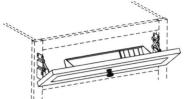

TILT-OUT TRAY
(SINKS & LAVATORIES)

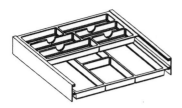

DOUBLE-TIER CUTLERY
DIVIDERS

SPICE DRAWER INSERT

CHOPPING BLOCK

TALL CABINET STORAGE ACCESSORIES

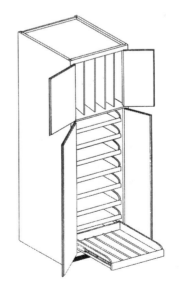

TRAY DIVIDERS ABOVE
ROLLOUTS BELOW

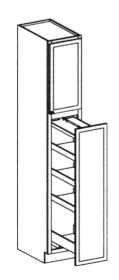

PULL-OUT PANTRY

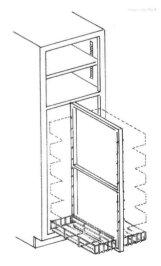

PANTRY WITH WIRE
BASKET PULLOUT

WIRE BASKET
KIT

"Many a small thing has been made large by the right kind of advertising." (Mark Twain)

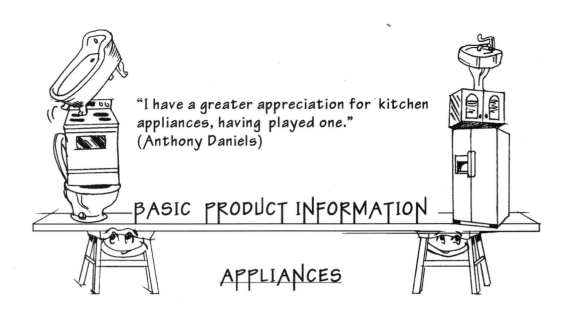

"I have a greater appreciation for kitchen appliances, having played one."
(Anthony Daniels)

BASIC PRODUCT INFORMATION

APPLIANCES

There are 182 major appliance manufacturers. Many of them manufacture and/or sell a full spectrum of appliances; some of them manufacture a limited spectrum of appliances. An excellent website with links to all of the major manufacturers is www.applianceadvisor.com. Another website to help you get particular information about products or manufacturers is www.aham.org. They list most, but not all, appliance manufacturers and products available.

Definite trends have evolved in kitchen appliances. Industry experts agree that we are about midpoint in these trends, which means they will continue for at least the next ten years or more. The trends that began in the late '80's are:

Stainless steel appliances. Most major manufacturers offer stainless steel finishes for cooktops, hoods, ranges, ovens, warming drawers, refrigerators, freezers, wine chillers, dishwashers, compactors, microwave ovens.

Integrated appliances. The trend started in the '70's when two major refrigerator manufacturers and several dishwasher manufacturers allowed trim kits to change the appearance of these appliances, to blend with cabinets or other appliances.

Specialty and high-end appliances. It started in the mid-1960's with downdraft cooktops that didn't require a conventional hood, and built-in refrigerators. Microwave ovens became popular in the 1970's. In the early 1980's, convection and micro-thermal ovens became popular. Since then, there's been an explosion of technology that has given appliance manufacturers the ability to offer advanced features for comparatively less, as the cost for technology has dropped over the years.

Every year, there's a major trade show for the kitchen and bath industry. The following product trends were shown:

> 2000: High-speed ovens. Knobless cooktop touch control. True white
> ceramic glass cooktops. Wide availability of warming drawers.

2001: Knobless cooktop touch controls; Ceran cooktops with pot sizing and pot sensing. New energy standards for refrigerators. French-made cooking equipment. Pitcher-sized refrigerator water dispensers. High-efficiency top-loader washers. Gas self-clean ranges. 1/2 load dishwashers.

2002: Ovens with ceramic glass broilers; 36" built-in ovens; Refrigerators with glass doors; Ice makers; Pro burners > than 15,000 BTU; 24" Pro Ranges; Stainless steel substitutes; Microwaves with big LED readouts; Wine refrigerators.

2003: Alternative finishes (nickel, platinum, high-fashion enamel). Outdoor barbecue units and all-in-one outdoor kitchens (including a sink, small refrigerator, and warming drawer).

The following information is a general description of individual appliance categories, to help you get started and to help you make informed decisions. No specific information about manufacturers, models, or operation is given in this guideline, and no specific safety information is offered (except for microwave ovens). Kitchen appliances are potentially dangerous if installed or operated improperly.

"Read the Owner's Manual to familiarize yourself with the appliance before you operate it."

Two PhD's had tried for hours to watch a rented movie on their new VCR -- no luck. They didn't take time to read the owner's manual (after all, one VCR is the same as any other VCR). So, they reboxed the unit and took it back to the appliance store, forgetting that the tape was still in the unit. The salesman hooked up the VCR, and verified that the rented tape wouldn't play -- not because the VCR was defective, but because the tape was jammed! Without saying a word, he simply pointed to the page in the manual that said, "If you can't play one tape, try another one."

COOKTOPS

First consideration: Fuel source. Is it electric, natural gas, or propane?

Electric cooktops are available with standard coils, smooth-surface ceran and glass which may have pot sensors and/or pot sizing. At least two manufacturers offer magnetic induction cooktops, which work by sending a magnetic impulse to steel pots and pans to heat them, and heat the food in them. Professional-type gas cooktops are available with high BTU rating; some are available with low-temperature settings for sauces, butter, and chocolate.

Second consideration: Size.

Cooktops are available in 12" modules, 30" units, 36" units, 48" units, and 60" units. Most cooktops are 22"-24" deep. If they are around 3" high, a shallow drawer can be placed directly below, which is convenient for cooking utensils.

Third consideration: Finish.

Cooktops are available in stainless steel, enamel, and glass. Enamel and glass are available in black or white as standard colors. Before you order a white cooktop, verify that the white blends with other white appliances. Enamel cooktops may be available in other colors, such as biscuit, red, green, blue, etc.

Fourth consideration: Investment.

Your investment in a standard coil-type electric cooktop will be no higher than $160. Your investment for a professional-type gas cooktop or a custom tile magnetic-induction cooktop could exceed $5,000.

Fifth consideration: Options.

Several manufacturers of glass cooktops have touch-sensor controls rather than knobs, which makes cleaning much easier. Gas cooktops are available with different grate sizes and shapes. Before you buy, verify that the grates are compatible with your existing pots and pans -- especially small saucepans. Many residential-type electric and gas cooktops have a downdraft option which eliminates the need for a hood. There is more information about downdraft venting in the next section.

At least one manufacturer has a modular design, where you can have one or more modules of gas, one or more modules of electric, a griddle module, and a deep-fryer module. Each of these modules sells for about $700.

VENTILATION SYSTEMS

First consideration: Downdraft or updraft.

Downdraft ventilation is meant for use with residential-type electric and gas cooktops, not for use with high-BTU professional cooktops. While downdraft ventilation is perfect visually for island and peninsula installation, it works better if the area for steam and cooking particles is limited to a full backsplash and wall cabinets on both sides. Without the backsplash, steam and particulates can escape into the room. The rating for downdrafts is 500 to 1,400 CFM (cubic feet per minute).

150

Updraft ventilation is more efficient for islands and peninsulas, because the hood can collect and exhaust a high percentage of steam and particulates, as the hot air rises.

Second consideration: Size.

Downdraft units are available in 30" wide and 36" wide. Updraft hoods should always be 6" wider than the cooktop, to provide a larger collection area, and to minimize potential damage to adjacent wall cabinets.

Standard hoods are available in 30" wide, 36" wide, 42" wide, and 60" wide. Standard hoods are about 21" deep; professional hoods are 24" to 27" deep. If you have a nine- or ten-foot ceiling, and you're planning to install a hood over an island or peninsula, you will have to order a duct extension, or your designer will have to creatively resolve the height difference.

NOTE: The bottom of the hood should be about 30" above the cooking surface.

Third consideration: Finish.

The downdraft unit should match the finish or color of your cooktop. Standard metal hoods are available in a wide variety of finishes: stainless steel, copper, brass, or enamel (black, biscuit, and white). Custom hoods can be anything you want them to be: metal, wood to match your cabinets (with metal liner), stucco (with metal liner), or tile (wood frame with metal liner).

Fourth consideration: Style.

Hoods can be any style to blend with your kitchen, or to add visual pizazz. Hoods are often used as focal points, because they are at eye level.

Fifth consideration: Investment.

Your investment in a standard hood can be as low as $200 or as high as $4,500. Your investment in a custom hood will start at $3,500 and increase exponentially based on the materials, design, and components (hood exterior + liner + duct + motor +installation).

"There is a peculiar burning odor in the room, like explosives. The kitchen fills with smoke and the hot, sweet, ashy smell of scorched cookies. The war has begun." (Alison Lurie)

OVENS

First consideration: Electric or gas.

Since manufacturers developed self-cleaning (compared to "continuous cleaning" used for many years) for gas ovens in the past three years, the choice between electric and gas ovens is a toss-up. If you use the broil feature more than once a week, you should use that feature as your main comparison.

Second consideration: Type.

Ovens are available as single (convection, conventional, halogen, or steam), single-with-microwave (convection or conventional oven), and double. One sub-category of double ovens is micro-thermal + convection on top, conventional or convection on the bottom.

About convection cooking. There has been ongoing discussion about what constitutes true convection cooking and baking. Any manufacturer can claim its ovens are convection. It's how the hot air is distributed evenly that will allow you to cook several different courses simultaneously, or multiple sheets of cookies, in less time with better results than conventional baking. Bread will rise higher, meat will be juicier, and cookies will be evenly browned.

Third consideration: Size.

Standard ovens are 27" wide and 30" wide. At least one manufacturer is producing a 36" wide oven, which can be installed below the same manufacturer's 36" wide cooktop, for an integrated look. Oven height is determined by the type of oven.

NOTE: Because ovens are heavily insulated for the self-cleaning feature, the interior dimensions are considerably smaller than they used to be. When you go shopping for ovens, take your largest cookie sheet, your largest roasting pan, and a pillow (which can be plumped to be the same size as a turkey). If you do this, you won't have the additional investment in new baking equipment.

Fourth consideration: Finish.

Ovens are available in stainless steel, white, black, or biscuit. At least one manufacturer offers other finishes to blend with its other high-fashion colors of red, blue, and green. Chrome and stainless steel are most often used for trim and handles, but some manufacturers have added polished brass or other metals for visual appeal.

Fifth consideration: Features.

Ovens can have analog (dials and standard buttons) or digital (buttonless) controls. Many models are available with thermometer probe, timed cooking, rotisserie, and low-heat features.

Sixth consideration: Investment.

You will invest about $600 for a standard analog oven, or you can invest $5,000 for a single digital convection oven. If you double these two numbers, that will give you the low-high investment for a double oven.

RANGES

"Range" is the generic term for a unit that combines the cooktop and oven.

First consideration: Fuel.

You can choose an all-electric range, an all-gas range, or a dual-fuel range (gas cooking surface and electric oven).

Second consideration: Type.

The range oven is either conventional or convection, whether it's electric or gas. If the cooking surface is electric, it can be standard coils or ceran.

Third consideration: Size.

Standard ranges are 30" wide or 36" wide. Professional-type ranges are 30" wide, 36" wide, 42" wide, 48" wide, and 60" wide.

Fourth consideration: Finish.

Standard ranges are available in stainless steel, biscuit, black, or white. Professional and specialty ranges are available in stainless steel, cast iron, high-fashion enamel colors, with stainless steel, chrome, brass, or other metal trim, handles, and accents.

Fifth consideration: Features.

See the Oven features. Several manufacturers also produce downdraft ranges.

Sixth consideration: Investment.

For a standard range, your investment will be around $1,000. For a large, imported specialty range, your investment will be over $15,000.

DISHWASHERS

First consideration: Type.

Before the dishwasher drawer was introduced, most dishwashers looked alike. They were interchangeable, because they were all the standard size of 24" wide (except for a very few apartment size which were 18" wide). At least one manufacturer is introducing a 30" wide dishwasher, to handle monstrous loads of dishes.   There are also new countertop and in-sink dishwashers, which are convenient for very small loads (at a fairly reasonable price). So, you have more choices than ever. Your decision will be based on more than bells and whistles.

Second consideration: Features.

All dishwashers can be integrated to look like cabinets. They also have interchangeable trim kits to blend with standard appliance colors. Several manufacturers have taken the integrated look to the top, literally, by putting digital controls on top of the door, so there are no visible controls on the front of the dishwasher. Many dishwashers have movable trays and racks, to accommodate large items. Some dishwashers have dedicated racks for silverware to keep them separated. Some have more than one dishwashing arm, for heavy-duty cleaning. Dishwasher interiors can be stainless steel or molded plastic; there's an ongoing debate which is best for residential use.

Third consideration: Investment.

For a standard 24-inch wide dishwasher with minimum features, or a countertop dishwasher, your investment will be as low as $300. For a pair of dishwasher drawers, fully-integrated dishwasher with multiple cycles and hidden controls, or a super-size dishwasher, your investment will be over $1,500.

REFRIGERATORS

Refrigerators, like other home appliances, have improved in the past five years because of technology. You have much more selection, and many more options than you used to have. This is a benefit, but it's also a challenge, because you have more choices. Here is a list of refrigerators you have available to you now:

Standard. 30" wide and 36" wide by approximately 68" high by approximately 32" deep. Available as side-by-side refrigerator+freezer, upper freezer+lower refrigerator, and upper refrigerator+lower freezer. Most side-by-side models also have ice and water compartments in the door. They are available in white and black; biscuit and stainless are available from some manufacturers, but not all manufacturers. Some manufacturers also provide trim kits so you can have panels made to match your cabinets.

The advantages associated with standard-size refrigerators is the storage space. This is also a disadvantage, because containers of leftovers can get pushed to the back, where they become laboratory experiments. Another disadvantage of the depth: it makes the refrigerator look and feel heavier than anything else in the kitchen -- especially if it's a galley or corridor kitchen.

Built-In. Because they are only 24" deep, which is flush with the base cabinets, these refrigerators blend in with the kitchen rather than overpowering the kitchen. They are available in the standard finishes, and most can be fully integrated with decorative panels and handles, so they don't scream "I'm an appliance!" Some manufacturers offer standard-height refrigerators that are only 24" deep, but the most popular built-in units are typically 84" high, with the compressor on the top.

Built-in refrigerators are available in widths from 27" to 48". Side-by-side units are available in 36" wide, 42" wide, and 48" wide; bottom freezers are standard in combination units that are 27" to 36" wide. It's been proven that bottom-mount freezers are better for two reasons: (1.) Food access is better (statistics show that we get into the refrigerator three to four times more often than we get into the freezer); (2.) Better energy efficiency (because cold air drops, it takes less energy to cool or freeze food).

A couple of manufacturers also make dedicated refrigerator and dedicated freezer units that are 27" wide, 30" wide, and 36" wide.

Special. Compact refrigerator or refrigerator+freezer units have been popular for over 25 years. Five years ago, one manufacturer introduced individual refrigerator and freezer drawers, which dramatically improved the flexibility of kitchen design. But these compact units are not restricted to kitchens or wet bars. Because of their size, they can be included in office, family room, living room, dining room, or master bedroom plans.

In the special category, you can also buy a refrigerator that has a retro look of the 1950's. Or, you can buy a refrigerator that blends with the look of a wood-burning range. These refrigerators have the same function as the others; the difference is the appearance (and your comparative investment).

 **"Why don't manufacturers offer side-by-side units with the refrigerator on the left and the freezer on the right? No one's been able to give a logical answer to this question! This would give kitchen designers more flexibility to design functional kitchen plans!"**

First consideration: Size.

After seeing what's available, you can decide what size you need, including how much storage you need. Your designer will also have valuable recommendations that should be considered.

Second consideration: Investment.

For a standard 36" wide refrigerator, your investment will be $700 to $1,600. For a built-in 36" wide refrigerator, your investment will be $3,000 to $4,500. You will pay extra for integrated cabinet panels and special pulls, and should allow at least $1,500 for these.

27" wide built-in refrigerator+freezer units, dedicated refrigerator or freezer units sell for around $3,500. 48"wide built-in refrigerator+freezer units sell for around $8,000.

For compact refrigerator+freezer units, your investment will be $1,000 to $2,500. Refrigerator and freezer drawers sell for around $2,600 each, not including integrated panels and decorative hardware.

Third consideration: Features.

If size and investment are equal for two different models, then a comparison of the features may help you decide. It's very much like buying a car -- getting the most for the smallest investment.

 "Times (and the economy) have changed. A 1978 Honda Civic was $3,200, and an complete kitchen remodel was $15,000. For $15,000 today, you can get two (or three) appliances, or a Honda Civic. A complete kitchen remodel is at least $45,000."

Features include:
    Adjustable climate zones
    Adjustable glass shelves
    Ice and water dispenser in the freezer door
    Adjustable door shelves
    Specialty storage compartments/bins
    Integrated computer that helps with shopping list
    Trim kits for integrated decorative panels
    Choice of handle styles
    Glass doors

MICROWAVE OVENS

Remember the early microwave ovens? They were big! Operating them was a challenge, because we needed to watch them constantly, to make sure our food was cooked uniformly.

Microwave ovens have gotten smaller (although there are still large ones being sold). Technology has made them smarter, and easier to use. One-touch cooking is available on most models, which has eliminated guesswork. You can purchase a microwave oven for as little as $129, or you can pay as much as $400, depending on the features, size, style, and finish you want. Most microwave ovens include a rotating shelf, which cooks the food more uniformly. The interior of a microwave should be able to fit a 9" x 13" dish, so the dish can rotate freely.

Several manufacturers offer microwave-hood combination units. Thousands of new homes, townhouses, and remodeled homes have these units, because they **seem** to accomplish two purposes. But, with a bit of closer inspection, they don't accomplish either purpose very well. If a microwave/hood is used in place of a standard hood, and if NKBA Kitchen Design Guideline #21 is followed (see Page 100), where the bottom of the appliance is a maximum of 48" above the floor, you will have only 18" between the bottom of the microwave and your cooktop. You could have difficulty with tall pasta pots or stewpots.

If the microwave/hood is placed higher to allow for tall pots, then the microwave is dangerously high. You should be able to see into the microwave at all times, especially when you're removing containers of hot food. The microwave height should be convenient (and safe) for the shortest member of the family that uses it.

"Safety and Function MUST come first in kitchen (and bathroom) design!!!!"

First consideration: Size.

> Standard microwave ovens are 21" to 24" wide, by 12" to 18" high, by 12" to 21" deep. Microwave/hood units are 24" to 36" wide, by 14" to 18" high, by 12" to 18" deep. When you're looking at microwave ovens, bring along your largest glass baking dish as a guideline to determine how large the interior needs to be (which will determine the overall size).

Second consideration: Features and Function.

> Technology offers you many bells and whistles:
>   Defrost cycle
>   One-button control for popcorn, baked potatoes, meat, frozen
>   entrees, etc.
>   Heat sensor
>   Automatic shut-off
>   Delayed start
>
> You may not need every feature offered, but it's good to know how each model compares with others in the same price range. Most microwave ovens are right-handed, with the door hinge on the left, but there are a couple of models that have drop-down doors that are usually meant for installation above standard ovens.

Third consideration: Price.

> After seeing what's available, you'll have a better idea of what your
> investment will be for a microwave oven.

Fourth consideration: Finish (color) and style.

> Most microwave ovens are available in white and black; many are offered
> in stainless steel, and a few are available in biscuit (light off-white) or
> high-fashion colors. A couple of manufacturers have taken style to a
> new level, offering a "retro" look that's gaining popularity. You might
> replace your microwave when the "retro" trend dies, or when you get tired
> of high-fashion colors.

GARBAGE DISPOSALS

This appliance is very important because it's used frequently, but your decision isn't as
critical or as difficult as other appliances.

First consideration: Power.

> Disposals are available with 1/2, 3/4, 1, and 1-1/2 horsepower motors.
> Select the one that most closely matches your needs.

Second consideration: Sound insulation.

> In the past five years, manufacturers have reduced the noise of
> disposals. Many models will have information about sound insulation in
> the sales brochures.

Third consideration: Price.

> Disposal units sell for $150 to $300.

TRASH COMPACTORS

Compactors had wide popularity in the 1960's to the late 1980's, but the need for compactors
has declined since more homeowners are actively recycling, and limiting the amount of trash
that goes to landfills. ("Hint, hint.") Several manufacturers still make compactors, in
sizes ranging from 12" wide to 18' wide; the most popular size (and highest availability) is
15" wide.

Trash compactors typically sell for $500 to $800, but one manufacturer sells its trash
compactor for over $1,500. Integrated decorative panels to blend with cabinets will be
more; allow at least $250 for cabinet panels.

WATER FILTERS

Homeowners are including water filters in their remodeling projects -- high on the *need* list, not just included on the *want* list. An internet search (google.com) for water filters retrieved a list of 956,000 sites! The information below is very basic; if you are interested in water filtration, you will have to do some homework.

One type of water filter is gravity-fed, where water flows through diatomaceous earth. These units sell for $250 (under-sink models) to over $2,000 (whole-house models).

Another type is reverse-osmosis which uses a semipermeable membrane that looks a lot like common household sandwich wrap. Under-sink models sell for $650 to $1,500 and whole-house models sell for $2,000 to over $10,000.

Another type of water filter is UV, ultraviolet energy. It works almost instantly, leaving no residuals or chemicals in the water. Under-sink models sell for $300 to $1,500, and whole-house models sell for $2,500 to over $10,000.

It is unsettling (ok, scary!) what our water can contain. There are about 60,000 community water suppliers in America. To help you decide what kind of water filter is best for your family, you may be able to obtain statistics about your local water quality. You can search at www.epa.gov/ceis, or www.wqa.org.

"Hint: If you're installing an under-sink purifier, remind your designer and contractor that you want a supply line from that purifier to the icemaker, or purchase a separate purifier for the icemaker."

"LUXURY" APPLIANCES

For most families' lifestyles and budgets, the following appliances are not a necessity, but they may be for you. To be a well-informed consumer, you need to know what's available before you make your decisions.

BARBEQUES

Indoor barbecue units have become more scarce since the explosion of outdoor professional barbecue islands. You can obtain one of these units for $2,500 or you can purchase one for over $25,000 that is a self-contained outdoor kitchen. Indoor barbecue grills are meant for occasional use only. They should have an exhaust unit (minimum 1,000 cfm) to reduce grease particles and lingering odors. Indoor barbecues sell for around $1,000.

DEEP FRYERS

One or two manufacturers of residential kitchen equipment make deep fryers, to be used in modular layout with other modules in a cooktop. Safety is an important consideration with these units; one minor mistake can lead to a serious burns or a kitchen fire. These units sell for around $1,000.

> "In department stores, so much kitchen equipment is bought indiscriminately by people who just come in for men's underwear." (Julia Child)

BUILT-IN ESPRESSO MACHINES

We love coffee! There are at least six manufacturers of countertop espresso machines, and at least one manufacturer of an espresso machine that is installed in a tall cabinet, with space below for a water filtration unit. That's *serious* caffeine! And so is the investment! You will pay from $500 to over $3,000 for one of these units.

Over 20 years ago, we thought our friend was more than "eccentric" when he installed a built-in restaurant-size espresso machine in his kitchen. It took up one entire countertop. He not only had it plumbed with filtered water, but he had it connected to a remote switch in his bedroom. When his alarm went off, he'd hit the switch and have espresso ready five minutes later. Didn't realize how far ahead of the times he was . . .

WARMING DRAWERS

Warming drawers are effective for the following purposes:

If dinner is often served in shifts because of unpredictable work hours;

If you entertain frequently;

If you really like to preheat dinner plates and serving dishes.

First consideration: Size.

Warming drawers are available in sizes from 24" wide to 30" wide, by 9" to 12" high, by 24" deep.

Second consideration: Finish.

Currently, warming drawers are available in standard white, black, stainless steel, biscuit, and high-fashion colors. Integrated models, with trim kits to allow cabinet fronts, are on the horizon.

Third consideration: Price.

These units sell for $700 to $1,300.

WINE COOLERS and WINE CELLARS

Wine coolers started gaining popularity in the 1980's. The early ones, which replaced wine racks in cabinets, were limited to about 24 bottles. Standard under-counter wine coolers are 24" wide. Several well-known manufacturers make residential wine coolers that can accommodate several hundred bottles in a 36" wide by 84" high unit with glass doors. Your investment in a wine cooler will range from $750 to over $5,000, depending on the size and features. Wine rooms (cellars) are often included in VERY upscale building and remodeling projects. These projects often include a media room or mini-theater room.

WOKS

Several manufacturers of residential kitchen appliances have wok rings that fit over high-btu gas burners. Commercial equipment shouldn't be used in the home, unless someone in the family is a trained professional chef. Commercial woks have one burner that's rated at 30,000 btu's or more, and requires a dedicated 3/4" gas line. These units will provide a flame almost one foot high!

"An all-purpose fire extinguisher should be considered standard equipment for every residential kitchen. I gave one to a client 15 years ago who demanded to have a commercial wok in her kitchen."

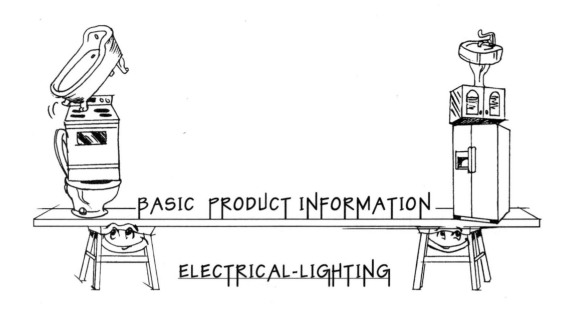

BASIC PRODUCT INFORMATION

ELECTRICAL-LIGHTING

Lighting is jewelry for your home. It creates the atmosphere. Hopefully, the days are gone when you walk into a room, flip a switch, and a single fixture in the middle lights up. Builders and electricians have become more educated about the importance of lighting as homeowners have become more sophisticated. Lighting, switching, and electricity are very technical; serious thought has been given how to make these subjects less threatening, and more user friendly. Instead of making you look in the glossary, a couple of specialized terms are defined below:

Lamp   Fancy word for "light bulb"
Incandescent lamp   Fancy word for standard light bulb, with
                             filaments that heat up

Energy laws and the electric code have gotten progressively more strict since the late 1970's. Most states have adopted regulations that California started imposing after the energy crisis. Even if your local building department doesn't have strict requirements, it's a great idea to include energy-saving ideas in your remodeling project, because in the long run you'll save money.

If you use fluorescent fixtures as the main source of light for your kitchen and bathrooms, you'll get more light for each penny than if you use incandescent fixtures. Example: A 12-watt fluorescent lamp will produce as much light as a standard 60-watt incandescent lamp. Your electric bill is based on the watts you use; if you pay $.10 for each kilowatt-hour you burn, and you leave this single light on every day, for 8 hours, then over a year, you will pay $3.50 for the electricity instead of $17.52, just for this one lamp. That's a savings of over $14.00.

The arguments that designers hear often from homeowners (their reasons for not wanting fluorescent lighting) are:

"The fixtures aren't as pretty."

While it's true that there are ugly fluorescent fixtures, manufacturers have worked hard to develop nice-looking fluorescent fixtures. Homeowners have a better choice now, and it's improving all the time.

"Some of the ugliest light fixtures on the market are incandescent! Ugly, and expensive to use!"

"The light makes me look sick; it's green."

Make an effort to visit the best lighting store in your city. They should have a display to show you the different colors available in fluorescent lamps. We've become accustomed to the warm color of incandescent lamps that flatters our skin tones (red-orange-yellow). You'll be pleasantly surprised when you see how close new fluorescent lamps are to that color.

"The flickering bothers me."

The flickering is caused by natural fluctuation of our electricity, when the "alternating current" alternates, at 60 to the second. Fluorescent lights turn on and off 60 times every second. Incandescent lights do, too, but because they have filaments in them, that are hot, the flicker is too slight for most people to notice. Technology has helped manufacturers develop fluorescent lamps that flicker less and provide better color, with improved phosphor coatings.

"The buzzing and humming bothers me."

Noisy fixtures are caused by inexpensive or defective ballasts, which can be replaced. Electronic ballasts aren't noisy; magnetic ballasts are the ones that usually cause the problems.

"Fluorescent lights can't be dimmed. They're either on full bright, or off."

Fluorescent fixtures can be dimmed, but it can get very expensive, because there has to be a dimmable ballast. Because there's an increased likelihood for humming when the fluorescent fixture is dimmed, it's a good idea to add an electronic filter, manufactured by at least two companies specializing in lighting controls.

Hints: How to Use Fluorescent Lighting

In kitchens, under-cabinet fixtures are a wonderful solution, because they provide soft, indirect lighting and great task lighting. The tubes are small, so the fixtures are only 1-1/4" high.

If you have several fluorescent under-cabinet fixtures, and if they're controlled by the first light switch, they meet the code requirement for fluorescent general lighting.

If you have an open soffit above your wall and tall cabinets, fluorescent fixtures bouncing light off the ceiling will brighten the whole room, make the ceiling float, and light objects or pictures above the cabinets.

Most manufacturers of bathroom exhaust fans have fan-light combinations that include fluorescent lighting. You can use incandescent fixtures for task lighting (makeup, shaving, etc.).

Fluorescent wall sconces are an excellent way to light not only kitchens and bathrooms, but every room in the house. There is an excellent selection of decorative wall sconces for living rooms, dining rooms, and hallways.

Fluorescent fixtures are wonderful for providing light in closets. If color-matching your clothes and accessories is important, spend the extra money to get full-spectrum lamps.

Having made an argument in favor of fluorescent lighting doesn't mean to imply that you shouldn't have incandescent or low-voltage lighting, too. To create a friendly atmosphere, lighting should be balanced and carefully blended. Most designers have the education, training, and experience to create the right light balance for your home. There are also lighting design specialists who can help you achieve the special feeling you want for your remodeled home.

 "The most beautiful home, poorly lit, is boring, overpowering, and sad. The modest home, beautifully lit, is exciting, happy, and peaceful."

Dimmer switches are wonderful tools to help you achieve dramatic effects for different situations. When you entertain, it's especially nice to have lighting at varying levels of brightness to create emphasis where you want it. You don't have to entertain company. You can entertain your immediate family for a special occasion -- or no occasion!

One area of the home where dimmer switches are overlooked is bathrooms. In the middle of the night, whether you're using the toilet or taking medication, it's nice to have enough light for what you're doing (especially reading medicine labels), without waking yourself or your partner with full-on lights. Dimmed lighting is nice, also, for taking a relaxing bath or shower.

Lighting controls have become more sophisticated in the last 15 years. A widely-accepted concept is to have two-, three-, or four-way switches control the same fixture(s). Separate switches to control certain fixtures -- especially if they're dimmer switches -- create a wonderful layered lighting effect.

Homeowners have become more knowledgeable about "smart" home controls featured on television and on the internet. Some of the systems must be installed in new homes; many systems can be installed during remodeling, and at least half a dozen systems can be retrofitted into existing homes with very little (if any) disruption to existing wiring.

One of the benefits of smart home controls is safety. Many of the systems have a panic switch that's usually located in the master bedroom. This switch allows the homeowner to turn on the house lights if they hear an unusual noise outside. Another safety feature offered by many of the smart systems is a preset program based on the way you normally use rooms before sunrise and after sunset, so when you are away, your home looks lived in. Some smart-home controls also offer remote switches that operate like your garage door, to turn on exterior and selected interior lights when you arrive home at night.

The list of possibilities is very long. A couple of good sites to do preliminary online research: www.getplugged.com, and smarthome.com.

> "Electricity is actually made up of extremely tiny particles
> called electrons, that you cannot see with the naked eye unless
> you have been drinking." (Dave Barry)

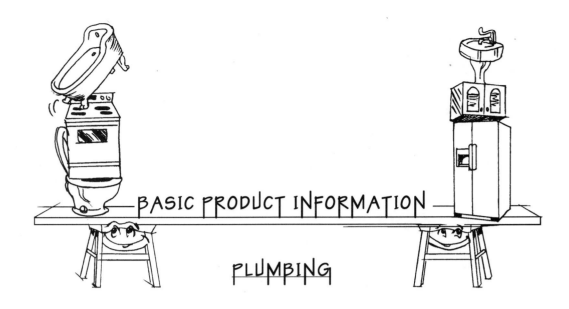

BASIC PRODUCT INFORMATION

PLUMBING

An internet search for plumbing products was very successful. One site (www.plumbingnet.com) links to major manufacturers directly and lists **all** manufacturers of plumbing products -- 302 pages, over 2,000 alphabetical names! The Plumbing Manufacturers' Institute (www.pmihome.org) has a shorter list. One of the best places to see a good selection of plumbing products is www.homeportfolio.com. You can easily spend days looking at websites, gathering product information. Your pre-selection process can be overwhelming. Can you imagine how difficult it was for homeowners **before** the internet became an effective tool?

You've read over and over throughout this book how important your budget is to your product selection. To become an informed consumer and make the best choices, you need to get current pricing for different alternatives. This chapter contains basic pricing guidelines to help you get started. Your potential investment in every product can vary 9:1! "What?" Yes, it's true.

Homeowners didn't listen to their designer's advice, and waited until construction to start buying bathroom plumbing. Choosing a toilet should be easy, right? Yes, they all have the same function. The homeowners discovered they could get a white, two-piece, round-front toilet from stock at the local plumbing store for $159, or they could get a similar toilet on sale from a major home remodeling chain store for $99. But they didn't want white; they had selected a high-fashion taupe color, which had to be special-ordered. They also wanted a one-piece, elongated-bowl model they'd seen in magazines. Their investment in the toilet was over $700; the fancy toilet seat was an additional $139, and the pewter trip lever was an additional $79. Same function, yes. Price? A range of $159-$918!

166

KITCHEN:

Most kitchen sinks are available in a wide variety of sizes, styles, materials, and prices. Farmhouse sinks have been popular for several years. Manufacturers have listened to designers and homeowners. In homeportfolio.com, you can see cast iron, stainless steel, quartz, solid-surface, copper, concrete, and stone farmhouse sinks. Practical hints to consider if you're interested in a farmhouse-style sink:

- Is the sink you selected compatible with the cabinets you're using?

- Will the cabinet support the weight?

- Are the cabinets finished to accommodate an exposed-front sink?

- Does the sink you've selected project beyond the front of the base cabinet to protect the cabinet from water damage?

- How smooth (or rough) is the front of the sink? Is there a potential for damaging your clothes when you rub against it?

- How deep is the sink you've selected? Is it going to hurt your back when you're bending over to do dishes or prepare food?

- Does the sink fit your budget? What hidden expenditures are there, if you stretch the budget (i.e., higher installation fee, more expensive countertop details, etc.)? These sinks sell for $500 to over $4,000.

For most kitchens, the typical sink has been 33" wide by 22" deep by 8" high, because it fits nicely into a 36" wide base cabinet. A 33" wide sink accommodates two bowls, whether equal or large bowl + small bowl. The increased popularity of the farmhouse kitchen has brought back the popularity of the large single sink. For smaller kitchens, 25" wide by 22" deep is a good size to accommodate broiler pans and roasting pans.

The 25" wide sink also makes a generous secondary (food preparation) sink. If space is limited, the next choice for an auxiliary sink is 19" round or square. A bar sink, typically 12" to 15" square, shouldn't be used as an auxiliary food preparation sink, because the drain isn't large enough for a garbage disposal, and the sink itself is too small to hold anything.

"**What kind of salad can you make in a bar sink?** **U**se your **head** to think of alternatives, 'cause you can't use a head of lettuce!"

As the example at left stated, your investment in every <u>kitchen</u> fixture or fitting can vary more than 400%.

You have a large selection of styles, finishes, and prices for your kitchen faucets, too. Chrome is still the most popular, because it's very durable. But stainless steel and powder coat finishes have become more popular in the past five years. A single-lever valve is better than a two-valve (hot+cold) faucet, because you can control the water temperature and flow with one hand (or an elbow, if both hands are full).

Until five years ago, most single-lever faucets looked very streamlined and contemporary. But more manufacturers are making traditional-looking single-lever faucets; this may be linked to the popularity of the farmhouse sinks.

Three basic factors affect your faucet investment:

- The internal workings (guts) of the unit
- The finish
- The style

The best faucets have ceramic cartridges, made from a similar material to the skin of the space shuttle. Sediment in the water will gradually grind away softer discs, which will lead to leaking and malfunction. If you purchase a cheaper faucet, it's a good idea to also purchase an extra cartridge or two -- remember the bathroom example earlier? Harder discs mean a longer lifetime, which means you may never have to replace the disc. Before you buy, figure out how much a cheaper faucet plus new cartridges will cost versus a more expensive faucet. You may be surprised!

Stainless steel, pewter, polished brass, and other special-order finishes will add at least $100 to your faucet investment. Traditional styling, with more curves, may be an additional charge, too. It's best to compare all of this, in writing -- back to the spreadsheet!

"I didn't promise that becoming an informed consumer would be 100% fun; I just said you would be a better consumer!! Saving money is fun, isn't it?"

Faucets with pull-out spray/aerator heads are very useful for food preparation and cleanup activities. Your building department may need to see written evidence from the manufacturer that the pull-out unit has an anti-siphon device, to prevent dirty water from being sucked into drinkable water.

BATHROOM:

Per square foot, your bathroom is the most expensive room in your home. If you take a minute to go back and revisit the "good-better-best" examples, you'll see that plumbing fixtures and fittings for the master bathroom (120 square feet) ranged from a low of $2,949 to a high of $37,083; the mid-range was actually $11,018, and the average was $20,016 --

skewed by the "best" numbers. So, your investment, per square foot, in bathroom plumbing fixtures and fittings will be approximately $150 per square foot. Add that together with your allowance for cabinets, countertops, backsplash, tub/shower walls, flooring, lighting-ventilation, your per-square-foot investment will jump to a minimum of $200 a square foot, PLUS labor.

The following information is similar to the Appliance Information chapter. Lots of information has been compiled and concentrated to give you good, reliable, basic information and many things to think about as you select what's right for you. Let's start with *heart* of the bathroom.

TOILETS

Most states are working to save our most precious commodity, water. Virtually every plumbing fixture or fitting related to water usage has been modified to require less water. Toilets are a primary example. Older toilets use three to seven gallons of fresh water per flush. New toilets require only 1.6 gallons of water per flush.

The technology has improved tremendously in the past three years. The first 1.6 gallon toilets would clog and overflow easily. One flush was fine for urine, but solid waste required two or three flushes. The plunger was always available, especially when guests arrived, and used new toilets for the first time.

 "My, how times have changed! When I was a girl, Jack Paar got into 'deep doo-doo' with a cute joke about a water closet. Now, we're talking openly about how many flushes it takes to clear solid waste from our water closets."

You can select from many types of toilets. Every manufacturer offers toilets with multiple combinations of features:

- One-piece or two-piece (close-coupled)
- Round-front or elongated bowl
- Gravity or pressurized flush (flushometer tank system)
- Trip-lever, top flush button, or proximity sensor flush
- Visible or concealed trap
- Standard seat height or ADA-compliant seat height

Toilets are available in a wide range of colors. Typically, white and off-white (and some gray) colors are standard. Any other color is usually considered high-fashion, and sells for a higher price.

One well-known manufacturer has two patented toilet accessories: A built-in hygienic washer, and a seat that closes slowly. Other manufacturers may offer similar accessories; if you're interested in them, ask your local plumbing supplier about these features when you're looking at toilets.

As stated earlier, you can buy a 1.6 GPF (gallon-per-flush) toilet for as little as $129 or as much as $1,500.

LAVATORIES

"Why is it called a 'lavatory' and not a sink? What's the difference?"

Eureka! The answer -- bartleby.com: From late Latin lavtrium, lavtor, lavre, to wash.

Random House Unabridged Dictionary: Middle English, sinc, a basin or receptacle, as in a kitchen or laundry, usually connected with a water supply and drainage system, for washing dishes, clothing, etc.

Of course, sinc was associated only with kitchens and laundries, because there were no bathrooms in England before the Victorian era! So, you are learning about home remodeling products and acquiring historical trivia at the same time.

For the past 30 or 40 years, standard lavatory/countertop height has been 30" or 31". Many homeowners have discovered the advantages of raising the height to 33" or 36":

> Reduces back pain, not having to bend so low;
> Allows more space for storage (usually one more drawer);
> Achieves better proportion between the lavatory cabinet, backsplash, and mirror.

You have a wide selection of style, size, color, and price when you shop for a lavatory. The styles and materials available are:

> Pedestal: These are freestanding units. They're available in all porcelain, porcelain bowl + metal base (or legs), all glass, glass bowl + metal base (or legs), glass bowl + wood base, pottery bowl + metal or wood base, metal bowl + metal base, metal bowl + glass base, metal bowl + wood base, stone bowl + stone base. There's a large selection of hand-painted and custom-glaze pedestal lavatories, as well as carved stone and solid-surface pedestal lavatories.

> Undermount (or integral): These permit the countertop to overlap the bowl, allowing you to wipe spills, etc. directly into the bowl. They're available in porcelain, glass, pottery, metal, and solid surface. You can purchase hand-painted and custom-glaze undermount lavatories, too.

> Integral bowls are usually associated with solid-surface materials, or composite materials, but they can also be made of glass. An integral bowl is part of the countertop, seamless, continuous.

Self-rimming: These bowls sit on top of the countertop, with the rim touching the countertop. They're available in the same materials as undermount bowls. Don't confuse them with the popular top-mount bowls.

Top-mount: These bowls were first introduced about five years ago, and they have been consistently growing in popularity, especially in high-end bathrooms. You have seen them featured in virtually every magazine for the past year or two. The bottom of the bowl around the drain sits on the countertop. The bowls are finished inside and outside. Most of these bowls require wall-mounted faucets.

THOUGHTS TO PONDER...

So many times in this book, you've read that your project should fit your lifestyle, needs, and budget. Before you buy any product that's popular, just because it's popular, try to analyze and weigh the benefits and liabilities. This is true with the top-mount bowls. The goal is to make **informed decisions.** Following are some questions to help you decide if a top-mount bowl is appropriate for you:

- How deep is the bowl?

- How high will the bowl be if you put it on a 36" high countertop?

- Does the overall height/depth of the bowl limit you to a 30" or 31" high countertop?

- How does the height of the bowl affect the height of the backsplash and mirror? If you're selecting a wall-mount faucet, will it be in the backsplash, or will it end up in the mirror? (Circular cuts in mirrors, close together, can get very expensive!)

- How difficult will it be to clean around the bowl?

- How much space will there be between the bottom of the bowl at the drain and the countertop? Can you easily fit a sponge or rag in this area?

- How much space will there be behind the bowl? How can you see what you're cleaning?

- Will you still be satisfied with a top-mount bowl when the trend changes? How much will it cost to change the faucet, bowl, countertop, and cabinets?

LAVATORY FAUCETS

To say that you can be overwhelmed by the selection of faucets is a gross understatement! If you take time to check the internet, your task will be much easier. homeportfolio.com again gets very high marks for a broad cross-section of good-better-best faucets available. Their website has an excellent way of categorizing these products. You can choose by manufacturer, style, type, etc., in the standard search. In the advanced search, you can select by your investment range or specific dimensions you need.

At this time, homeportfolio.com shows a total of 1,180 bathroom faucets from 53 manufacturers. They show the following quantities in four price ranges:

Less than $325	=	174
$325 - $550	=	420
$550 - $1,000	=	333
More than $1,000	=	174

They show the following quantities in four styles:

Contemporary	=	600
Country	=	300
Traditional	=	577
Victorian	=	47

The following descriptions follow the logical format that homeportfolio.com uses to help you select your preference.

TYPE:

4-inch center: From the centerline of the hot valve to the centerline of the cold valve is four inches, with the spout between them and an escutcheon (or base plate) below. If the faucet has two valves, it is harder to clean than a single-lever valve (which is mounted on top of the spout).

Basin: This is a very interesting faucet. Each valve has its own spout.

Bridge: A pipe connects the hot and cold valves to the center spout. Some of these faucets are designed to be wall-mounted, and some are designed to be countertop- or lavatory-mounted.

Minispread: This faucet looks like to the 4-inch center, except that the valves are separate from the spout, not mounted on an escutcheon. Again, it is more difficult to clean around the components of this faucet than other types of faucets.

Single hole, single handle: This faucet looks similar to the 4-inch center with the single valve, except the base of the spout is more tubular-shaped than the other faucet type.

Single hole, two handles: The base of this faucet is tubular, but the hot and cold valves are attached to the side of the spout, and raised above the countertop approximately one inch, which makes cleaning very easy.

SPOUT:

"C" design: If you imagine the letter "C," that's what many of these spouts look like. Some are more elongated; they're often referred to as "modified 'C' spouts."

"Aladdin's Lamp": Also known as "S" or "modified 'S' spouts." A couple of manufacturers make faucets that really look like "Aladdin's Lamp;" you'll know them when you see them!

Faceted: The tubular spout usually has five sides or more. Many valves in this type of faucet have a bell shape. They have a wide appeal because of their graceful appearance.

Gooseneck: This type of faucet gets its name from the long, straight appearance before the top curve.

> **"Be careful! If you select a tall gooseneck lavatory faucet, you probably won't be able to have a medicine cabinet directly above and behind it."**

Swivel: Just as the name implies, this spout swivels. There are at least two faucets with swivel spouts that become drinking fountains when the spout is turned upside-down.

Teapot: This spout looks similar to the "Aladdin's Lamp" ("S" or "modified 'S'").

Victorian: This spout is very elongated. It is often high and curvy, with a comparatively fragile appearance.

Waterfall: Instead of a tubular-shaped stream of water, this spout is often wider and open on top, producing a stream that may look like liquid plastic wrap. Cleanability could be a problem, especially with hard water deposits.

HANDLES:

Cross: The top bars form an "X," and often have a porcelain plate for "H" and "C" in the center of the cross. Several manufacturers are making contemporary-style cross handles.

Curved lever: One single bar at the top of each valve, in a graceful "S" curve.

Cylindrical : The handle appears to be solid from top to bottom. If it has no ridges or finger dimples, it may be very difficult to operate with wet hands, or arthritic fingers.

Lever: Generic term for any handle that projects out from the top of the valve, in a straight line, curved, or crossed. Most lever handles are approved for people with physical limitations, and are highly recommended for *aging in place* bathroom designs.

Oval: This type of lever is oval-shaped at the top.

Porcelain lever: The top of the valve is porcelain; it may be any shape, i.e., cross, oval, straight, or curved. It may also have a porcelain escutcheon, or bottom.

Round: This ball-shaped handle may be very difficult to operate, even with ripples or different textures. A good way to test whether it will be a problem or not is to wear white gloves when you make your final selection.

Square: This cube-shaped handle may be easier to grasp and control than the cylindrical or round handle.

Touchless: The popularity of this faucet is growing, especially in high-tech and *aging in place* bathrooms. The water turns on automatically when you place your hands under the spout. Controlling temperature for drinking water may be a challenge with some models; it's best to ask questions of a knowledgeable salesperson.

Wrist blade: This lever is elongated, often looking like the hot-cold valve in a doctor's office. The advantage of this valve control is it can be operated with an elbow, or wrist, which is advantageous for someone with extremely painful arthritis, or very poor eyesight.

SHOWER UNITS

You can choose from several types of manufactured shower units:

> One-piece base only
>
> Modular, base and walls separate
>
> All-in-one (with or without fittings and enclosure)
>
> Custom

You have a choice of materials for shower units:

> Acrylic (alone or with tile)
>
> Composite: cultured stone, terrazzo
>
> Concrete
>
> Fiberglass
>
> Solid surface

Your selection of shapes and sizes includes:

> Square and round: 32x32 to 60x60
>
> Rectangular: 32x48 to 48x60 and 48x72
>
> Neo-angle: 32x32 to 60x60

Your investment range:

> Under $500. Shower bases only (may not include all sizes and materials). homeportfolio.com lists 17 in this range.

$500-$1,500. This range includes all types of shower units, but the size may be limited to smaller units. homeportfolio.com lists 40 units in this range.

$1,500-$4,500. Includes fully-plumbed shower walls, multiple shower sprays, enclosures, some with integral seats. A couple of the units have steam. The most expensive unit shown is over $13,000. homeportfolio.com lists 18 units in this range.

CUSTOM SHOWERS

You can combine manufactured shower pan with any wall surface, or you can have a totally-custom shower designed and built for your space, in any shape or size (as long as it complies with the Uniform Plumbing Code). Your designer will talk with you about many details, and help you make important decisions about your shower, if your project includes a bathroom. Below are details and basic information about safety features, shower equipment, accessories, and finishes.

SAFETY FEATURES:

These should be included in your remodeled bathroom:

- Nonslip flooring. Highly-polished tile, stone, vinyl, etc. should not be used for the main floor or the shower floor.

- Grab bars. These should be in showers <u>and</u> tubs, to help you enter and exit, as well as help you get your balance or help you stand up if you fall.

- Safety glass. All glass in the bathroom (tub/shower enclosures, and windows) should be tested and approved by UL and/or ASTM, and it should have the appropriate etched label.

- Anti-scald tub and shower valves with lever or other easy-grip handles.

- Nonskid area rugs. They are nice, but they're not recommended for occupants who use a wheelchair or walker, or who have trouble navigating and might trip.

EQUIPMENT:

Shower Sprays: Of course, you can buy an inexpensive showerhead that provides one kind of spray. For a little more money, you can buy a showerhead that provides three (or more) kinds of spray. The next logical increase in investment will provide you a personal shower with a hose that sits in a holder until you remove it to rinse more precisely. The next level of investment will buy a personal shower that sits in a holder on a slide bar, so you can adjust the height of the showerhead. For a larger investment, you can have body-spray bars and individual body sprays in addition to other types of showerheads. Some people consider the ultimate shower experience to include a large overhead spray, plus personal shower and body sprays. Combinations like this will exceed $3,000. At least one manufacturer makes a showerhead that looks and feels like a waterfall.

> HINT: A standard (fixed-arm) showerhead should be installed at a comfortable height for you. Consider the angle of the arm and the height of the showerhead. If the pipe comes out of the wall at six feet above the floor and the overall height of the arm and head are six inches high, the bottom of the showerhead will be only 5'-6" above the floor. If you're 5'-8" or taller, you're going to have a potentially dangerous situation.

Shower Valves: With increased emphasis on safety, most manufacturers make valves that will maintain the water temperature (+/- 3 degrees) while hot and/or cold water is being used somewhere else (toilet flushing, washing machine, dishwasher, or landscape watering). Every style and finish is available in single-lever valves, which are the safest to operate in an emergency situation. If you've ever gotten soap in your eyes, or had the water change temperature suddenly, you know how difficult it can be to fumble trying to find the separate hot and cold valves.

 "When you're selecting a shower valve, close your eyes and try to feel where the controls are. If it's logical for you in the plumbing store, then you have a better chance of using it successfully in your home."

Diverters: These are used when you have a shower/tub combination, or multiple shower sprays, and you need to divert the water from one source to another. Diverters are often attached to wall tub fillers (a knob on top that you raise or lower), but they can be a handle on the shower wall that you turn to switch the water flow from one device to another.

ACCESSORIES:

Shower accessories include:

Soap dishes. Many choices for size and finish are available.

Shelves: These are usually triangular-shaped to fit into corners. They can be metal wire, porcelain, stone, solid-surface, cultured stone, solid metal, or glazed tile.

Shampoo-soap niches. These custom units are built into the wall following your designer's plans.

Seats: These can be custom units that your contractor builds, or they can be factory-made (i.e., wall-mount drop-down seats or portable waterproof benches).

Foot rests. These custom-made or factory-made units are meant for women to rest one foot while they shave their leg. It's very important to also have an adjacent grab bar to maintain balance and prevent falling.

Fogless mirrors. Manufactured for men to use, if they like to shave in the shower.

Soap and lotion dispensers. Wall-mount push-button containers that eliminate the need for separate bottles.

Waterproof electronics. Radios, cd players, and telephones are made especially for shower use.

SHOWER FINISHES:

Any material that is water-resistant can be used for shower walls. Different materials can be combined to create the look you want. There are only two limitations for your choice of materials: The creativity of your designer, and your budget. Shower wall (and floor) finishes include:

Concrete and aggregate.

Solid-surface sheets (i.e., manmade acrylic, polymer, and polyester composite material). These include:

"Avonite"	"Silestone"
"Corian" (DuPont)	"Staron" (Samsung)
"Cultured Granite"	"Surell" (Formica)
"Cultured Marble"	"Swanstone"
"Cultured Onyx"	"Topstone"
"Durastone"	"Transolid"
"Earthstone" (Wilsonart)	"Zodiaq" (DuPont)
"Gibraltar"	
"Gibraltar SSV" (Wilsonart)	

Stone slabs (and tiles), including:

Granite
Limestone
Marble
Onyx
Quartzite
Slate
Soapstone

Tile (including ceramic, porcelain, glass, and stone), available in a wide range of sizes, colors, and finishes. Tile should be mud-set (i.e., kraft paper, chicken wire, concrete base) over water-resistant wallboard (also known as greenboard), NEVER thin-set directly onto the wallboard. Mud-set tile will last longer, and provide better protection for wood framing from water damage.

"A well-known TV celebrity and author has stated it's okay to glue tile directly to wallboard (especially for tight-budget bathroom projects). Don't believe it! Don't do it!"

When you're selecting the finish products for your shower, consider the following questions:

- How durable is the surface?

- Does it stain easily (i.e., skin care and hair dye products)?

- Does it require special maintenance?

Abrasive cleaners should not be used on most surfaces, especially acrylic and fiberglass. Anything with acid can damage many stone surfaces, especially limestone and marble; many skin-care products contain Vitamins A and C, which are acidic. Acetone and other solvents will damage acrylic and polyester products. You'll be happier if you carefully select and use your bathroom products. It's important for everyone to know how to take care of your valuable investment, including family members, guests, and cleaning helpers.

A new cleaning company was highly recommended to homeowners who had just remodeled their master bathroom. The company's literature proudly stated, "We save you money because we use our own equipment and cleaning supplies." One evening, after a challenging day at the office, the wife was filling the new whirlpool tub when she noticed circular scratches all over it. The next day, she called the owner and asked what cleanser had been used. He said that everyone was trained to use only nonabrasive cleanser on acrylic products, but the crew did have abrasive products for heavy-duty stains. The following week, the wife made arrangements to work from home, so she could see what products the crew used. To her horror, not only did she see someone using the heavy-duty abrasive on her tub, but she heard that person accidentally turn on the whirlpool motor and leave it running, with the tub empty, which would eventually burn out the motor. She called the company's owner; he paid to have the tub repaired professionally, but it was never the same.

"A common mistake that people make when trying to design something completely foolproof is to underestimate the ingenuity of complete fools." (Douglas Adams)

BATHTUBS

You can choose from several styles of bathtubs: Freestanding (includes clawfoot and pedestal), one-piece, and modular, and custom.

FREESTANDING. You've seen pictures of these tubs. They evolved from the washtub which was brought in and filled by hand (when people didn't bathe very often). Indoor bathrooms became more common in the Victorian era, and the tub became a permanent fixture.

"How were washtubs emptied? Always been curious about this, but haven't ever found an answer. No matter how it was done, it was a lot of hard work!"

Freestanding tubs are very elegant to look at, and they can be fun to use. But there are problems to think about before you purchase one:

Space. Freestanding tubs should have enough floorspace around them to have access for cleaning.

Safety. It's very hard to enter and exit these tubs without balancing on one foot, which will put you in a potential slip/fall situation. Also, it's very difficult to install useful grab bars around these tubs without losing the visual charm.

Plumbing. Fittings are readily available for freestanding tubs. The main plumbing issue is the showerhead-valve-diverter configuration. Again, it becomes an issue of safety if you don't have a single-lever temperature valve to control the shower easily. It's better to have a personal hand-held shower that's part of the tub valve and filler unit, so you can rinse off before/after your bath.

Standard freestanding tubs can be manufactured from cast iron, acrylic. Custom freestanding tubs can be manufactured from virtually any material. You will have difficulty purchasing a freestanding tub for less than $1,500. Many more are available in the $2,000-$5,000 range. Custom freestanding tubs sell for $6,000 - $60,000. A company well-known for manufacturing luxury plumbing fixtures has a tub that's been touring the country. It's manufactured from solid gold, valued at over $1,000,000.

ONE-PIECE. One-piece tubs are available in three styles: Alcove, corner, and deck-mount. Alcove tubs are surrounded by three walls. Corner tubs are surrounded by two walls. Deck-mount tubs are like islands, often in the middle of an area (similar to freestanding tubs); the tub can be top-mounted or undermounted.

TUB SAFETY HINTS

➤ Floor-mount or sunken tubs are actively dangerous and should **never** be used.

➤ Steps up to a tub should be avoided, if possible. If steps are necessary, handrails must be installed -- and used. The steps should be slip-resistant material.

➤ All glazing in and around tubs should be certified safety glass, including mirrors.

➤ Light fixtures and exhaust fans should be UL-approved for wet locations, and installed on GFI breakers. (There are code limitations about the proximity of light fixtures to the water source.)

➤ Grab bars should be included in the tub installation, using blocking in the wall for stability. Molly and toggle bolts should not be used to install grab bars.

➤ Flooring surfaces in the bathroom should be slip-resistant.

➤ **Never stand with one foot in the tub and the other foot on the floor!!!!!**

WHIRLPOOL TUBS

Until about five years ago, you had a choice between non-jetted regular bathtubs and jetted tubs, which were called whirlpool or hydrotherapy tubs. Now you have an additional choice, often called air baths. Air baths pump air through jets or channels in the bottom of the tub, instead of (or in addition to) pumping bath water through jets located in the sides and ends of the tub. The advantage you get with air baths: There is reduced chance of algae or mold buildup inside pipes, like there is with piped whirlpool or hydrotherapy tubs. For this section, "whirlpool" will be used as a generic term for all jetted tubs.

When you are selecting a whirlpool tub, consider the following alternatives:

> The purpose for a whirlpool (i.e., relaxing overall massage by bubbles, or
>   vigorous massage for problem areas)
> The size of the whirlpool -- for one or two bathers
> The size of the motor
> The number of jets
> The location of the jets
> The location of the tub filler, valves, controls, and pump

The whirlpool tub you select should be large enough to completely immerse your body up to the top of your shoulders in an inclined position, without bending your knees. If possible, you should try different tubs to see how they fit and feel, especially if you're purchasing a tub for two people.

Whirlpool tubs are available with 1/2-horsepower to 2-horsepower motors. Many have fixed jets. Some have adjustable jets, where you can aim the flow and pressure of aerated water, and some have special jets for the neck and shoulder area. Less-expensive whirlpool tubs (often referred to as "builder models") often have only four jets. More expensive whirlpool tubs and air baths have more than eight jets.

The physical location of your whirlpool tub is important, not only for safety reasons, but also cleaning. If the tub you select has built-in head rests, and the tub is going to be an alcove installation, there should be a minimum of three inches from the wall to back of the head rest. This will prevent you from bumping your head, and it will make the area easier to clean. Often, this will mean a small platform, because many head rests are within 1/2" of the tub edge; so, a 72" tub with head rests will require the alcove to be at least 79" wide.

The physical location of the pump is also important. There are code requirements for pump access repair/replacement, minimum 18" wide x 18" tall. Pump access shouldn't be on an outside wall, especially if the tub is on the second floor!

Couldn't believe my eyes and ears one day at a plumbing showroom. A well-known interior designer was working with a salesperson to help her client select a whirlpool for the new master bathroom. When the salesperson asked, "Where are you planning the pump access to be?," the designer just stood there, wide-eyed, and shrugged her shoulders! It was clear she hadn't thought about the technical details. I often wondered how the project went, if the technical and safety requirements were ironed out before the project went into construction.

Many whirlpool tubs have integral fillers. Some of these fillers look like water falls; it's nice if these fillers can be a focal point. But, keep in mind the location of the tub valves. They should be located where you can easily reach them from inside and outside the tub, to turn the water on and off. Also, the location of the drain is important. You shouldn't have to lean across the tub to engage the drain stopper.

Safe entry into and exit from all tubs is very important. You should sit on the tub ledge (or skirt ledge) and swing both feet into the tub, while you hold onto a convenient grab bar with one hand and balance your weight with the other hand as you turn your entire body to face the tub. Then you can ease yourself into the tub, balancing your weight with both hands on either side, or holding onto integral grab bars. Exiting should be the reverse of this procedure.

Your investment in a whirlpool tub is a very wide range: $1,500 to over $15,000.

"A fashion [i.e., trend] is nothing but an induced epidemic." (George Bernard Shaw)

BASIC PRODUCT INFORMATION

COUNTERTOPS

Many products are appropriate for bathroom countertops. Most, but not all, of the same products are appropriate for kitchen countertops, except those with a (*) code. These materials shouldn't be used in kitchens for sanitary reasons related to food preparation, or safety reasons. The following is an alphabetical list of countertop materials:

Butcher block	Granite	Slate (*)
Concrete	Laminate	Soapstone (*)
Copper	Lavastone	Solid surface
Cultured granite (*)	Limestone (*limited)	Solid surface veneer
Cultured marble(*)	Marble (*limited)	Stainless steel
Cultured onyx (*)	Onyx (*limited)	Tile
Glass (*limited)	Quartzite	Zinc

Butcher block. These are usually made from laminated hardwood strips, 1/4" - 1" thick. Butcher block countertops can be sealed with a non-poisonous oil to maintain the wood color, but they should be sanitized regularly. Raw fish, meat, and poultry should never be prepared on porous countertops of any kind (*), especially wood countertops. If they're installed near a sink, the wood will eventually become a silvery gray until they're refinished and resealed. Your investment in a butcher block countertop will be approximately $35 - $150 per square foot.

Concrete. These have become very popular in the past three years. Like other materials, concrete countertops must be manufactured by an individual or company who has taken special training to know what raw products to use, how to pour and finish the concrete so it's safe for food preparation and maintains its appearance. Remember, concrete will crack, and the edges will chip with regular everyday use. Your investment in a concrete countertop will depend on the thickness, color, finish, and inclusion of stamped patterns or other materials. Generally, the investment range is $85 - $250 per square foot, but it can go as high as $400 per square foot.

Copper. This is a wonderful material, if you have the time, energy, and motivation to keep it looking nice. It is soft, and will scratch, but that's part of its beauty. Your investment in a copper countertop will be approximately $75 - $200 per square foot.

Cultured granite, marble, and onyx (*). These materials should be used for bathroom countertops only. They will not withstand the daily use and care required for kitchen countertops. Abrasive cleaners and sharp implements should never be used; once the surface seal is broken, the material is prone to discoloration. Also, personal-care products containing acetone or other solvents (including semipermanent hair color) should not be used anywhere near these surfaces. Your investment in these countertops will be approximately $55 - $75 per square foot, plus lavatory bowls (approximately $125 each).

Glass (*limited). Glass countertops are being used more frequently for bathroom countertops; they are gorgeous (and a bit pricey)! Glass should be used sparingly for kitchen countertops, but they have great potential for visual interest at eating bars and table tops attached to islands. A custom 10-square-foot etched- or textured-glass countertop will be in the range of $2,500 - $4,000 (or more).

Granite. Granite countertops have been the luxury standard for more than ten years. The slabs are available in a wide range of colors and patterns. Earth tones (i.e., gold, brown) tend to be less expensive per square foot than other colors; blue and blue-green are the most expensive per square foot. A word of caution: All stone is porous. Because it is more dense, granite is not as porous as limestone and marble. Olive oil stains are very difficult to remove. The investment range for granite countertops is $200 - $600 per square foot ($2,400 per square foot for blue and blue-green).

Laminate. Laminate is the least-expensive option for kitchen countertops, and tied with cultured marble for least expensive bathroom countertop option. Laminate has the widest range of solid colors and patterns available, to fit any decor. It is not as durable as other materials, but it can last a long time if you never use anything abrasive or sharp, and you never set anything hot directly onto the surface. The investment range for laminate countertops is approximately $125 per square foot.

Lavastone. This glazed and fired stone is a good alternative to other stones. It's available in a wide range of colors, manufactured in France to your designer's specifications. It has a comparable investment range to other stones, approximately $210 - $600 per square foot.

Limestone (*limited). Because limestone is so porous, it is not recommended for high-use countertops. It will stain even when it's sealed, and every stain will show because of the inherent pastel colors. No denying it's a beautiful product, with the same square-foot investment as other stones.

> Homeowners chose a lovely beige-grey limestone for their kitchen floor. The installation included a durable surface sealer. About six months after completion of the project, a bottle of fruit juice fell on the floor. Although the homeowner wiped up the spill immediately, the acidic juice had already etched and stained the floor.

Marble (*limited). In the earth's crust, marble is found between limestone and granite. Because it, too, is made up of calcium, anything acidic will attack it. Marble makes a wonderful countertop for baking preparation and candy making, because it remains cold to the touch. Like other natural stone products, it is a wonderful material for bathrooms (as long as harsh chemicals aren't used). Same investment range as granite, slate, and limestone.

Onyx (*limited). This material can have a very strong pattern of lines and swirls; most people either love it or hate it. It is the most glass-like material of all the stones, that will allow light transmission. Imagine a back-lit countertop that glows! It is very brittle, like glass, and etches easily, so its use in kitchens should be limited. Your investment in an onyx countertop may be a bit higher, because the material is harder to fabricate (approximately $250 - $600 per square foot).

Quartzite. This is a very hard, durable stone, available in a wide range of colors -- from nearly white to earth tones and brilliant gem colors. It is usually a higher investment than most standard granite and marble, in the same range as onyx.

Slate (*). Slate has great appeal because of its inherent texture, but that texture can be a problem when working on kitchen countertops. It is difficult to find in slabs; more readily available in a wide range of colors in tiles. Glasses with long stems and small bases will tip over and break more easily. Cleaning crumbs, flour dust, and other spills from the crevices is very difficult, at best. It makes a beautiful backsplash. Slate is considerably less than other stones, approximately $85 - $150 per square foot.

Soapstone (*). It is not recommended for high-use kitchen countertops because it is so soft and porous. It is wonderful for baking stones (pizza and bread), and natural hotplates. Installed price is $70 - $150 per square foot.

"Stone is fine for desks and tables -- if you like cold forearms, and uneven writing. Before you commit to having a stone desktop or tabletop manufactured, get a 12x12 sample and rest your forearm on it for about 10 minutes; write a note to yourself on plain paper that's sitting directly on the stone. That will give you the evidence to make an informed decision."

Solid surface. This material has been popular since its introduction in the mid-1970's. Solid-surfacing material was available in limited colors at first, manufactured only by DuPont under the brand name "Corian;" now there are hundreds of colors and styles of solid-surface material available from DuPont and other manufacturers. There is a list of solid-surface products on Page 172. The appearance may be the same, but the durability and function may vary based on the chemical composition of the material (i.e., acrylic in a polymer base or polyester in a polymer base). The advantage with all solid-surface material is that the colors/patterns go all the way through, so they can be sanded and repaired as needed. Another advantage is the unlimited fabrication possibilities. Solid-surface countertops are approximately $80 - $200 per square foot, installed.

"1984. We'd just remodeled the kitchen, using Almond Corian countertops. I was making a traditional flower arrangement, using an antique porcelain footed container. Place a flower, turn the container, place another flower, turn the container. This went on for almost an hour. When I was finished, the arrangement looked beautiful, but the countertop had a circular rut! Immediately, I called the fabricator and explained my dilemma. He stopped by the next day on his way to another appointment and sanded the area, blending the rut so it was only visible if you laid your head on the countertop."

Solid surface veneer. Several solid-surface manufacturers are offering this as an alternative to 1/2"-3/4" thick solid-surface material. It's definitely something to think about if your budget is limited but you want the look, feel, and function of solid surfaces. Countertops fabricated with these materials will be approximately $25 - $60 per square foot.

Stainless steel. These countertops have been popular since their introduction in the mid-1930's. Inherently nonporous, stainless steel is one of the safest materials to use with food preparation, but it does scratch easily. Many people think of restaurants or hospitals when they see stainless countertops, and prefer to use materials that have a less-industrial appearance. Your investment for stainless steel countertops will be in the range of approximately $60 - $125 a square foot, manufactured and installed; integral sinks and lavatories will require a custom quote.

Tile. Tile continues to be a very popular material, because it is available in so many colors, sizes, and patterns. A couple of cautionary words, though, about selecting tile, especially for kitchen countertops: 1. High-gloss finish is not as durable as a matte or crystalline finish; 2. Try to find tile that has all of the necessary trim pieces (i.e., V-caps, quarter rounds, bullnose, and surface bullnose); 3. If you are using two different sources, i.e., one for countertops and another for backsplash, verify that the tiles are **exactly** the same size (6x6 isn't always 6" x 6" -- it can vary +/- 1/4"); 4. If you intend to use a decorative insert from another company, double-check the comparative thickness of both tiles.

Zinc. This material is similar to stainless steel in overall appearance, but it will oxidize and develop a soft patina with time and use. It is considerably softer than stainless, and will scratch easier. Also, some chemicals will alter its appearance, so it should be used with discretion. The investment range for zinc countertops is approximately the same as stainless steel; custom integral sinks are also available, which require a custom quote.

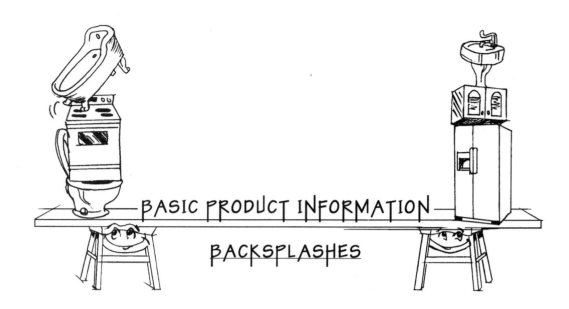

BASIC PRODUCT INFORMATION

BACKSPLASHES

This section is not a design how-to; it's written to reassure and inspire you. Virtually every product mentioned in the Countertops section can be used for bathroom and kitchen backsplashes. Providing functional protection for walls and other surfaces, backsplashes can also add visual pizzazz to your environment. Try to be open and receptive to new and interesting ways to use these materials; don't be afraid to mix and match, to do something daring and different. As you look through books and magazines, notice what designers have done to create visual interest. There are hundreds of great examples, to get the creative juices flowing freely!

All you need to do is communicate with your designer, to let her or him know you want something unique. Then you can work together to achieve something really special for your home. You don't have to <u>copy</u> what's in magazines and books; very likely, your designer has lots of great ideas -- that's why you hired him/her.

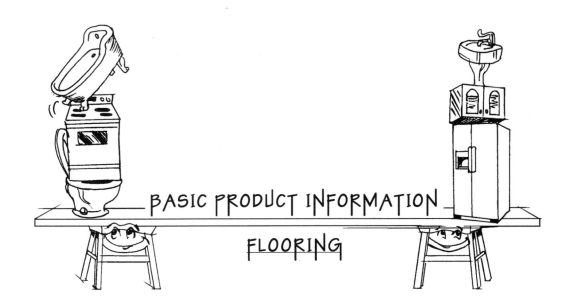

BASIC PRODUCT INFORMATION

FLOORING

For this book, discussion of flooring surfaces will be limited to "hard" materials; carpeting and decorative rugs are not included. Choices! You have hundreds of choices, maybe thousands of choices, if you consider color and style variations within each type of flooring. You can choose from:

Cork
Laminate
Linoleum
Rubber
Tile
    Unglazed pavers
    Glazed pavers
    Porcelain
    Stone
Vinyl
    Sheets
    Tile
Wood
    Domestic hardwoods
    Domestic softwoods
    Imported hardwoods
    Specialty woods

Cork. This product has been used for flooring in America since the 1930's. Lately, it has regained the popularity it had in the 1970's. Several manufacturers have figured how to pre-finish the cork so it isn't as porous, yet maintains its healing ability, sound absorption, and buoyancy. Cork is now available in a wide range of colors and styles. After installation, it can be jobsite-finished with a water-base urethane to protect it. The investment range for cork flooring is $11.50 - $20.00 per square foot, installed.

"What about the natural grooves in cork? Can crumbs, dust, and spills get into the texture, like V-grooves in wood plank flooring, adding time and effort to the maintenance? To make an informed decision that's right for you, you need to weigh all the facts equally."

Laminate. This type of flooring has been popular for residential use for about seven or eight years, but it's been used in commercial applications for more than twice that long. Laminate flooring is often referred to as a "floating floor," because it isn't installed tightly against walls; it's usually spaced about 1/4" from the wall, so there's room for it to expand, contract, and move. It's very durable, and available in a wide range of colors and patterns. Before you decide to install laminate flooring, however, walk on it. People have complained that it is noisier than standard wood flooring which is nailed to the subfloor. The investment range for laminate flooring is $7.50 - $15.00 per square foot, installed.

Linoleum. This product has recently become popular again. Several companies are manufacturing it; you can get a list from an internet search of "linoleum floors." Because it doesn't contain any vinyl, it is a more environmentally-friendly product. Linoleum is manufactured from linseed oil, rosins, and wood flour on a jute (or polyester) backing. It's available in about 150 colors and patterns, with the possibility of interesting borders, medallions, or decorative inserts. The investment for linoleum flooring is approximately $8.50 per square foot, installed (sold by the square yard).

"Technical information says that the linseed oil is constantly oxidizing. No technical information talks about the effect of breathing linseed oil particles, especially if someone suffers from asthma, chronic bronchitis, emphysema, or other health problems. Just something to think about . . ."

Rubber. This product has been popular for commercial and residential applications for over 25 years. It's available in sheets or tiles, with or without texture, in a wide range of colors. Because it's softer than other materials (except cork), rubber is great for kitchen floors; it will make standing and walking less painful for your feet, knees, and back. One advantage that rubber flooring has over many other types of flooring: It is classified as a "green" product, because it can be manufactured from reclaimed raw materials. The investment range for rubber flooring is around $13.50 per square foot, installed.

Tile. Tile is appropriate for every room of the home, not just wet areas. The style of your home and furnishings determines whether tile is appropriate for living rooms, dining rooms, and bedrooms. Also consider the noise and safety factors, and the members of your family (anyone under the age of 2 who's prone to falling, or over the age of 70 who's prone to tripping on area rugs). Whether the tile is unglazed or glazed, or stone, it must be as nonslip as possible, especially in bathrooms, kitchens, laundry rooms, and entries where standing water can be a problem.

If you're thinking about stone floors, most of the tiles are polished, so you'll pay extra to have them honed, sandblasted, or acid-washed to make them safer for wet areas. Any of these applications changes the physical appearance, so it's wise to pay for a sample before you commit to having all the material for an entire floor changed.

Tile -- particularly stone tile -- is heavier per square foot than most other flooring materials, so your designer or contractor needs to calculate the additional load and beef up the floor joists as needed. The last thing you want is a tile floor that cracks because the floor supporting it is flexing.

The investment range for tile flooring (not including any structural changes) is around $15 - $45 per square foot, installed.

Vinyl. The vinyl material we've used for years in our homes has been sheets and tiles. Most sheet and tile vinyl is printed, then coated with a heavy vinyl layer. There is also solid vinyl flooring. The color and pattern are an integral part of the material, so if it ever gets damaged, the damage isn't as obvious. Vinyl flooring has the widest investment range, from $14.50 to $58.00 a square yard ($1.61 to $6.50 a square foot), installed.

Wood. Wood flooring continues to be the most popular choice for most homes. You have many types of wood to choose from:

Domestic hardwoods

Alder	Cottonwood	White Oak
Ash	Cypress	Pecan
Aspen	Elm	Poplar
Basswood	Hackberry	Sassafras
Beech	Hickory	Sycamore
Birch	Maple	Walnut
Cherry	Red Oak	Willow

Domestic softwoods
Chestnut
Fir
Pine

Imported hardwoods*

Bunnark**	Makahmong**
Ebony	Padauk**
Ironwood**	Purpleheart
Mahogany	Rosewood**
Makaleung**	Teak**

Specialty woods
Bamboo

Wood flooring is available in several thicknesses. Thinner material is installed by gluing it down or top-nailing it in place. Thicker material (3/4") often has tongues and grooves which are appropriate for blind-nailing. In addition to this, wood flooring is available pre-finished or unfinished. The advantage you have with pre-finished flooring is the ability to use it immediately after installation.   It usually takes at least one week to stain and urethane a wood floor after it's installed. The dust and solvent fumes can be a health hazard, but the advantage jobsite-finished flooring has over factory pre-finished flooring is that it is less prone to damage by spills seeping between the boards.   Your investment per square foot is very similar for both pre-finished and unfinished flooring.

You have already heard and read about the impact of deforestation, especially exotic trees from rain forests. If you are interested in imported hardwoods, there are companies that sell reclaimed and farm-grown exotic woods, similar to farm-grown domestic hardwoods that don't destroy old-growth trees and disturb the natural balance of our ecology. Bamboo has become very popular in the past several years, because it is an easily-renewable resource. Thinking about all aspects of your choices makes you the best consumer.

Your investment in domestic hardwood and softwood floors will be $7.50 - $25.00 per square foot. Imported hardwood floors will be a higher investment, $12.50 - $45.00 per square foot. Bamboo floors are $10.50 - $17.50 per square foot. Medallions and borders will be an additional investment, and require a custom quote which depends on the wood used, the complexity of the design, and the size or quantity (square feet or lineal feet).

You can search the internet for more information about wood flooring: www.homeportfolio.com, www.hardwood.org, www.nofma.org, www.woodfloors.org.

"Think positively about the possibilities that lie ahead." (Dr. Robert Schuller)

It was a "hooky" kind of fall afternoon, sunny with a little breeze. But there was no time to play hooky -- typical Monday. The day had been filled with phone calls and interruptions, on top of two important deadlines. I got a call from my favorite contractor, Bruce, around 4:30. "Hey, I've got the perfect clients for you. I think you and the wife will hit it off."

"What makes you say that?"

"You two have so much in common. She's an animal lover, too."

"What about her husband?"

"Tom. Don't worry. He's very shy. Lets her make all the decisions."

"Do you want to give me her phone number so I can call her?"

"I gave her your phone number. She's going to call you."

I'd heard that same thing many times before, from different people, "They're going to call you." Yeah, maybe in six months, or whenever they get around to it; maybe never.

Bruce and I talked about other projects for a couple of minutes before his cell phone clicked off -- dead zone. When the phone rang again, I assumed it was him. "What's the matter, forget to pay your phone bill?" I shouldn't have said that.

"Excuse me. I must have the wrong phone number. I'm calling D.P. Design."

"Oh. I'm sorry. I'm D.P. -- uh, Diane Plesset. I was just talking with a contractor and ..."

"Bruce? Did he call you already?"

"Yes, he did. Oh, no, you're not Patty, are you?"

"Yes, I am. Bruce came by today, and told me I needed to work with you. He said we'd get along, that you can help me. What kind of cats do you have?"

Bruce was right! Patty and I chatted for almost an hour about many things, including their home remodeling goals. We set an appointment to meet on Thursday afternoon. Tom couldn't attend the meeting, but Patty assured me that he would have very little input except for his bathroom and den/studio.

Thursday was another beautiful fall day. I allowed time to drive around the neighborhood, to familiarize myself with the area, particularly the architectural style. All of the homes looked about the same age, built in the 1930's and 1940's. They had the popular "cottage" look of that era, with large front gardens and mature trees. Several had been remodeled, with second-story additions that maintained the look and feel of the neighborhood.

I parked in the narrow driveway, because the street already had parked cars on both sides, barely wide enough for one car to pass through. As I approached the house, I could see Patty walking from the kitchen through the dining room to welcome me at the front door. "Hello, I'm Diane."

"Hi, I'm Patty, and this is one-half of our greeting committee. His name is 'Furball.'"

"Good name for a Persian cat. I know all about furballs." His curiosity quenched, Furball sauntered into the living room to take his early mid-afternoon nap.

Patty and I went into the kitchen. "This is one of the rooms that needs attention, but there's more. Would you like to see the rest of the house?"

I pulled out my sketch pad to take notes as we walked around the house. The first notation I made was "lots of stuff."

Patty recognized the look on my face; obviously she'd seen it on other visitors, too. Paintings were stacked at least three deep along the baseboards. Dust couldn't get to tabletops, because of the decorative accessories and collectibles.

"Tom's an artist. We go to estate sales and garage sales. We like to collect unusual things."

"It's going to be a challenge when you remodel. You'll probably have to box and store everything for several months."

"I was afraid you'd say that. Same thing Bruce has been telling us for months."

192

The house was much larger than it appeared from the street. The living room and dining room were exceptionally large. Tom's den and the hallway felt like a cave, but the rest of the rooms had great daylight, which gave the house a cheerful feeling. Two bedroom doors were closed. "You can see the kids' rooms when they get home from school." I made another notation, "linens." Neatly-folded towels, sheets, and blankets bulged out of the small linen closet.

All three bathrooms spoke loudly to me, "Repair me! Fix me! Make me beautiful again!" One wall of the master bathroom shower was bulging -- probably dry rot. If the wall was rotted, it wouldn't be long before someone fell through the floor!

The master bedroom was almost as large as the living room, with an adjoining sitting area. I made another notation, "more closet." Clothes were packed onto single rods in the two small closets. I imagined Tom and Patty pulling out one hanger with hangers on either side coming out, too. The family's English sheepdog was lying in a patch of sun, taking a nap; he looked up sleepily as we approached the french doors. "This is 'Furface.' He sleeps all day long until the kids get home." Patty and I stepped over Furface to get to the back garden.

"You've got a lot of property here."

"Yes, the lot is almost half an acre. But Tom and I are the only ones who can really enjoy this area. It's awkward to entertain back here, because the only way to get here is from our bedroom, or the back door by the kitchen. I don't want guests to have to walk down the driveway to get here. We've been thinking about turning the master bedroom into a family room."

"That would definitely work. Then you'd add a master suite upstairs?"

"Right. And maybe it could be large enough to move Tom's den upstairs, where the light would be better."

"That's a great idea. Looks like several of your neighbors have already done something like that."

"Yes. We saw the house down the street last Christmas, and that's what got us to thinking about doing something similar."

The house seemed to be in pretty good shape for its age and years of deferred maintenance. "I'd recommend that you have a gardener come in and thin out some of the old plants that are too close to the bathroom with the bulging wall. They're probably damaging your foundation, which could be more expensive when you get into construction."

We went back into the house through the back door. I could understand the problem Patty had described. The driveway was so narrow, and so close to the house, there was no room to plant anything to soften the appearance.

Patty invited me to sit at the kitchen table, so we could talk about kitchen details that were very important to her. I could only see the edge of the old laminate countertop; the countertop itself was covered with jars of flour, bottles of vinegar, containers of utensils, and every electrical appliance available (plugged into a single outlet with multiple adapters). Patty confirmed that she was passionate about cooking, but frustrated by the original mid-1940's kitchen layout, which had been poorly remodeled by the previous owners.

"Why did they pay good money for plank flooring with such large grooves? I have to vacuum the floor every day, to keep ahead of the crumbs and pet hair. I have to get down on my knees to clean spills out of the grooves."

Our discussion in the kitchen was cut short when Tom and Patty's children got home from school. As Patty had predicted, Furface came running into the kitchen to greet the kids, skidding the last five feet and almost hitting the cabinets.

Chuck, the 17-year-old son, stopped long enough to pat Furface, then made a beeline for the refrigerator, without saying a word. Cindy, the 14-year-old daughter, wasn't shy about interrupting, "Can I spend the night at Pam's house?"

I sat patiently, trying to review my questionnaire while Patty and Cindy had a heated discussion about the last time Cindy spent a weeknight at a friend's house. Cindy stayed with us while I showed Patty my portfolio. Cindy's mouth dropped open and her eyes got big when Patty and I started talking about their remodeling budget. Chuck was oblivious to everything. He was standing at the sink, focusing on the jar of pickles and hero sandwich .

"Kids, I hope your rooms are clean, because I'd like Diane to see them. At least pick up your dirty underwear off the floor, please."

"Don't worry about it," I said. "I've had many clients with kids."

The childrens' rooms were large, by today's standards, but like the master bedroom, the closets were very small. Clothes were packed on hangers as tightly as possible, and there were as many clothes lying on the floor, with pathways from the door to the closet and the bed. I felt sorry for Patty on washdays.

As I was walking back to the kitchen, Tom arrived. "Sorry, I'm late. Wanted to be here sooner, but traffic was pretty bad today."

"Patty, you can tell Tom about most of our discussion, but while we're here, I'd like to get Tom's input." The three of us talked about their budget, and specific challenges they'd face during construction. With both of them there, I explained how we'd use the "good-better-best" categories to help them stay within their budget.

"Oh, yeah, I can just see us buying something 'good' when we want 'best.'"

"Oh, Tom," Patty sighed, "If we need to do it to finish the project, we'll do it."

"You know I'm going to hold you to it! "

"So you think we ought to store all our stuff and move out while they're working on the house."

"Yes. If it was just you and Patty, you might be able to live here and camp out. But with the kids, too, it's going to be difficult."

"You're saying almost word-for-word what Bruce has said."

"That's what I told Diane during our discussion, Tom."

"It's going to be expensive to find a place to rent."

"Yes, but think of it as an investment in your sanity."

"What do we do with the animals? That's another challenge."

Patty added, "I wouldn't want to rent to a family with two teenagers, a cat, and an English sheepdog. And, we never board our pets."

"It's important to discuss all of these things before you start, so you can make good decisions." Tom asked me to explain my services, and how much I'd charge them. As I was finishing my explanation, Chuck came into the kitchen. "What's for dinner? I'm starving!"

"I think Chuck would like a walk-in refrigerator the size of our kitchen."

"That's my cue to leave. I'll get a written proposal to you by the end of next week. Call me if you think of anything else we didn't discuss." The sun had set. I walked to my car in the dark, and carefully backed onto the narrow street, coming within inches of a neighbor's car. "Oh, boy," I thought, "the neighbors are going to love all the trucks here for months."

When I got back to my office, after reviewing new phone and e-mail messages, I started to prepare the written proposal, to get it out of the way while the information was fresh. Jay arrived home half an hour later. "Do you want to finish that before dinner, or after?" he asked. After 18 years, he had become accustomed to my long hours. If he relied on me for regular meals, he'd starve to death, and learned to cook out for self-preservation.

"I'll finish it later." Later was 5:00 the next morning, after my alarm went off. I'd discovered years ago, it's much easier to concentrate and get things done before and after business hours, when the phone isn't ringing.

I finished the proposal, and asked Jay to drop it in the mail on his way to work. Four days later, Patty called. "We got your proposal and looked it over. Do you have a couple of minutes to answer some questions?" Although I was in the middle of product research, I took time to talk with Patty because her phone demeanor was friendly and considerate. At the end of the conversation she said, "Tom and I like the way you work. We've talked with several other designers. I'll talk with him tonight and one of us will call you tomorrow or the next day."

As promised, Patty called the next afternoon. "Hello, Diane. Is this a convenient time for a quick phone call?"

"Sure."

"I've called the other designers and told them we've selected you to work with us. When would you like to start?"

"I have time next Saturday, if that's convenient. I'd like to review my agreement with you and Tom before I start, and I'd like to confirm what you want to do. I'd like the kids to participate, if possible."

"Chuck's got football practice at 9:00, and Cindy usually sleeps in until after 10:00 on Saturday. I'll see what we can do. How about Saturday, around 9:30?"

"Sounds great."

After I hung up, I dialed Bruce. "Hello, there, Mr. Referral-man!"

"How's it going? I heard you had a great meeting with Patty. I knew it was a good match."

"Yes. Thank you for remembering me."

"What's this 'remembering me' stuff?"

"Okay, okay. You know what I mean. They've hired me! You're going to be stuck working with me again."

"I hope so. They haven't given me the go-ahead yet. It's okay if they want to talk with other contractors, too. They know me, and they know how I work."

"Yeah. And I'll tell them how good I think you are."

Bruce and I became acquainted at a project seven years earlier. It took him a long time to admit that he was apprehensive when he first met me; I looked like a typical "designer." Once we got into construction, though, Bruce and his crew discovered that although I dress like a lady, I can communicate like one of the crew (as long as homeowners aren't around!).

I could rely on Bruce to follow my plans, and call me if he had any questions. He was one of very few contractors who wanted to understand the homeowners' decisions. Without him and his crew, my plans were just wallpaper.

Saturday morning -- another beautiful fall day. Perfect for taking measurements. I double-checked all of my tools and arrived at Tom and Patty's house at 9:32. When Tom answered the door, I was expecting "Furball" to greet me; I was totally unprepared for "Furface" when he stood up on his hind legs to greet me eye-to-bangs, nose-to-nose, almost knocking me down.

"I'm sorry! He's only a year old, still a frisky pup. Get down, Furface! The only one around here who can control him is Furball." I was hoping for help taking measurements, but not from "Furface."

I saw Patty putting breakfast dishes away, so I went into the kitchen. "Good morning!"

"Good morning, Diane. Are you ready to take measurements?"

"Yes, of course. Let's review the agreement first, and finish the questionnaire." We'd have to sit at the dining room table, because Cindy was sitting at the kitchen table, eating a bowl of cereal. She was either still asleep or following her morning routine; the cat was sitting on the table, lapping milk from her bowl. "Good morning, Cindy! Good morning, 'Furball'!"

After I reviewed the agreement with Tom and Patty, I asked if Cindy could join us, so I could include her in the discussion about the new kitchen, the family room, and her bathroom.

For the next two hours, we all discussed what they needed, and what they wanted. Their wish-list was extensive. The goals for their project would be to borrow space from Tom's den, to make the kids' closets larger, and create a guest bedroom. The existing master bathroom would become Cindy's bathroom, and the master bedroom would become the family room where the kids could entertain their friends.

Tom and Patty wanted a more private master suite with a new den and studio for Tom. It made sense to create a new retreat for them upstairs. Patty desperately needed a new and larger kitchen -- without grooved floors.

As we went through the wish list, I put a star by items for later discussion, when there would be more time to discuss the pro's and con's. A major issue between Tom and Patty was a bidet for the master bathroom.

"Seems like a frivolous waste of money to me," Tom said sternly. "I thought it was discussed and decided."

"It was discussed, but not decided," Patty responded.

"This may be one of your compromise items, or a tradeoff to stay on budget. You're going to get tired of hearing this from me, but you're going to have to make many tradeoffs before you're ready for construction."

"This is getting boring for me. May I go to my room now?"

After three final questions for Cindy, she disappeared into her room and shut the door. I assumed she was going to take a mid-morning nap. Tom and Patty smiled at each other, then Patty said, "We have an agreement that Cindy can spend private time on Saturday morning, primping and trying on makeup, but nothing that she can't wash off to go out in public."

"And no body piercing until she's at least 16," Tom added.

"When you need to take measurements in her room, just knock. Don't be surprised what you see. Last week she went 'Gothic.' Oh, boy."

I was glad that Tom and Patty arranged to be home on Saturday, to help me. Measuring a whole house is challenging for two people; it takes more than twice as long for one person to measure accurately.

"I hope you don't mind. Here's a small pad and pencil for you. If you'd write down any questions while we're taking measurements, I'll answer them before I leave."

After I showed Tom how I like to take measurements, I sketched the house. We started outside with overall dimensions, then took measurements of each room.

Two hours later, I knocked on Cindy's bedroom door. "May I come in?"

"Sure."

I opened Cindy's door and walked in. "I wonder if you'd . . . Oh, my gosh. How cute! Can I take a picture?"

"Uh, I guess so."

I went to the dining room to get my camera. "Patty, Tom, you've got to see this. In Cindy's room. It's so cute!"

Again, I knocked. "Okay if I come in with your parents?"

"Only if they promise not to get mad."

198

Patty and Tom looked at each other, puzzled. What had Cindy done that would make them mad, short of blue spiked hair?

"Oh, my God! Cindy, how could you?"

"Mom, I didn't mean to do anything wrong. Please, don't get mad."

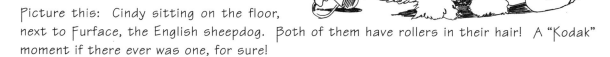

I tried to break the tension. "Years from now, you'll all laugh and remember this. I want to get a picture of all of you, but first, I want to get a picture of just Cindy and Furface."

Picture this: Cindy sitting on the floor, next to Furface, the English sheepdog. Both of them have rollers in their hair! A "Kodak" moment if there ever was one, for sure!

We finished the measurements just as the afternoon light was disappearing. We ended our marathon meeting with a discussion about the questions that Tom had written down, and set an appointment for an evening appointment, a week from the following Wednesday.

"If you have time, I'd like you to look at this list of websites before our next meeting. E-mail a list of what appeals to you, and my assistant, Rosanne, will start getting estimates for your products."

I wanted to start work on the plans Monday morning, but it turned out to be an "interrupt-driven" day with phone calls and meetings. Rosanne set up files for Tom and Patty's project, and established an account for invoicing and payments. I finally started working on their as-built plans late Monday afternoon.

The as-built plans took only nine hours to create, but with phone calls, interruptions and meetings, I didn't finish the plans until Thursday evening. Friday morning, Rosanne and I went to the building department and the assessor's office to verify lot coverage limitations, setback requirements, and get other information that would affect the project.

I was happy when the Planning Department verified that Tom and Patty didn't <u>have</u> to add a second story to get their master suite. On the way back to our office, Rosanne asked me, "Why do you think they asked for a second-story master suite?"

"Could be they talked with someone, maybe Bruce, who told them it would be cheaper to add a second story. Maybe they saw something in a magazine, like an article about a 'private retreat' that inspired them. I won't know until I ask them."

"Are you going to go ahead and draft the second story, or are you going to give them options?"

"Of course, I'm going to give them options. But before I do, I need to do some further investigating."

"Like what?"

"Talk with Bruce, and the structural engineer. In any case, we know that the city requires a soil test, whether they decide to add out, or up. I've got to think about the roofline, the foundation, plumbing and heating first. And the most logical location for the stairway that won't rob too much real estate."

"Huh?"

"Most homeowners who talk about a second story are shocked when I tell them how much space a stairwell takes up, especially if we make the stairs comfortable."

"Like Frank Lloyd Wright used?"

"Right! A two-to-one ratio, with lower risers and deeper treads than builders use now."

"Makes a difference for someone with bad knees, right?"

"It's so right because it's so 'Wright'!"

As soon as we got back to the office, Rosanne made our to-do list for Monday. It included phone calls with Bruce, the structural engineer, the soils engineer, and a heating contractor.

"Task Master!," I said sarcastically when Rosanne showed me the to-do list.

"Excuse me?"

"Before I can talk knowledgeably with all of these people, I've got to work on a couple of preliminary plans first. You've got me making these calls on Monday. Do I REALLY have to work all weekend?"

"I guess you can take one day off, if you have to," she said with a wink and a smile.

Sunday afternoon, I decided to work on Tom and Patty's plans for an hour or so while Jay was running errands. When Jay returned, he came into my office. "How's it going?"

"Very well. Just finishing the basic space for the second-story addition. The stairs were challenging, but now they're okay. I'd like to work a little longer."

"Sure. I'm going to go install the new software I bought. Half an hour?"

"Okay."

Half an hour later, we were still involved in our respective tasks. An hour later, same thing. Almost three hours later, Jay came into my office again. "How's it going now?"

"Half an hour already? Just a few more minutes, and I'll put it away."

"Actually, it's almost time for 'Emeril Live'. How about a dinner break while we watch TV?"

I printed out the preliminary plans while Jay prepared dinner. When Rosanne arrived the next morning, the plans were taped to the front of her monitor with the note, "Dear Task Master: Ready to make phone calls."

Rosanne and I played phone-tag with everyone all day Monday, and part of Tuesday. On Wednesday, the effort yielded results I'd hoped for: There wasn't a distinct advantage that either plan had over the other; both involved tradeoffs of one kind or another. Tom and Patty's decision would be personal preference, whether their master suite was on the main level or a new second floor.

Wednesday afternoon, I called Patty go give her an update. I'd mentioned the possibility of a soils engineer needed for their project during my meeting and in my agreement. After we chatted for a minute or two, I said, "We've confirmed that you are going to need the soil engineer first, before the structural engineer can start to work. His fee is going to be about $3,500. He's sending a proposal directly to you and Tom."

Patty asked, "How about the structural engineer?"

"He needs to come see your home and look at the preliminary plans before he can give you an estimate of his fee. Can I ask him to call you directly?"

"Of course!"

"Have you had a chance to look at the websites?"

"Yes, Tom and I surfed the internet over the weekend. Would you like us to send you what we've got so far?"

"Yes, so Rosanne can put information into a preliminary spreadsheet."

"Okay. Will do."

"See you a week from today."

"Can't wait to see what you've got for us!"

For the next four days, Rosanne began to gather product literature and preliminary estimates. I worked on details of the kitchen plans, the alternate additions, and the existing bathroom upgrades. With other projects before, Rosanne and I would be working on these things up to the last minute before a meeting. Sometimes, the pieces of the puzzle would fall into place, like Patty and Tom's project. It feels really good when this happens.

It also feels good to have productive meetings with positive results. Tom and Patty arrived at my office on Wednesday evening at 6:30. Rosanne had put everything I needed on the table in the reference room, where I have bookshelves full of product literature and drawers full of samples.

After Tom and Patty left at 8:45, when Jay and I were having dinner, he asked me how the meeting went.

"Wonderful. They were excited about the preliminary plans. They loved seeing the quick perspectives, every time we talked about a change."

"How many changes did you make?"

"We now have four alternate kitchen plans, two or three master bathroom plans. They decided that Cindy doesn't need a tub in her bathroom -- a large shower with lots of room for all of her bottles. You thought I had a lot of hair and body care products, and makeup; you ought to see what Cindy has!"

The next morning, I told Rosanne all about my meeting with Patty and Tom, especially about the products they'd chosen.

Rosanne looked at the list. "Uh-oh. They're already starting to go over budget. They know that, right?"

"Oh, yes. We talked about that for almost an hour. That's why I'd like you to get the preliminary spreadsheet finished ASAP, so you can send them a copy. I want them to think about their options. They both agree it's hard to draw the line between what they need and what they want. I set another appointment with them for next Wednesday, same time, at their home. I'd like to recommend some alternatives then that might help the budget."

By the following Wednesday, Rosanne had entered all the data into the spreadsheet, and we'd completed the list of alternative choices for my meeting with Patty and Tom.

"You can see how the different products compare," I said as the three of us were studying the spreadsheet. "There's not that much difference between the fancier 'professional' gas cooktop and the 'regular' gas cooktop. Higher btu's and heavier look. Difference of $500 for that one item."

"Wow! Anything is going to be better than that old electric cooktop I use now."

"Right. And then, you're not locked into the more expensive hood. That's another thousand dollars or so you can save."

"Geez, when I saw this stuff in the magazine, I wasn't aware how much it'd cost. Magazines

really don't give price breakdowns, do they?"

"No. They might tell you the brand name, and you're supposed to do the homework, to get prices. You're supposed to do homework about quality and reliability, too. Almost everything is based on appearance."

Tom voiced his opinion, "That's one thing that bothers me. Patty gets all excited about something she sees in a magazine, like the cooktops. Not much difference between the way they cook?"

"Nope. Everyone thinks they've got to have high btu's, but they don't. It's only a difference of three or four thousand btu's per burner -- 12,000 versus 15,000. That means a difference of maybe a minute or so to boil pasta water. I've had a couple of clients who wanted a professional wok. It puts out 32,000 btu's -- a flame about 9 inches high. I mean, how fast do people want to burn their food?"

We were making good progress on the products until the bidet subject came up again, just as Chuck was walking through the dining room, munching on his evening snack.

"Let's see how much this thing costs, then we can decide," Tom said matter-of-factly.

"The one I selected, with the faucet, is only $550. . ."

"$550? Wow, Mom, what's it for?"

"Personal hygiene, Chuck. It's called a bidet. Your father will tell you what it's about."

"I don't have a clue about how it works, and I don't care!" Tom snapped. "You're always complaining about Furface drinking out of the toilet. What's he going to do with the bidet?"

I had to choke back my laughter -- not laughing at them, but the mental picture that flashed through my mind, when Tom and Patty were filling out the detailed survey.

By the end of our meeting, Patty and Tom had made several decisions, except the final decision about the bidet. They had shaved thousands of dollars from their investment. We refined their plans a little. After two or three more meetings, we'd be ready to send the preliminary plans to Bruce and two other contractors for preliminary labor estimates.

It surprised me when Tom said, "Every meeting, you have us initial and date new stuff in our file as we go over it. Don't you trust us? I'm not used to this."

"I'm sorry, Tom. It's just standard procedure for me. It's not that is mistrust you, or any of my other clients. It just helps to keep everything straight, in case a question comes up in the future and we can't remember exactly when we talked about it."

"Okay. Now I understand."

"I'm glad you brought it up."

I couldn't believe how smoothly everything was going with Patty and Tom. It had been only two months since my first discussion with Patty. There was still a lot to do before we could submit the plans for permits, but the steady progress was reassuring.

The soil engineer hadn't been to the jobsite to get samples yet. Although Patty and Tom had signed the structural engineer's proposal, he couldn't start work on their project until he had information from the soil engineer. It was almost a month later before Richard and I could start talking about foundation, framing, and roof details.

The time wasn't wasted, though. Tom and Patty spent the time shopping, physically seeing and touching products they'd liked on the internet and in brochures. During this time, I finished the preliminary plans to get labor estimates, and Richard had enough information so the contractors could estimate the foundation and framing.

Patty and I talked about their project several times a week. During one of our conversations, she said something I'd heard from other clients -- but I still found it amusing.

"I've got to tell you, Tom and I felt really stupid going to the appliance store with a cookie sheet, and roasting pan with a pillow in it."

"It helped you select your oven, though?"

"Oh, yes. The minute we walked in, the salesman knew we were your clients. Took several hours to show us everything and explain the difference between this one and that one. Now I know why you gave them such a high recommendation."

"They've always treated my clients well. Great knowledge, great customer service."

"Tom's a little concerned about what you're going to have us do when we shop for the whirlpool tub."

"Wear comfortable clothes, and slip-on shoes."

"It won't involve undressing, will it?

"No, not at all."

"I guessed that one right!"

It took a month to get preliminary labor estimates. Bruce and one of the other contractors sent proposals after they got estimates from electricians, plumbers, painters, roofers, and supply yards. The third contractor met with Tom, got a couple of sets of preliminary plans from me, then seemed to fall off the face of the earth.

Patty confided to me in one of our phone discussions, "I just don't understand it. Steve was highly recommended by one of our neighbors. He did a beautiful job on their home. His estimate was very low, ended up being about the same as the high estimate, but within their budget. Has he returned your phone calls?"

"No. We've tried to reach him early morning, during the day, and evening. No luck."

"What do we do now? It's been a long time. Tom and I don't want to wait another month or two. We want to be ready to start in the spring."

"You have several options. You can choose between Bruce and Dennis now, or you can wait to get another estimate. The two estimates we got are very similar, right?"

"Yes, I was surprised at how close they are."

"Okay. And you've checked all the references, even for Bruce?"

"Yes."

"Why don't you and Tom talk about it and consider your options? Think about, and talk about, how you feel about Bruce and Dennis. Trust your gut feelings."

"Okay."

Three days later, Patty called to talk about the two contractors again. "Tom asked me to ask you if you'd be willing to meet with us and the two contractors."

"Gee, I've never done that. You mean the five of us, at one time?"

"No. I'm sorry. The three of us with Bruce and Dennis individually."

"Great idea! Sure."

Dennis was available first. The four of us met at the jobsite to review plans, and discuss the project. It was clear he had studied the plans, and prepared a list of questions about the alternative plans, and who would be responsible for ordering products. "I saw the list of products you've selected. I really don't want to be chasing all over to get most of them."

I replied, "Tom and Patty will be ordering most of the products, but I'd like all of us to go over the specifications and verify everything, especially quantities."

Tom had also prepared a list of questions. Again, he asked, "Do you think we can live here during construction? It's going to be difficult to find a place for all of us, including Furball and Furface. And, it's not going to be cheap."

"You should rent a house. It's going to be a real mess here for several months. What's your opinion, Diane?"

"I agree."

When Tom asked Dennis, "Can you see any way we can save more money without sacrificing what we really want?," Dennis' answer was textbook perfect -- clear he'd answered similar questions from other homeowners. "I have some ideas about the foundation and framing that may save a couple thousand dollars. You could get cheaper windows, but the selection would be limited. I can't think of anything other than that. It's clear you've really thought about everything. The major difference is going to be your products at this point."

I didn't know Dennis as well as I knew Bruce, but Dennis proved to all of us he was comfortable collaborating with a designer, as well as working with Patty and Tom. It was going to be a difficult choice for them.

Two days later, we met at the jobsite with Bruce. There was less discussion about the

plans, and fewer questions from Bruce about them. I could count on him to study and understand my plans. After seven years and several dozen jobs together, Bruce understood that I had reasons for my recommendations. He never tried to second-guess me or change anything, unless it saved money for the homeowners.

Tom asked the same questions he'd asked Dennis, and got essentially the same answers. There was more chatting with Bruce than there had been with Dennis, because Bruce had worked with Tom and Patty before, and he was a more chatty person naturally.

The next day, I sent Patty an e-mail, "Working with the structural engineer on the framing details. You and Tom have a lot to discuss; call me if you have questions or want my input. I'll wait to hear from you."

I asked Rosanne to call Richard to let him know that Tom and Patty would be making the decision about their contractor soon. We'd call him to schedule an appointment to discuss the final framing details and get input from the contractor.

Patty called two weeks later. "Sorry we didn't call sooner. Cindy came home with the flu, and we all got it from her."

"How are you feeling now?"

"Better, but not 100% yet. I wanted you to know we've been talking about the project a lot. The kids have even participated."

"Even Chuck?"

"Especially Chuck. He thought of several things that could save us money. One of them is pretty far out there."

"What is it?"

"First of all, both kids agree that we don't need a fireplace in the family room. Yeah, it would be nice, but it's not necessary."

"Okay. What else?"

"Chuck's 17 going on 18. He's been working summers and part-time at Burger King for a couple of years, putting aside money for college."

"That's great!"

"He offered to go to work with the contractor, if the contractor will hire him, in exchange for a discount to us on the labor. He can be the errand boy, the carpenters' assistant, and the clean-up boy."

"Sounds like a good idea. I don't know what the contractor will say, though. And, speaking of contractor, have you and Tom made your decision?"

"Yes. It was a difficult one, but we decided to hire Bruce. We wanted to be fair to Dennis."

"Have you called Bruce and Dennis yet to let them know?"

"No. I wanted to call you first, to get your opinion about Chuck working with Bruce. Don't you dare call him before I get a chance! You've probably got his number on quick redial!"

"Actually, I've got it memorized. I'll wait until you call him, and he calls me."

"Okay."

"How about the project? Have you and Tom decided whether you want to add your master suite on the main level, or add a second floor?"

"I think we're going to have to focus on that at our next meeting. We're leaning towards the second floor, but we're not sure. We like the idea of the patio being accessible from the new family room, without many changes to the existing doorway that's in our bedroom. We went over the spreadsheet, plugging in the labor estimates, to see how much we're going to borrow against the equity."

"How did it go?"

"Tom's the computer specialist in the family. He did an electronic spreadsheet, and I did an old-fashioned one on paper. He had some trouble with the computer, and I actually finished before he did!"

"Did you both arrive at the same numbers?"

"Within a couple hundred dollars."

"And you both added the bidet in your calculation?"

"Uh, I'm going to have to check on that one. I'm not sure. One thing Tom mentioned to me, though."

"What's that?"

"He's been a lot more involved in the decisions than both of us thought he'd be."

"That's great. You'll both be happier with the results if everything's discussed and decided openly. Makes the design go faster and smoother."

"That's what we think, too."

"Great! Let's make the bedroom addition the number one item on our agenda, then."

"Okay. See you next Wednesday."

The phone rang 20 minutes later. I guessed it was Bruce. When Rosanne transferred the call, I'd guessed right.

"We're going to be working together again. Now, quit crying and be brave. Working with me isn't the end of the world!"

"I'm not crying. I'm laughing, 'cause you have to work with me again!"

Bruce and I talked about a few of the project details, including Chuck's offer. "I told Patty it would be best if Chuck didn't come to work with me. Couldn't forgive myself if he got hurt. Isn't worth the money they might save."

"Give some thought to the master bedroom addition. I'd like Patty and Tom to make that decision next, so Richard and I can focus on that framing. Your input is going to be a key factor in their decision."

"Geez, I haven't received my deposit yet, and already you're putting me to work!"

"Talk to Rosanne about that. She's taught me all I know about being a tough task master."

The next three weeks were busy for all of us, headed for the finish line of the design phase. All of us wanted to get the plans finalized before the holiday crunch. Rosanne scheduled me to meet with Patty at least twice a week, to help her finalize the product selection.

Murphy's law prevailed, and three other clients decided to move ahead more quickly with their projects, too. One of the clients was actually surprised when I told her I had four clients in different phases of the design process, plus two clients in the construction process.

"You mean I'm not the only one you're working with now?"

"No. Six clients at one time is a comfortable workload, as long as everyone isn't at the same point in their project."

I knew Mrs. Brooks was starting to get nervous. "What if I need you to answer a question or solve a problem immediately?"

"That's why I have an administrative assistant. She always knows how to get ahold of me. If you have an emergency, other clients will understand. I'll explain that it could be them on the other end of the phone and not you."

"Well, okay. I guess it's all right."

I told Bruce about my conversation with Mrs. Brooks, and the explosion of work.

"Yep, it never fails. Feast or famine."

"Right now, I feel like a one-armed juggler, with cleavers and paring knives."

"Hey, that's a good one. I'll have to remember it. One of my favorites from Joe at the lumber yard, "Busy as a one-legged man in an ass-kicking contest."

"That's a great one, too. I wish there was a way to even things out more."

"Yeah, time AND money."

I was thankful that Tom and Patty were excellent communicators, and understood the importance of staying in the information loop. They didn't become pests with me, or Richard, or Bruce, but they knew exactly what we were doing, and what to expect. They finished their product selection very soon, so Rosanne could finish the specifications.

Patty and Tom also made quick, logical decisions about the design, so Bruce could finalize his estimate and Richard could finish the structural details for their second-story addition. Their diligence paid off. Patty and Tom were able to order all of their products by the middle of December and avoid the end-of-year price increases.

The plans were also finished by the middle of December. When we got together for them to approve and sign the plans, I told Tom and Patty not to expect their plans to be approved before the end of January at the earliest.

"You told us we'd feel like movie stars, signing so many autographs," Patty said as she flipped another page. The entire set of originals totaled 11 pages, 24 by 36 paper, plus seven pages of spreadsheets.

"Yeah, reminds me of last week, when we signed all the refinance papers."

"You think you've got it bad! After the blueline copies are made, I have to stamp and sign three sets!"

Our final design meeting was a celebration at Patty and Tom's home the week before Christmas. Plans were submitted, products were selected and ordered. Even Cindy and Chuck had a good time; Patty had cooked a lot of food.

210

"Diane, did you see the cookies?"

"Yes, they're beautiful. You made so many different kinds!"

"I didn't think I was going to get any made. The oven element burned out, and the first batch were charred on the top and raw on the bottom. I didn't want to waste the money to have it fixed, but the kids were insistent."

Chuck nodded. "Yeah, what's the holidays without food -- and gifts?

With Patty and Tom's project on hold until the building department completed their plan check, I was able to accomplish many of the tasks that Rosanne had added to my to-do list for several months.   She was counting on fewer client meetings during and immediately after the holidays. She assigned nightly reading for me, to eliminate the tall stack of trade magazines in my "to read" inbox.

January 17th, about four weeks after I'd submitted the plans, I got a letter from the building department, with a list of revisions and information they wanted to be included in the plans. Patty called that afternoon. "Is this a convenient time for a quick question?"

"Yes."

"Did you get a letter from the building department?

"Yes."

"We did, too. What's it mean? What do they want us to do?"

"You don't have to do anything. They sent a copy to you as a formality, to make sure you're notified that they've requested me to make some changes."

"Can they do that? Will it affect what we want to do?"

"No, it's all right. Everything they're asking for is information covered by codes. They just want to make sure that Bruce doesn't do anything that's outside the scope of the codes. When I've made the revisions, I'll make a new set for you and Tom. You'll see a lot of 'clouds' around information that's already on the plans."

"If the information is there already, why do you have to put clouds around it?"

"The plan checker may not have seen the information, or the plan checker may want to assure that the contractor sees it. I don't know."

"Seems like a waste of time and money to me. Tom and I are paying you to do these revisions, right? And we'll have to reimburse you for the additional copies, right?"

"Unfortunately, yes, you're right."

"Does this happen to everyone who submits plans?"

"Yes, virtually everyone. I don't have statistics. Bruce would be a good person to ask because he's been in the business so long and he's seen hundreds of plans from architects and designers."

The next afternoon, after I'd finished the revisions on my portion of the plans, I called Richard to get a status report on revisions the building department asked him to make.

"I won't have the revised plans finished until next Monday at the earliest. We're sort of hammered here, deadline for the new library. If I get them done before Friday, I'll give you a call, but don't count on it."

"No, problem. I'll give Bruce a call with an update." I hung up and called Bruce on his cell phone. "Hate to do this to you, but the building department hit me with a <u>ten-page</u> comment letter filled with revisions they want. It's going to take weeks to make all the modifications. Probably take at least another month to go back through plan check."

"WHAT? Patty called me and said she'd received a copy of the letter, sounded a little upset. Your plans normally don't have more than five comments, total! Must be a new plan checker. A <u>blind</u> plan checker! I think we can arrange the schedule, but this puts me . . ."

"Gotcha!"

"Oh, you . . ."

"Yes?"

"I'm going to get back at you <u>Big Time</u> for this one!"

After Bruce calmed down, we talked more seriously about comment letters and plans he'd seen. I didn't want to know particular names, just Bruce's feeling about how many plans he'd seen with no clouds or bold revisions. "Not very darn many," he replied. "Only a small handful, and mostly small projects, without structural changes."

"When do you want to get together with Patty and Tom to develop the critical path calendar?"

"Very soon. Two weeks, maybe three. Then I'll call the subs to pull it together. How are the deliveries coming?"

"Well, some of the stuff has come in. I expect more to be delivered by the end of this month. Holidays really foul up the delivery schedule."

"Yeah. Remember that one job? Think it was the third one we did together. The couple who had to have two bathrooms finished by Christmas?"

If Bruce started reminiscing, we'd end up talking for hours. Both of us had work to do. "Bruce, I'd love to talk with you more, but I've got to go take care of these plans. Sorry to cut you off."

"Yeah, old 'motor mouth' doesn't know when to stop."

"It's fun to talk with you, but we've both got things to do. Let's plan to get together for lunch during construction."

"See 'ya!"

Two-and-a-half weeks later, Bruce and I met with Tom and Patty, to begin developing the calendar for construction. It was right after dinner, so everyone was there -- including Furball and Furface.

"I've got a question for all of you. Have you been to an amusement park recently?"

"Tom went to a computer tradeshow in Orlando a couple of years ago, and we decided to turn it into a family vacation. Why do you ask?"

"Did you get on a wild ride?"

Tom's eyes lit up. "Oh, yeah. They had rebuilt an old rollercoaster. Safe as a new one, but looked and sounded old. Man, it was one of the best rides I've ever been on!"

"Speak for yourself! That thing scared me to death! I knew we were doomed -- and being in the front car! Tom and Chuck had just eaten spicy hot dogs with all the trimmings. No way!"

"Yeah, Dad and I loved it. You and Cindy were wimps!"

"Who are you calling a wimp? I wasn't afraid! I didn't want to have my hair go all frizzy. You weren't aware you were even on a ride. You talked with Sheila the whole time on your cell phone!"

"Okay, okay. I think we've touched a raw nerve here -- right, Bruce?"

"Yeah, but what's with the rollercoaster?"

"Well, in July, when Jay and I were at the county fair, I noticed how people reacted to the rollercoaster. The idea hit me then, that remodeling is like a rollercoaster ride -- an emotional rollercoaster. You're the first ones I'm sharing this with, so be patient with me.

"Everyone approaches a rollercoaster with anticipation. You guys -- Tom and Chuck -- were pumped up to have a great time. You ladies were more apprehensive. Human nature.

"You've just gotten on the ride. It's starting out, slowly. Climb, climb, climb, until you reach the top. Then, Whoosh! You're speeding down the steep slope, towards twists, turns, ups and downs.

"Okay. You got on this ride about four months ago. You've been climbing, climbing, climbing -- slowly. You're almost to the top, but not quite. The first week of construction will be like that first big drop. It'll be so exciting. It'll also be scary. You've never been on this ride before."

"Oh, boy. Hope I like it better than that rollercoaster in Orlando."

"Hang on tight. Here we go!"

Bruce really understood the emotional rollercoaster. He pulled out the preliminary schedule he'd prepared, and sketched the ups, downs, turns and twists that happen during construction, on top of Tom and Patty's schedule. Tom was really impressed with the computer bar graphs and calendar that Bruce prepared to show how long each phase of construction would take.

"So, you're saying that our project will take about eight months?"

"That's the way it works out, Tom."

"Between two and three thousand a month for the rental place and storage of our stuff. That's a chunk of change. No way to speed it up?"

"If everything goes perfectly, we might be able to trim off one month, but don't count on it."

214

"I've seen them build new homes faster than that. Why does it take so long?"

"If you're seeing a single home built, it's going up faster because there's less prep work. A little grading, set up and pour the foundations, then build the walls. It's easier to build new foundation and walls than it is to remodel."

"Okay. I understand. What about that new development just off the freeway?"

"There, they have whole crews who move from house to house doing the same thing. It's really a production line."

"Yeah, I've seen six new homes pop up in the last couple of weeks. Before we just go ahead, maybe we should investigate buying a new home and selling this one."

"We did that, remember, Tom? Those new homes, for example. They're selling for about $100,000 more than our remodeling is going to be. But the houses are small compared to this, and they're on small lots. And there are no mature trees like we have."

Bruce was getting a little fidgety. I'd learned over the years that although he loves to talk, he hates indecision, so I intervened. "You did a list of pro's and con's as part of your initial survey. I think now is a good time to review it. You can scrap the project now, but you've already got a pretty large investment of time and money into this project. It's normal to feel nervous when you're starting something so large."

"Nervous -- I'm petrified!" Tom responded.

"Me, too. And overwhelmed with all we have to do first, and everything that's going to happen over the next year."

"Bruce and I are here to help you. I brought a copy of our 'Remodeling Preparation List' that will help you. Remember the emotional rollercoaster. I think that will help. And remember, you can always call, even if you just need a friendly voice of reassurance."

We agreed to meet again in one week, to finish the conversation and talk more seriously about the start date, after Tom and Patty had reviewed the pro's/con's list and looked at the preparation list. I'd learned over the years to give homeowners time to make decisions, wait patiently in the background until they contacted me, or wait until a scheduled meeting.

The following week, the feeling was more relaxed. Bruce gave me a 15-minute head start to chat with Tom and Patty before he arrived. He understood (and appreciated) that designers are often marriage counselors, too.

Patty started the conversation. "It's been one of the toughest weeks in our marriage."

"I'm sorry to hear that, but I'm not surprised. It's a normal part of the process."

"Yeah," Tom added, "I thought everything was going to blow up two days after our meeting.

I almost called you and said, 'Forget the whole remodeling thing; it's not worth losing Patty and the kids.'"

"Wow! But you worked everything out?"

Patty nodded her head, looking guilty. "I should have never said what I did. It was the final straw for Tom."

"It's okay now. At the time, it just seemed like a low blow to my ego. Now, I think it's rather funny. Patty accused me of getting my degree in frugality at the local hardware store."

The three of us were still laughing when Bruce arrived. "Care to tell me the joke?"

"It's not a joke, Bruce. But it is funny. Tom and Patty will have to tell you, though."

"Patty, it's okay with me if you want to tell Bruce. Only if you're comfortable."

"Now I feel better about it, 'cause we laughed." Patty did a good job of telling her story. I'd never seen Bruce laugh so hard. I knew he'd be telling the story to everyone at the lumber yard the next morning. I could hear all the guys laughing, and teasing each other about their degrees. Typical guy stuff.

"Okay, folks, I hate to break up the party, but we've got to get back on track." Rosanne would be proud to hear me say this.

For the next three hours, we looked at Bruce's proposed schedule and calendars. We could start the project as early as the middle of March, but we finally arrived at a starting date of June 1st. This would give Tom and Patty almost four months to find a rental home, pack everything for storage, and move necessities into the rental home. It would be late enough in the school year so the kids would have to be shuttled to school for only two weeks.

Patty and I talked about once a week during those four months. I appreciated her natural organization ability. She related to lists easily, and used them effectively. I helped her develop the list of kitchen equipment to be stored. With Tom's computer skills, she developed a program that would show the contents of every box on demand. The information was cross-referenced, so it could be retrieved by an easy search.

Tom was in charge of finding a rental home. Chuck and Cindy were invited to help, and eagerly gave their opinions. It was a good lesson in financial planning, especially for Chuck, who would be leaving for college in a year or two. But it made a strong impact on Cindy, too. One afternoon, when I called to see how Patty was doing, Cindy answered the phone, and we had a nice chat.

"I didn't know what a big deal this thing is."

"That's right, Cindy. It's a lot of money. It's also a lot of people."

"What? I don't understand."

Well, there's your family. Then there's Bruce, and his crew of about 15 people, and Bruce's suppliers. And there's me, and Rosanne. Then there are about five or six places your parents went shopping to get products. For every single product, there's the manufacturer, the warehouse, the warehouse employees, truck drivers. Add it all up, you've probably got four hundred people working to make this project a success."

"Oh, wow! You sure?"

"You bet!"

"I can't wait to tell my friends about this!"

The following week, Patty called me to ask if I would give my opinion about a rental house Tom had found. This was one of those times I'd mentioned that she needed reassurance. While we were in the car, I let her do all the talking while I drove. When we arrived at the house, I knew immediately why Patty wasn't enthusiastic about the rental house. It had absolutely no curb appeal.

As we walked through the house, I let Patty continue to vent about everything she didn't like. When we got to the master bedroom, I said, "I know this house isn't your style at all. It's old, and shows its age."

"It needs remodeling more than our home does!"

"I won't disagree. But it's clean and well-maintained. It's only two miles away from your home, and it's $1,000 less a month than the one you and the kids liked better."

"I keep telling myself that. If we're here a year, that's $12,000 more in our pocket, or to put towards the new mortgage. But I don't know if I can live here a year, and spend the holidays here."

"You won't be here that much. You'll be over at your place, watching construction. Even when you're here, you'll be actively thinking about your new home. "

"Yeah, you've got a point."

"About the holidays. I saw your decorations last year. You didn't store them, did you?"

"No, we're bringing them with us, wherever we move to."

"Okay. You'll be so caught up in decorating this place, baking, and celebrating, it'll be fun." Then I felt it was time to play my trump card. "How long did you say you've lived in your home, wanting to remodel it? When you get home, look at your kitchen, and think about how long you've lived with that awful electric cooktop. I bet you and Tom and the kids will make the most of this place, and have fun."

"When you say it like that, I have to agree with you."

The next day was one of the most memorable in my career. Patty called to tell me they were going to sign the rental agreement for the "ugly house" that night. A few minutes after our phone call, the doorbell rang. When I answered the door, a delivery boy handed me a basket with beautiful plants and flowers. Jay never sends flowers. I was puzzled, and read the card. "Don't know what you did or said, but it worked. Thanks a million -- Tom."

Two weeks later, Tom and Patty, Chuck and Cindy -- and their furpersons -- moved from their home into the ugly house. I stopped by to take pictures of them moving, and their empty house. In three days, Bruce and his crew would start tearing their house apart; it would never be the same again . . .

I'm not as good at telling a story as Diane is, but she asked me to take over from here. Construction is my baby. I really don't care about the products people use, as long as my guys can figure how to install them, and they don't give us problems. It's all about time and money. And satisfied clients who'll give us referrals.

I start new projects on Monday, so my crew can put in a full week. Before we start, though, I meet the electrician and plumber with my lead carpenter and the designer at the house so we can fine-tooth the plans.

We take double-check measurements and look at anything suspicious. Sometimes, we need to make a hole in the wall or ceiling to see what's going on. Better to do that than have a crew standing around drinking coffee while we figure out what to do, after we've started construction.

I knew Tom and Patty's house well. Been up in the attic and down in the crawlspace several times. The house has good bones. But I've seen evidence of standing water, and the neighborhood is known to have a network of underground streams. Beefing up the foundation is likely to strike one of those streams, so I've planned for a french drain system, with a backup sump pump, just in case. It's like insurance -- if you pay for it and don't use it, you really don't miss the money. But if you don't pay for it and need it, you're going to end up spending more. Lots more.

My three guys have worked with Diane before. Gary, the electrician, knows she's nuts for all kinds of lighting and fancy switches. Now, he just shrugs when he sees her plans. The first job, though, that was different. I remember when he called me. "What the *&^%? Do you know what that crazy decorator did? She's got more $%^&^% wiring in the kitchen than I normally put in whole houses! And what's with all these fancy multiple switches? Do the clients know how much they're paying for each one of those suckers?"

Yeah, he moaned and griped through the whole project. But when it was done, and he saw the results, he was bringing prospects to the job, to talk them into doing the same thing. Like it was his idea. Now he looks forward to her jobs, even if there's something new she's put in. And he no longer calls her "That @#$%^&*() decorator."

Al, my plumber, had issues, too. Can't remember which job it was, but he also read me the riot act when I told him he had to put the shower fittings exactly where they were shown in the elevations. He was used to doing everything the same way. Never had to think about how his plumbing affected the tile setter before he saw elevations with the tile laid out to scale. He's not a whiner or complainer like Gary, but I have to watch him and oversee what he does to make sure he follows the plans. If he doesn't, he knows he's going to pay for it.

Sorry. I get carried away sometimes. Back to Tom and Patty's project.

Okay. First week. We're in demolition. Everything going okay. Little bit of dry-rot in a

219

couple of places, but nothing out of the ordinary. Then one of my guys discovers termites -- a whole established colony inside a bearing wall. Fair amount of damage. Potential structural problems. I called the structural engineer and Diane first, to get their opinion. We met at the house that afternoon, to see the problem. Richard and I came up with a solution that wouldn't affect the job, and wouldn't cost more than a couple hundred dollars above what I'd figured for dry-rot and termite damage. The extra tear-out and framing would add three days to the job. First week, and already three days behind the schedule I'd laid out.

I called Tom that evening. "Can you meet me at the house tomorrow on your way to work? I have something to show you."

"Oh, no. Is it bad? How much is it going to cost?"

"It's not as bad as it could be. A little termite problem, nothing really serious for a house like yours. Just want to show it to you and talk about what we're going to do."

The next morning, Tom and Patty came to the house in separate cars, on their way to work. First time they'd been to the house since they moved out. I know they were shocked to see just the shell. Tom seemed to take it in stride, but Patty was hit pretty hard. I wished then I'd asked Diane to be there, too. I don't know how to act when women cry. I focused on Tom, hoping he could keep Patty calm.

"Here's the termite nest one of my guys found yesterday morning, inside this bearing wall. The colony has spread up to the ceiling joists in that area. We can take care of it, no problem."

Tom asked the same question, "How much is it going to cost?"

I had no time to answer. Patty jumped in, "Why didn't you see the termites when you went under the house and into the attic?"

I hate it when women's voices get higher. Reminds me of screeching birds at the zoo. I have to remember to delay, and take a deep breath.

"Okay. I understand. I feel bad 'cause I didn't see the termites. You can't really see termites. You see the sawdust they leave, or their poop, then you go looking for them. Everything was hidden inside the wall. I've already figured for dry-rot and termites, so it's only going to be a couple hundred more than I figured."

"Yes, but a couple hundred here, a couple hundred there, pretty soon you've got a thousand." Tom sounded more like a bean-counter than a computer geek.

"You're right. That's why I listed everything I've included in your project, and gave you and Patty a computer printout of the budget for each item. I'm not going to nickel-and-dime you to death. I keep a running total of everything -- debits and credits. We review it every week, to see where you stand budget-wise. Okay?"

220

"Patty, are you okay with this?" Tom asked.

"I don't like it, but I can deal with it."

"There's one other thing . . ."

"Oh, shoot. Now, what?"

". . .the extra work, I figure will take about three days. I'll see how that fits into the schedule I gave you, and if it causes a problem, I'll print out a revised schedule. I usually pad the schedule for stuff like this, anyway."

"Oh, if that's all it is, no problem."

"Okay. I'll have Larry get started on it right now."

I said good-bye to Tom and Patty and went back to work.

"Bruce?"

I turned around. Patty was walking towards me.

"We just hit the first sharp corner in our rollercoaster ride, didn't we?"

"Yep."

"And we didn't fall out!"

"Yep."

I don't understand women. They can be screeching at you one minute, and hugging you the next. They cry when they're mad, they cry when they're hurt, they cry when they're happy.

It took only two days for my guys to clean up the termite problem, and the rest of the framing was going up fast. I gave Diane a heads-up call that we'd be installing the roof in about two weeks. If Tom and Patty wanted to change their minds, now was the time to do it. Diane called back the next day to tell me that Tom and Patty still wanted the same product they specified, so I went ahead and ordered it. She asked about the termite problem. "You're not giving Patty and Tom a change order for the extra work and lumber?"

"Naw, it was only a couple hundred dollars more than I'd estimated. But if we run into more termites, or serious dry-rot, I'll have to give 'em a change order."

"Okay. Just wanted to make sure I understood what Patty told me."

After I talked with Diane, I checked with my subs, to make sure they'd be at the house on schedule. My guys are pretty reliable, but anyone can make an honest mistake. One job I had, the electrician wrote the wrong date in his calendar, and couldn't fit me in. It set the job back over a week. It's hard to find a substitute on short notice. So I pulled my crew off the job until we could get back on track. It was an expensive lesson. Haven't made that mistake since!

The next time I saw Tom and Patty at the house was right after we framed the stairway to the new second floor. I took the time to walk around the house with them. We stopped several times to look at the plans. It's hard to see what's what when all you've got is rows of studs. Glad I did this with Tom and Patty, 'cause they thought one of the closets was their master bathroom. At first, I didn't understand, until Patty asked, "where's the toilet going to be?"

I left to get back to my guys when they started talking about furniture and stuff like that. That's not my department. Before they left, Tom and Patty asked me a couple of questions about windows, and the view they'd get from their bedroom. I told them I'd be talking with Diane that evening, so I'd ask her. I wrote a reminder to myself and got back to work.

Diane had an evening appointment, so I left a message with her husband, and kept the reminder with my cell phone, so I'd remember to call Diane in the morning. I've learned that Jay sometimes forgets to give Diane her messages. Then I called Tom and Patty, to tell them I'd talk with Diane in the morning before work.

6:45 a.m., next day. On my way to the lumber yard, I called Diane. Jay answered. "Can I speak with the boss?"

"Sure. Just a second. I **did** give her the message. She said she'd call you around 7:30."

"That's bankers' hours!"

"No, normal person's hours!"

"Okay, you guys, I'm on the line. I heard the phone ring, and figured it was you, Bruce."

"Yeah, it's me. Just wanted to give you an update, and pass along a coupla questions from Tom and Patty."

She put me on hold while she went to her office upstairs, and had the plans up on her monitor. It's more convenient for me when architects and designers work from home. I don't have to wait for answers, when they get to their office, which sometimes is a day or more.

So, we talked about the windows and Diane said she'd talk with Tom and Patty, to reassure them that they'd have a great view of the garden from the bedroom without losing privacy. I knew she had some tricks up her sleeve that didn't affect my work. I just want to do what I'm hired to do, and leave all that foo-foo stuff to others.

When everything's going well, and we're on schedule, I don't remember many of the details. One job is like the others. It's the problems I remember. That's the difference between the different jobs. Try to learn from the problems.

I'll never forget a big problem Diane and I had with a job, about five years ago. Whole-house remodeling, similar to Tom and Patty's project. The homeowners took time to get all their products chosen, and Diane finished the plans in mid-August. As soon as the permits were approved in early October, they wanted us to start. We tried to talk them into waiting until early spring, but they wouldn't listen. Wanted their house finished and decorated by the next Thanksgiving, so they could have holiday parties. So, we went ahead.

Weather in October and early November can be nice, but it can be horrible. Don't get ahead of me! You know what's coming. As soon as we got the roof off and the studs exposed, it got nasty. Heavy rain, and wind like I never remember -- for over two weeks solid. Couldn't keep tarps on the house. Wouldn't have mattered, but we were trying to save most of the original wood floors, to save money. Yeah, the wood warped and the floors buckled. Looked like an old washboard.

Right away, the homeowners started talking liability and lawsuit. That makes me angry. I was just trying to help them. So I called my attorney, to see what I could do.

"The first thing you should have done, Bruce, was to have the homeowners sign a simple acknowledgment that you advised them to wait until better weather."

"Yeah, rub my nose in it, Arthur. It's too late for them to sign anything now, except lawsuit papers."

"Not necessarily. You have damage insurance?"

"Of course."

"And the homeowners have property insurance. I bet we can get this thing split four ways, between you, the homeowners, and the insurance companies."

"Hey, sounds good."

Sometimes, attorneys are worth what they charge. Just kidding. But a coupla hundred dollars for Arthur saved me thousands, and saved the job. The homeowners were happy, 'cause they got new wood floors for one-quarter what they would've paid. And I learned to take the time to write this thing Arthur called an acknowledgment. If homeowners ask me to do something I know I shouldn't do, they'll have to sign the form. No verbal agreements. Period.

And then there was this other job, about a year later. Diane referred me to a couple who wanted a wiz-bang master bathroom. When I met them to go over the preliminary plans, they got into a pretty heavy disagreement about the guy who'd remodeled their kitchen. The husband got along with the contractor, and seemed pretty satisfied. The wife couldn't stand the contractor, and didn't want him back in her house.

The best I can do in these situations is change the subject, or leave. I get real nervous when I'm caught in the middle. I made it clear to them that I won't get into a bidding war with any other contractor. No one wins. When I spend time doing estimates, they're as accurate as can be. I'll answer questions and provide details, but I won't give anyone my estimate breakdowns. That's another lesson I learned a long time ago. But that's another story.

I did a preliminary estimate for the couple. They were almost maxed out on their electrical service, and I knew they'd need new service, especially with a whirlpool tub. So I figured the amount for trenching alongside their driveway -- about 150 feet -- to bring in another 200-amp panel. That alone amounted to some serious coin. The project also included structural changes, and major plumbing changes. The total labor added up to over $35,000. Didn't have to worry about products, 'cause they were buying everything.

About a month after I sent the estimate, I was talking with Diane about another project. I asked her about how things were going with the fancy master bathroom.

"Uh, ok. They're going to use the other contractor again. I'm sorry."

"I figured that when they didn't return my calls. Hope they get what they want."

"Me, too."

About three months later, Diane called me. I knew there'd been problems with the fancy bathroom project, but none of the particulars.

"Bruce, they fired the contractor. He wasn't showing up regularly. We've got major problems with the wiring. And there are some other problems, too. Do you feel like helping, or would you rather pass?"

I told her I'd have to think about it. And I'd have to look at the job before I'd commit. Sticky situation. I don't like going in after another contractor's left. To do it right, I'd have to pull everything out and almost start from scratch. Like another job recently. Oh, yeah. Lost my train of thought for a second.

So I went back to the fancy bathroom project. The homeowners were real friendly, and very embarrassed. I usually have a joke or two, to break the tension. It was really bad. Some of it was so bad it was funny. But most of it just made me sick, to think they'd actually paid this guy for that kind of work. I felt guilty about charging them to redo most of the other guy's work, but I'm not rich enough to give my services away. I'm not a non-profit organization. My financial advisor says I am, but that's just his opinion.

I really didn't want to do this project. It could turn into a nightmare for me. It was already a nightmare for the homeowners. If it had been any other project, any other designer, I'd have told 'em I'm too busy. Something like this could spoil the working relationship Diane and I'd had for several years. I knew anyone coming into the project now would have two strikes against them. The homeowners were decent, honest people. They had a right to mistrust all contractors. This was one case where they had a right to sue the other guy, or at least collect money from his insurance company. They decided to just let it drop, and move on.

Man, what a situation! Against my better judgement, I took on the project. I dreaded going to work every morning. I didn't sleep hardly at all until the job was finished. But I had to put on my smiley face every morning for the homeowners, like I wasn't worried about anything. I'd arrive an hour before work sometimes, park about a block away, to drink my coffee and think about what I'd say and do to reassure them. For two months solid, I lived with a fireball in the pit of my stomach. My wife and kids wished I'd never agreed to do this job. When I'd get home, all I wanted to do was watch TV. Didn't want to talk to anyone. Even the guys at the lumber yard noticed. Of course, they'd tease me about not being my usual self. I wanted nothing more than to finish this !@#%$ job and get back to normal.

The turning point was when we got the new electrical service installed. Then my guys and I could button everything up like it'd been one of our own projects from the start. I was still on guard, though. It helped to get positive feedback from the homeowners and Diane. As well as she knew me, I don't think even she knew how bad it was. I couldn't tell her, 'cause I knew she'd feel guilty about pressuring me to do it. As we got closer to finishing, I was able to talk with her more about the job and things in general.

Actually, everything went pretty smoothly, until the granite fabricator fouled things up. He knew about the problems. I don't know why he didn't come to take the measurements himself, instead of sending one of his guys. Just when we could see daylight ahead, it took him an extra two weeks to straighten out the mess. I know it cost him two sheets of granite. The expensive stuff, imported from Brazil. But as the general, I was the one who had to explain the situation to the homeowners, not him, although they were paying him directly. I had no control over him, 'cause I didn't hold the purse strings. I think down deep, he enjoyed watching me squirm.

Finally, the granite was done, and the homeowners never knew what the problem was, only that there'd been a delay. Me and the guys finished the trim work, then the cleaning crew came in and spiffied up the place. Gotta admit, it turned out to be one heck of a beautiful bathroom. Something we were all proud of.

Time for final walk-through with the homeowners, after the inspector'd signed the last line on the permit card. Everyone was in a good mood. At least, I thought they were, until the husband came out of his den with a stack of computer paper, looking stern. I couldn't see anything but the first coupla lines that said, "Punch list -- Master Bathroom." Slowly, he unfolded the paper. He'd made a list of everything that was wrong with the bathroom after the other contractor left. One by one, he checked off each item. Slowly, the frown turned to a slight smile, then a big smile. He must've had 25 pages or more by the time he finished the list. The last page was my favorite. In bold letters it said, "Thank you, Bruce. You did good!"

We popped a bottle of champagne open. They gave me a ten-pound box of expensive chocolates for me and my guys. Ten pounds of Hershey bars would've been fine for us. This was overkill. Didn't want my crew to expect it every time we have a difficult job. Then the husband handed me an envelope. Said it was my final check, well-deserved. Told me to open it. Inside was not only my final check, but a gift certificate for a weekend getaway for my wife and me, at one of the fanciest resorts in this area. I don't like to get emotional, but their kindness choked me up. Had to take a big gulp of champagne to clear my head.

That kind of experience is a confidence-builder. Yeah, it doesn't hurt the bank account, either. I've gotten so many tasty referrals from the homeowners, it was worth the several months of hassle.

I'd better finish Tom and Patty's story before I get sidetracked again. Compared to the fancy bathroom project, theirs was a cakewalk. We had a few minor problems with a coupla products, but nothing major. No major delays that I can remember. The project was finished just about when I figured it would be, and right on the money.

I had to get used to Patty's quirks, though. She's a hugger and a toucher -- the kind who'll pat you on the hand or arm while they're talking. I know it's real friendly, and a sign of trust, but I don't care for it. Patty shows her appreciation with a hug. All I need is kind words. Tom's just the opposite; typical computer geek. I never knew where I stood with him. Never says much, unless he gets all fired up about some new computer gadget. Then he'll talk your head off. Ram, rom, bits, bites. Don't know one from the other. Guess that's how it sounds when a bunch of us contractors get together and talk shop. No one else is interested in what we're saying except us.

Diane was right about the emotional rollercoaster. I'd never given it much thought, but every job has predictable ups and downs. In fact, I've used her description with several clients already. It's something that everyone can understand.

Well, I'm about finished with my part of the story. Think I'll hand it back to Diane, so she can wrap up the loose ends ......

Bruce is right when he said that Patty and Tom's project fell into place. Of course, there were questions along the way, and a few minor setbacks. One of the lavatory faucets arrived defective, and the replacement valve was also defective. As much as Tom and Patty paid for the faucets, I expected better quality, and better service from the manufacturer. The distributor and the plumbing supplier were wonderful to work with, but I felt like the manufacturer was stonewalling, expecting us to accept anything they shipped. But it got resolved. The results are all that matter.

I remember there were some challenges with the color scheme. Tom prefers cooler colors, and Patty likes a warmer palette. But that, too, was resolved with compromise. Color and lighting are two of the most difficult things for people to choose, because they both evoke an emotional response. It's hard to select color without relying on how you feel about it, or how it makes you feel. And, without light, there's no color. Light affects color, and vice-versa. I spent several weeks during the final stages of construction, helping Patty and Tom finalize the color scheme. But they're happy with it. That's the most important thing. If it wasn't for the inspector's comment about the color scheme to Patty . . .

Patty and Tom and the kids are settled into their new home now. Furface and Furball have gotten over the stress of moving twice in the same year, and they're both fine. Everyone's looking forward to the holiday season this year, and Chuck's graduation party. Oh, by the way, they thoroughly enjoyed last Christmas. Patty did decorate, and the house looked very nice. And as usual, she baked hundreds of sweet treats. People can adapt to almost anything, especially if they know it's a temporary situation.

I was pleasantly surprised a couple of weeks ago. Patty invited me over for coffee and to chat. She said she couldn't wait to tell me about a conversation she had with one of their neighbors when they bumped into each other in the grocery store. Their conversation went something like this:

"Hi, Deborah!"

"Oh, hi, Patty." (Sigh)

"How's your remodeling coming along?"

227

"I'd rather not talk about it. It isn't going as well as yours did, and we're not doing as much, either.   I get really upset every time I think about it or talk about it."

"I'm sorry to hear that. Is there anything I can do to help?"

"You tried to help by referring Bruce, and giving us other advice. We didn't listen to you or Bruce. It's our own fault."

I hate to hear stories like this, but I hear them all the time. Patty proceeded to tell me what she knew personally, and what Bruce told her.

Deborah and her husband, Phil, empty-nesters, decided to do as much of their project as possible, to save money. Deborah took a basic design course for one semester. She and Phil bought a CAD program at the local office supply store, and learned how to use it fairly proficiently. They watched all the do-it-yourself shows on television, and took classes at the local building supply store. They acquired and read every homeowner "how-to" book about drawing plans, being your own general contractor, etc. They did as much as homeowners can do, with limited time and resources.

They talked with Bruce several times. He knew they were headed for disaster. They were partially-informed consumers. They knew mostly what they wanted, but they really didn't know how to achieve it. They had so much input, so much conflicting information, they were confused but didn't know how confused they were. They had lots of advice, but no real-time feedback. Most of their ideas came from pictures of other projects in magazines and books, but none of the pictures bore a direct resemblance to their home. What looked good in pictures didn't look good in real life, but they didn't realize it until they saw it and had to tear it out and start all over.

Several of the TV home remodeling programs showed one aspect of a major project being completed in a one-hour segment. Like laying a hardwood floor. Or installing kitchen cabinets. Or setting tile in a master bathroom. Deborah and Phil got inspired by these programs. They didn't realize -- nor did anyone tell them -- that it takes weeks, often months, to record and edit a one-hour segment. They had no idea how long it would take to remodel their home once the work had started. They really believed that they could remodel their kitchen and master bathroom during a three-week vacation plus a month or so after that, working on the house in the evening and on weekends.

No one told Deborah and Phil about the months of preparation that goes into EVERY remodeling project. Untold hours drafting and refining the plans, shopping for products, making each decision in the proper order. Setting a realistic budget and updating the figures regularly, to verify that everything fits financially as well as dimensionally.

No one prepared Deborah and Phil for the differences that would arise between them, often causing arguments and hurt feelings. Without the real-time feedback about compromise, they would have to resolve their differences -- or scrap the project. Al they heard (and read) was how easy it would be, and how much money they would save.

They knew there were codes and requirements, but they didn't know which ones would affect their project, until they submitted their plans to the local building department. No one had offered the advice to check with the building officials before they started drawing plans, to ask which codes would be pertinent. Deborah and Phil thought they knew what they were doing. They thought they knew what they wanted. The plans they prepared made perfect sense to them, but there wasn't enough information for the building department to issue permits. There wasn't enough information to get estimates from the cabinet distributor, plumbing and lighting suppliers, or tradespeople. Phil and Deborah didn't know how to estimate quantities of tile, and their plans didn't clearly show where tile would be.

And so it went. The three-week vacation sped by. The first week was spent demolishing the existing kitchen and master bathroom. The other two weeks were spent installing rough electrical wires and plumbing pipes. They didn't allow whole days off work, waiting for the building inspector. Some evenings were spent doing the work, but not much could be accomplished after sunset when they were tired. They were lucky if one day each weekend was spent working on the house. Most products were bought at the local home improvement store, last-minute -- not by choice, but necessity. They were living in a constant state of chaos, with no end in sight. They were lucky to still be married.

What about the money Deborah and Phil wanted to save? They never really knew how much the project was costing, and didn't want to know. Instinctively, they did know that it was much more than they had budgeted. They had to get a second mortgage to fund the balance of their project.

"I've heard enough!" I said. "There's nothing we can do now for Deborah and Phil. Let's change the subject a little and put more emphasis on the positive."

"Sounds good to me. You have something in mind?"

"Sure do."

"Is it anything like your rollercoaster analogy?"

"Yes, you might say that."

"Okay. I'm ready."

"There are two couples looking for a yacht. One of the couples is Deborah and Phil. The other couple is you and Tom."

"Okay."

"Both couples do research, but with different emphasis. Deborah and Phil know they want to travel, but they don't have a specific destination in mind. They think they can navigate the vessel themselves, and hire part-time crew members only as needed. You and Tom look for a yacht that precisely fits your needs. But you're also flexible, willing to explore alternatives. You know you want to travel up and down the coast. You know that to enjoy it, you're going to need a professional crew.

"Phil and Deborah don't acknowledge the value of a navigator, captain, and crew. They just want a boat that looks good. You and Tom decide how much you can afford for your yacht, your crew, and your traveling expenses. You make allowances for additional expenditures along the way. You hire the best crew you can afford: The navigator, the captain, the deckhands, and specialists.

"Deborah and Phil haven't got a clue. They're not relaxed, and they're certainly not enjoying the trip they've been dreaming of for a long time. You and Tom keep a running ledger for every investment or expense associated with your new yacht. You know at any given time whether you can afford a luxury trinket, or how much you have put aside for emergencies. When you set out on your voyage, everything is planned. You can relax and enjoy it."

"I see the analogy clearly," Patty said. "We're the owners of the remodeling vessel. You're the navigator. Bruce is the captain. His employees and subs are the crew."

"Don't forget the suppliers. They're crew members, too. Wow! I'm glad you understand. I wish more people did. Can you figure out what's the best name for your boat?"

"I suppose you have the perfect answer that's part of the analogy?"

"I think so. The name of **your** yacht is 'REALISTIC EXPECTATIONS.'"

"That's great! I can't wait to share this with Tom. I know he'll enjoy it."

Patty walked me to the front door of her new home. We were both smiling, and hugged before I departed. It had been a great voyage for all of us, the team members of the "Realistic Expectations" project. We arrived at the destination relaxed, happy, and satisfied. It's a voyage none of us will ever forget.

GLOSSARY

ABRASION RESISTANCE: A quality of withstanding mechanical action, such as rubbing, scraping, or scrubbing, which may tend to remove material progressively from a surface.

ABS: Acrylonitrile Butadiene Styrene. Black plastic used in the manufacture of DWV (drain, waste, and vent) pipe.

ABSORBENTS: Materials that absorb sound readily; usually building materials designed specifically for the purpose of absorbing acoustic energy.

ABSORPTION: The ability of a fiber, yarn, or fabric to attract and hold gases or liquids within its pores.

ABSORPTION FACTOR: The ratio of light absorbed by a material to the incident light.

ABSORPTION, SOUND: Conversion of acoustic energy to heat or another form of energy within the structure of sound-absorbing materials. Acoustic Used in conjunction with a basic property of sound.

ABSTRACT OF TITLE: A summary of all deeds, wills, and legal actions to show ownership.

ABUT: Joining the end of a construction member.

ACRE: A unit of land measurement having 43,560 sq ft.

ACOUSTICAL: Used in conjunction with apparatus or sound control

ACOUSTICAL TILE: Acoustical absorbents produced in the form of sheets or units resembling tiles.

ACOUSTICS: The science of sound. In housing, acoustical materials used to keep down noise within a room or to prevent it from passing through walls.

ACRYLIC: A glassy thermoplastic vacuum-formed to cast and molded shapes to form the surface of fiberglass bathtubs, whirlpools, shower bases, and shower stalls. Do not confuse with gelcoat.

ADA: Americans with Disabilities Act. A government criteria mandating how buildings must be constructed in order to serve the needs of disabled people.

ADHESIVE: A natural or synthetic material, usually in liquid form, used to fasten or adhere materials together.

ADOBE CONSTRUCTION: Construction using sun-dried units of adobe soil for walls; usually found in the southwestern United States.

AERATOR: A device at the end of a faucet spout which mixes air into flowing water.

AIR, AMBIENT: The air surrounding an object.

AIR CHANGES: A method of expressing the amount of air moving into or out of a building or room in terms of the amount of air in the space volumes exchanged.

AIR CIRCULATION: Air movement.

AIR CLEANER: A device for the purpose of removing airborne impurities, such as dusts, gases, vapors, fumes, and smokes. This is accomplished by washing, filtering, or electrostatic precipitators.

AIR CONDITIONER: An apparatus that can heat, cool, clean, and circulate air.

AIR CONDITIONER, ROOM: A unit designed for independent installation in a space without ducts. It may be mounted in a window or through a wall.

AIR CONDITIONER, UNITARY: One or more factory-made assemblies which include cooling and may also include a heating function; the separate assemblies are designed to be used together.

AIR CONDITIONING: The process of treating air so as to control simultaneously its temperature, humidity, cleanliness, and distribution.

AIR COOLING: Reduction in air temperature due to the abstraction of heat.

AIR DIFFUSER: An air-distribution outlet to discharge air-conditioned air.

AIR-DRIED LUMBER: Lumber that has been dried by unheated air to a moisture content of approximately 15 percent.

AIR DUCT: A pipe, usually made of sheet metal, that conducts air to rooms from a central source.

AIR TRAP: A U-shaped pipe filled with water and located beneath plumbing fixtures to form a seal against the passage of gases and odors.

AIR WASHER: Device for cleaning, humidifying, or dehumidifying the air.

ALCOVE: A recessed space connected at the side of a larger room.

ALKALI: A caustic substance such as lye soda or lime. Alkalies or strong alkali solutions are highly destructive to oil paint films

ALTERATION: A change in, or addition to, an existing building.

AMORTIZATION: An installment payment of a loan, usually monthly for a home loan.

AMPERE: The unit used in the measure of the rate of flow of electricity.

ANCHOR BOLT: A threaded rod inserted in masonry construction for anchoring the sill plate to the foundation.

ANCHORS: Devices, usually metal, used in building construction to secure one material to another.

ANDIRONS: Fireplace accessory. A pair of decorative columns attached to iron bars to hold logs above the level of the hearth.

ANGLE BLOCK: A small block, usually shaped like a right-angled triangle, glued and tacked into the corner of a frame to stiffen it.

ANGLE IRON: A structural piece of rolled steel shaped to form a 90° angle.

ANGLE STOP: A shutoff valve between the water pipes and a faucet. Its inlet connects to the water supply pipe in a wall and its outlet 'angles' up 90 degrees toward the faucet, toilet, or bidet.

ANTIMICROBIAL: A property or treatment applied topically or fused into carpet fiber. The process resists the growth of odor-causing bacteria and mildew.

APPRAISAL: The estimated evaluation of property.

APPRECIABLE CHANGE: A change that is noticeable in comparing the tested specimen with a sample of the original specimen under standard viewing conditions.

APRON: (1) a panel or board below a window board projecting slightly into a room. (2) vertical asphalt on a fascia or overhang of a roof. (3) a part of the driveway that leads directly into the garage.

ARABESQUE: Elaborate scroll designs, either carved or in low relief

ARCADE: An open passageway usually surrounded by a series of arches.

ARCH: A curved structure designed to support itself and the weight above.

AREA: The length multiplied by the width determines the area.

AREA WALL: A wall surrounding an areaway.

AREAWAY: Recessed area below grade around the foundation to allow light and ventilation into basement window.

ARRIS: (1) An external angular intersection between two planes; the sharp edge of a brick. (2) The sharp edge formed by two surfaces; usually on moldings.

ASHLAR: A facing of squared stones.

ASH PIT: An enclosed opening below a fireplace to collect ashes.

ASPHALT: Bituminous sandstones used for paving streets and waterproofing flat roofs.

ASPHALT SHINGLES: Composition roof shingles made from asphalt-impregnated felt covered with mineral granules.

ASSESSED VALUE: A value set by governmental assessors to determine tax assessments.

ASTM: American Society for Testing and Materials.

ASTRAGAL: T-profiled (rabbeted) molding usually used between meeting doors or casement windows.

ATRIUM: An open court within a building.

ATTIC: The space between the roof and the ceiling in a gable house

AWNING WINDOW: An outswinging window hinged at the top of the sash

AXIS: A line around which something rotates or is symmetrically arranged.

BACKFILL: Earth used to fill in areas around foundation walls.

BACKHEARTH: The part of the hearth inside the fireplace.

BACKPLATE: An applied decorative moulding used on ceilings above a chandelier or ceiling fan.

BACK PRIMING: Applying a coat of paint to the backside and edges of woodwork and exterior siding to prevent moisture absorption.

BACKSET: The horizontal distance from the center of the face-bored hole to the edge of the door.

BAFFLE: A partial blocking against a flow of wind or sound.

BALCONY: A deck projecting from the wall of a building above ground level.

BALLCOCK: A fill valve device in a toilet tank. A "Cock" is activated by a float "Ball" to refill tank water after a toilet is flushed.

BALLOON FRAME: A type of wood framing in which the studs extend from sill to eaves without interruption.

BALUSTERS: Small, vertical supports for the railing of a stairs.

BALUSTRADE: A series of balusters supporting the railing of a stairs or balcony.

BANK: A setting-machine yarn creel.

BANNISTER: A handrail with supporting posts on a stairway.

232

BARGEBOARD: The finish board covering the projecting portion of a gable roof.

BASE, or BASEBOARD: The finish of a room at the junction of the walls and floor.

BASE COURSE: The lowest part of masonry construction.

BASE LINE: A located line for reference control purposes.

BASE PLATE: A plate, usually of steel, upon which a column rests.

BASE SHOE: A molding used next to the floor in interior baseboards.

BASIN: A circular vessel with slopping or curving sides for holding water for washing.

BATT: A type of insulation designed to be installed between framing members.

BATTEN: The narrow strips of wood nailed vertically over the joints of boards to form board-and-batten siding.

BATTER: A masonry or concrete wall which slopes backward from the perpendicular.

BATTER BOARDS: Horizontal boards at exact elevations nailed to posts just outside the corners of a proposed building. Strings are stretched across the boards to locate the outline of the foundation for workmen.

BAYS: Uniform compartments within a structure, usually within a series of beams, columns, etc.

BAY WINDOWS: A group of windows projecting from the wall of a building. The center is parallel to the wall, and the sides are angular. A bow window is semicircular.

BEAM: A horizontal structural member that carries a load.

BEAM CEILING: A ceiling in which the ceiling beams are exposed to view.

BEARING PLATE: A metal plate that provides support for a structural member.

BEARING WALL: A wall that supports a weight above in addition to its own weight..

BED MOULDING: Cornice moulding

BENCHMARK: A mark on some permanent object fixed to the ground from which land measurements and elevations are taken. This is the reference point to determine lines, grades, and elevations in the area.

BENDING MOMENT: A measure of the forces that break a beam by bending.

BENT: A frame consisting of two supporting columns and a girder or truss used in vertical position in framing a structure.

BEVEL: A surface meeting another surface at an angle that is not a right angle.

BEVEL SIDING: Shingles or other siding board thicker on one edge than the other. The thick edge overlaps the thin edge of the next board.

BIB: A threaded faucet allowing a hose to be attached.

BIDET: A plumbing fixture used for washing genitals and posterior areas of the body. It is floor mounted, usually next to a toilet, and incorporates a washing basin, faucet and sprayer.

BILL OF MATERIAL: A parts list of material accompanying a structural drawing.

BINDER: A film-forming oil or resin.

BLANKET INSULATION: Insulation in rolled-sheet form, often backed by treated paper that forms a vapor barrier.

BLIND NAILING: Method of nailing to conceal nails.

BLOCKING: Small wood framing members that fill in the open space between the floor and ceiling joists to add stiffness to the floors and ceiling.

BLOCKING RESISTANCE: A quality of resisting adhesion or sticking between any surfaces which touch under uniform loading and temperature conditions for a specified time.

BLOW (THROW): A term used to describe the distance an airstream travels from an outlet.

BLUEPRINT: An architectural drawing used by workers to build from. The original drawing is transferred to a sensitized paper that turns blue with white lines when printed. Also, prints of blue lines on white paper.

BOARD MEASURE: The system of lumber measurement. A unit is 1 board ft. which is 1' sq by approximately 1 thick.

BOLT: A rolled length of wallcovering containing an area specified by the wallcovering manufacturer.

BONDS: The arrangement of masonry units in a wall.

BOOKED: Folding back of pasted wallcovering so that pasted sides are touching.

BOOKMATCHED: Paneling that has been split in two and unfolded to give a symmetrical grain pattern.

BOOT: A projection from a concrete beam or floor slab to carry the facing brickwork.

BRACE: Any stiffening member of a framework.

BRACED FRAMING: Frame construction with posts and braces used for stiffening.

BREEZEWAY: A roofed walkway with open sides. It connects the house and garage.

BRICKMOLD: Exterior wood moulding to cover gap between door or window frame.

BRICK VENEER: A facing of brick on the outer side of wood frame or masonry.

BRIDGING: Thin wood or metal pieces fastened diagonally at midspan between floor joists to act as both tension and compression members for the purposes of stiffening and spreading concentrated loads.

BROKER: An agent in buying and selling property.

BTU: Abbreviation for British Thermal Unit; a standard unit for measuring heat gain or loss.

BUCK: Frame for a door, usually made of metal.

BUCKLING: A carpet that does not lay flat on the floor and contains ridges. Can be caused by uneven beam tension, dimensional instability, and putting together mismatched carpet. Failure to stretch wall-to-wall installations sufficiently will also contribute buckles.

BUILDING CODE: A collection of legal requirements for buildings designed to protect the safety, health, and general welfare of people who work and live in them.

BUILDING LINE: An imaginary line on a plot beyond which the building may not extend.

BUILDING PAPER: A heavy, waterproof paper used over sheathing and subfloors to prevent passage of air and water.

BUILDING PERMIT: A permit issued by a municipal government authorizing the construction of a building or structure.

BUILT-UP BEAM: A beam constructed of smaller members fastened together.

BUILT-UP ROOF: A roofing composed of layers of felt impregnated with pitch, coal tar, or asphalt. The top is finished with crushed stone or minerals. It is used on flat or low-pitched roofs.

BULLNOSE: The rounding of an arris; in general, any rounded edge or end of a brick, a step, a joiners plane, etc.

BUTT: Type of joint having the pieces edge to edge or end to end. Also a type of door hinge allowing edge of door to butt into the jamb.

BUTTERFLY ROOF: A roof with two sides sloping down toward the interior of the house.

BUTT HINGES: Two metal plates joined with a pin, one fastened to the door jamb or frame and the other to the door.

BUTT JOINT: A joint formed by placing the end of one member against another member.

BUTTRESS: A projection from a wall to create additional strength and support.

BX CABLE: Armored electric cable wrapped in plastic and protected by a flexible steel covering.

CABINET WORK: The finish interior woodwork.

CALL OUT: A note on a drawing with a leader to the feature.

CANDLE POWER: The unit of light intensity. One candle power is the light given off by a standard candle whose composition, size and burning rate have been specified. The modern method of measuring the candle power of light is to compare its brightness with that of an electric light of fixed candle power, rather than with that of a standard candle. A 40 watt electric lamp is rated at about 32 candle power.

CANOPY: A projection over windows and doors to protect them from the weather.

CANTILEVER: A projecting member supported only at one end.

CANT STRIP: An angular board used to eliminate a sharp, right angle, usually on roof decks.

CAP: Covering for a wall or post.

CARPET: The general designation for fabric used as a floor-covering. It is occasionally used incorrectly in plural as carpets or carpeting. The preferred usage today is carpet in both singular and plural form. It may be used as an adjective as in carpeted floors.

CARPORT: A garage not fully enclosed.

CARRIAGE: The horizontal part of the stringers of a stair that supports the treads.

CASEMENT WINDOW: Window with one or two sash that hinge on their sides. They may open either in or out.

CASING: (1) the exposed frame or trim around a door or window. (2) a timber or similar enclosure on the face of a wall, floor, or ceiling, made to accommodate pipes or cables in a chase or other duct.

CAST IRON: Metal which is formed by casting on molds to make some plumbing fixtures such as bathtubs, lavatories and sinks. The iron form is then coated with enamel. Also DWV sewer pipe.

CATCH BASIN: An underground structure for drainage into which the water from a roof or floor will drain. It is connected with a sewer drain or sump pump.

CAULKING: A soft, waterproof material used to fill open joints or cracks.

CAVITY WALL: A masonry wall having a 2 airspace between brick wythes.

CEDAR SHINGLES: Roofing and siding shingles made from western red cedar.

CEILING OUTLET: An air diffuser located in the ceiling.

CEMENT: A fine, gray powder made from lime, silica, iron oxide, and alumina that when mixed with water and aggregate produces concrete.

CENTERSET: A style of bathroom lavatory faucet having combined spout and handles. Handles are 4" from center of handle-to-handle. Also a single handle faucet installed on 4" center-to-center faucet holes.

CENTIGRADE: A thermometric scale in which the freezing point of water is called 0 degrees and its boiling point 100 degrees at normal atmospheric pressure. Indicated with a C.

CENTRAL HEATING: A single source of heat that is distributed by pipes or ducts.

CERTIFICATE OF TITLE: A document given to the home buyer with the deed, stating that the title to the property named in the deed is clearly established.

CESSPOOL: A pit or cistern to hold sewage.

CHAIR RAIL: Strip of wood or moulding placed on the wall at the same height as the back of a chair to protect the wall from damage

CHALKING: Powdering of the paint film on the film surface. Mild chalking may be desirable. Heavy chalking should be removed prior to repainting.

CHALK LINE: A string that is heavily chalked, held tight, then plucked to make a straight guideline against boards or other surfaces.

CHAMFER: The beveled edge formed by removing the sharp corner of a material.

CHANGE OF AIR: Introduction of new, recirculated or cleansed, air to conditioned space.

CHASE: A vertical space within a building for ducts, pipes, or wires.

CHECKS: Splits or cracks in a board, ordinarily caused by seasoning.

CHECK VALVE: A valve that permits passage through a pipe in only one direction.

CHIMNEY: A vertical flue for passing smoke and gases outside a building.

CHIMNEY STACK: A group of flues in the same chimney.

CHINOISERIE: (French) Chinese designs or style. Cobble.

CHORD: The principal members of a roof or bridge truss. The upper members are indicated by the term upper chord. The lower members are identified by the term lower chord.

CINDER BLOCK: A building block made of cement and cinder.

CIRCUIT: The path of an electric current. The closed loop of wire in which an electric current can flow.

CIRCUIT BREAKER: A safety device used to open and close an electrical circuit.

CISTERN: An artificial reservoir for storing water. A toilet tank. This term is usually used in England.

CLAPBOARD: A board, thicker on one side than the other, used to overlap an adjacent board

CLEARANCE: A clear space to allow passage.

CLEAR FINISH: A material that is transparent in nature. Usually referred to if and when an application of the material is applied overall on a finished surface.

CLEAR TIMBER: Wood that is free from defects and knots; usually obtained from the bottom section of trees.

CLEAT: A small board fastened to another member to serve as a brace or support.

CLERESTORY: A set of high windows often above a roof line.

CLINCH: To bend over the protruding end of a nail.

CLIP: A small connecting angle used for fastening various members of a structure.

CLOSE-COUPLED (TOILET): A modern style two-piece toilet which is configured of a separate tank and bowl. The tank is "coupled" "closely" (directly) to the bowl by bolts and a gasket. This term is to distinguish from old style low-tank toilets where the tank mounted on the wall, above and behind the bowl and was connected by a pipe called a flush ell.

CLOTH-BACKED: Wallcovering having a backing of woven or knitted yarns

COATING ADHESION: A measure of the strength of the bond between the surface coating and the backing or substrate of a wallcovering

COATING SYSTEM: A combination of specific coating materials and their sequential application to an appropriately prepared surface to impart color or protect the surface.

COCK: A faucet or valve for regulating the flow of water.

COCKHOLE COVER: A round cover-plate or disk installed on a sink to cover an unused faucet hole.

COFFER: A panel in a ceiling, deeply recessed to make a decorative pattern.

COIL: A cooling or heating element made of pipe or tubing.

COLLAR BEAM: A horizontal member tying opposing rafters below the ridge in roof framing.

COLORFASTNESS: A quality of resisting change or loss of color resulting from exposure to light.

COLUMN: In architecture: a perpendicular supporting member, circular in section; in engineering: a vertical structural member supporting loads

COMFORT ZONE: The range of effective temperatures over which the majority of adults feel comfortable.

COMMERCIAL MATCHING: Matching of colors within acceptable tolerances or with a color variation that is barely detectable to the naked eye.

COMMODE: An archaic style of toilet. "A boxlike structure holding a chamber pot under an open seat."

COMMON WALL: A single wall that serves two dwelling units.

COMPOUND CURVE: Curving in two different directions at the same time.

COMPRESSION: A force that tends to make a member fail because of crushing.

CONCAVE: Hollow or inward curving shape.

CONCRETE: A mixture of cement, sand, gravel, and water.

CONCRETE BLOCK: Precast hollow or solid blocks of concrete.

CONDEMN: To legally declare unfit for use.

CONDENSATE: The liquid formed by condensation of a vapor. In steam heating, water condensed from steam; in air conditioning, water extracted from air, as a condensation on the outside of a cold beer glass on a hot day.

CONDENSATION: The formation of frost or drops of water on inside walls when warm vapor inside a room meets a cold wall or window.

CONDUCTANCE: Transfer of heat through a material.

CONDUCTOR: In architecture: a drain pipe leading from the roof; in electricity: anything that permits the passage of an electric current

CONDUCTOR PIPE: A pipe used to lead water from the roof to the sewer.

CONDUIT: A metal, plastic, or fiber tube fitted to a wall, ceiling, or other part of a building and used as an encasement to cables.

CONDUIT: A channel built to convey water or other fluids; a drain or sewer. In electrical work, a channel that carries wires for protection and for safety.

CONDUIT (METAL FLEXIBLE): Spiral-wound interlocking tubing that is flexible.

CONDUIT, ELECTRICAL: A metal pipe in which wiring is installed.

CONSOLE LAV: A table-like fixture with an integral lavatory. The back is fixed to a wall and the front is supported by consoles (brackets) or legs.

CONSTRUCTION LOAN: A mortgage loan to be used to pay for labor and materials going into the house. Money is usually advanced to the builder as construction progresses and is repaid when the house is completed and sold.

CONTINUOUS BEAM: A beam that has no intermediate supports

CONTROL: Any device for regulation of air-conditioning equipment.

CONVECTION: Transfer of heat by movement of fluid or air.

CONVECTOR: A heat-transfer surface that uses convection currents to transfer heat.

COPED: Shaped or cut to fit an adjoining piece of moulding.

COPING: A cap or top course of masonry on a wall to prevent moisture penetration.

CORBEL: A projection of masonry from the face of a wall, or a bracket used for support of weight above.

CORE: The inner layer of plywood. It may be veneer, solid lumber, or fiberboard.

CORNER BEAD: A metal molding built into plaster corners to prevent the accidental breaking off of the plaster.

CORNER BOARD: Vertical board forming the corner of a building.

CORNER BRACE: Diagonal brace at the corner of a wood-frame wall to stiffen and prevent racking.

CORNICE: (1) a molding at the top of an outside wall that overhangs the wall and throws drips away from it. (2) a molding at a junction between an inside wall and the ceiling.

CORNICE RETURN: The short portion of a molded cornice that returns on the gable end of a house.

COUNTER FLASHING: Flashing used under cap flashing.

COUNTERSUNK: Hole prepared with a bevel to enable the tapered head of a screw to be inserted flush with the surface.

COURSE: A continuous row of stone or brick of uniform height.

COURT: An open space surrounded partly or entirely by a building.

COVE: A concave molding usually used on horizontal inside corners.

CRAWL SPACE: The shallow space below the floor of a house built above the ground. Generally it is surrounded with the foundation wall.

CRICKET: A device used at roof intersections to divert rain water.

CRIPPLE: A structural member that is cut less than full length, such as a studding piece above a window or door opening.

CROSS BRACING: Boards nailed diagonally across studs or other boards to make framework rigid.

CROSS BRIDGING: Bracing between floor joists to add stiffness to the floors.

CROSSHATCH: Lines drawn closely together at an angle to show a section cut.

CROWN MOLDING: A molding used above eye level, usually the cornice molding under the roof overhang.

CULL: Building material rejected as below standard grade.

CULVERT: A passage for water below ground level.

CUPOLA: A small structure built on top of a roof to provide ventilation.

CURB: A very low wall.

CURE: To allow concrete to dry slowly by keeping it moist to allow maximum strength.

CURTAIN WALL: An exterior wall that provides no structural support

DADO JOINT: A recessed joint on the face of a board to receive the end of a perpendicular board.

DAMP COURSE: A layer of waterproof material.

DAMPER: A device used to vary the volume of air passing through an air outlet, inlet, or duct.

DATUM: A reference point of starting elevations used in mapping and surveying.

DEADBOLT OR DEADLOCK: Hardened steel bolt with a square head operated by a key or turn piece

DEADENING: Construction intended to prevent the passage of sound.

DEAD LOAD: The weight of the structure itself and the permanent components fastened to it.

DECAY: The disintegration of wood through the action of fungi.

DEHUMIDIFY: To reduce the moisture content in the air.

DEPRECIATION: Loss of value.

DETAIL: Information added to a drawing to provide specific instruction with a drawing, dimensions, notes, or specifications.

DIFFUSION: (1) When parallel rays of light strike a smooth surface they are reflected uniformly or parallel, but when they strike a rough surface they are reflected in all directions. The reflected light is diffused. This results in a soft light. Light reflected by smooth surfaces often results in uncomfortable glare. (2) Dispersion of sound within a space so that there is uniform energy density through-out the space.

DIMENSION BUILDING MATERIAL: Building material that has been precut to specific sizes.

DIMENSION LINE: A line with arrowheads at either end to show the distance between two points.

DIMENSION LUMBER: Framing lumber, such as "2 x 4", which is nominally 1-1/2" by 3-1/2" in actual size.

DIRECT CURRENT: A flow of current that takes place at a constant time rate, practically unvarying, and in the same direction around the circuit

DISPERSION: The scattering or distribution of sound or light in a space.

DISTORTION: Any change in the transmitted sound that alters the character of the energy-frequency distribution so that the sound being received is not a faithful replica of the source sound.

DISTRIBUTION: The pattern of sound-intensity levels within a space.

DIVERTER: Valves which direct water to various outlets. They are used in showers, tub & shower combinations, bidets, Roman tub fillers and kitchen faucet sprayers.

DOME: A roof in the shape of a hemisphere used on a structure.

DOOR AND HARDWARE INSTITUTE: DHI represents the industry.

DOOR JAMB: Two vertical pieces held together by a head jamb forming the inside lining of a door opening

DOORSTOP: The strips on the doorjambs against which the door closes

DORMER: A structure projecting from a sloping roof to accommodate a window.

DOUBLE GLAZING: A pane made of two pieces of glass with air space between and sealed to provide insulation.

DOUBLE HEADER: Two or more timbers joined for strength.

DOUBLE-HUNG: A window having top and bottom sashes each capable of movement up and down.

DOWNSPOUT: A pipe for carrying rainwater from roof to ground.

DOVETAIL: A joint often used in the corners of boxes or fine joinery. It differs from the combed joint in that the interlocking tenons are fan-shaped, like a pigeon's tail. They are thicker at the end than at the root and therefore cannot be easily pulled out from the corresponding mortise.

DRAIN: A pipe for carrying waste-water.

DRESSED LUMBER: Lumber machined and smoothed at the mill. Usually 1/2 inch less than nominal (rough) size.

DRIP: A projecting construction member or groove below the member to prevent rainwater from running down the face of a wall or to protect the bottom of a door or window from leakage.

DRY ROT: A term applied to many types of decay, especially an advanced stage when the wood can be easily crushed to a dry powder.

DRYWALL CONSTRUCTION: Interior wall covering with sheets of gypsum board rather than traditional plaster.

DRY WELL: A pit located in porous ground and lined with rock that allows water to seep through the pit. Used for the disposal of rainwater or the effluent from a septic tank.

DUCTS: Sheet-metal conductors for warm and cold-air distribution.

DWV: Drain, Waste and Vent. The pipes in a plumbing system that remove waste water.

DUPLEX OUTLET: Electrical wall outlet having two plug receptacles.

EARTH BERM: An area of raised earth.

EASEMENT: The right to use land owned by another, such as a utility company's right-of-way.

EAVES: The lower portion of the roof that overhangs the wall

ECHO: Any reflected sound that is loud enough and received late enough to be heard as distinct from the source.

EFFLORESCENCE: Whitish powder that forms on the surface of bricks or stone walls due to evaporation of moisture containing salts.

EFFLUENT: The liquid discharge from a septic tank after bacterial treatment.

ELASTIC LIMIT: The limit to which a material can be bent or pulled out of shape and still return to its former shape and dimensions.

ELBOW: An L-shaped pipe fitting.

ELECTRICAL CLOSET: Electrical equipment grouped in a small room.

ELEVATION: The drawings of the front, side, or rear face of a building.

ELL: An extension or wing of a building at right angles to the main section.

ELONGATED: The optional shape of the front of some toilet bowls. About 2" longer than the standard "round front" bowl.

EMBELLISH: To add decoration.

EMINENT DOMAIN: The right of the local government to condemn for public use.

ENAMEL: (1) Paint with a considerable amount of varnish. It produces a hard, glossy surface.
(2) An opaque vitreous composition applied by fusion to the surface of metal fixtures such as cast iron tubs, lavs and sinks.

EQUITY: The interest in or value of real estate the owner has in excess of the mortgage indebtedness.

ERGONOMICS: The study of human space and movement needs.

ESCUTCHEON: (1) The decorative metal plate used around the keyhole on doors or around a pipe extending through the wall. (2) A flange or shield beneath a faucet handle. This part covers the faucet stem and the hole in the fixture or wall.

EVACUATED: Air is removed.

EXCAVATION: A cavity or pit produced by digging the earth in preparation for construction.

EXHAUST OPENING: Any opening through which air is removed from a space being heated or cooled, humidified, dehumidified, or ventilated.

EXHAUSTER: A fan used to withdraw air under suction.

EXPANSION JOINT: A flexible joint used to prevent cracking or breaking because of expansion and contraction due to temperature changes.

FABRICATION: Work done on parts of a structure at the factory before delivery to the building site.

FACADE: The face or front elevation of a building.

FACE BRICK: Brick of better quality used on the face of a wall

FACING: A surface finish material used to cover another surface.

FAHRENHEIT: A thermometric scale in which 32 degrees denotes freezing and 212 degrees, the boiling point of water under normal pressure at sea level.

FASCIA BOARD: (1) a wide board set vertically on edge, fixed to the rafter ends, wall plate, or wall. It carries the gutter around the eaves. (2) the wide board over a shop front.

FAST PIN: Pin that is permanently in place. Nonremovable.

FATIGUE: A weakening of structural members.

FEATHERING: Tapering off to nothing.

FEDERAL HOUSING ADMINISTRATION (FHA): A government agency that insures loans made by regular lending institutions.

FELT PAPERS: Papers, sometimes tar-impregnated, used on roofs and sidewalls to give protection against dampness and leaks.

FENESTRATION: The arrangement of windows.

FIBERBOARD: A building board made with fibrous material-used as an insulating board.

FIBERGLASS: Glass in a fibrous form used in making the body of products such as boats and bathtubs.

FIDELITY: The faithful reproduction of the source sound.

FIELDSTONE: Rounded stone.

FILLER: Fuller's earth or clay, or similar material, used in the mix of latex and attached cushion.

FILL: Sand, gravel, or loose earth used to bring a sub-grade up to a desired level around a building

FILLED INSULATION: A loose insulating material poured from bags or blown by machines into walls.

FILTER: A device to remove solid material from air or fluid

FINISH LUMBER: Dressed wood used for building trim and cabinet work.

FIP: Female Iron Pipe. Standard internal threads on pipe fittings.

FIREBRICK: A brick that is especially hard and heat-resistant. Used in fireplaces.

FIRECLAY: (1) A grade of clay that can withstand a large quantity of heat. Used for firebrick. (2) A variation of vitreous china having greater amounts of quartz and feldspar in the clay material beneath the vitreous surface.

Fireclay is heavier (30%), denser, and thicker than regular clay. These properties insure smooth, flat surfaces on large fixtures which is not achievable with standard vitreous china.

FIRECUT: The angular cut at the end of a joist designed to rest in a brick wall.

FIRE DOOR: A door that will resist fire.

FIRE PARTITION: A partition designed to restrict the spread of fire.

FIRE STOP: Obstruction across air passages in buildings to prevent the spread of hot gases and flames. A horizontal blocking between wall studs.

FISHED: A splice strengthened by metal pieces on the sides.

FITTING: A broad based term usually referring to faucets, shower valves, and tub fillers. Also refers to various piping parts such as tees and elbows.

FIXED LIGHT: A permanently sealed window.

FIXTURE: (1) A piece of electric or plumbing equipment that is part of the structure. (2) A broad based term usually referring to sinks, tubs, toilets, basins, etc.

FLAGGING: Cut stone, slate, or marble used on floors.

FLAGSTONE: Thin, flat stones used for floors, steps, walk, etc.

FLASHING: The material used for and the process of making watertight the intersections on exposed places on the outside of the building.

FLAT: A finish having no luster or gloss.

FLAT-PLATE COLLECTOR: A solar energy collector made from metal piping with glass over.

FLAT ROOF: A roof with minimum pitch for drainage.

FLITCH: Portion of a log from which veneer is cut.

FLITCH BEAM: A built-up beam formed by a metal plate sandwiched between two wood members and bolted together for additional strength.

FLOATING: Spreading plaster, stucco, or cement on walls or floors with use of a tool called a float.

FLOOR JOIST: Structural member of a floor.

FLOOR PLAN: The top view of a building at a specified floor level. A floor plan includes all vertical details at or above windowsill levels.

FLOOR PLUG: An electrical outlet flush with the floor.

FLUE: A pipe used for exhaust of hot gas.

FLUE LINING: Terra-cotta pipe used for the inner lining of chimneys.

FLUSH SURFACE: A continuous surface without an angle.

FLUTTER: A rapid reflection or echo pattern between parallel walls, with sufficient time between each reflection to cause a listener to be aware of separate, discrete signals

FLUX: The rate of flow of energy across a surface.

FOCUSING: Concentration of acoustic energy within a limited location in a room as the result of reflections from concave surfaces.

FOOTCANDLE: The illumination of a surface produced by spreading one lumen uniformly over an area of one square foot.

FOOTING: Poured concrete base upon which the foundation wall rests.

FOOTING FORM: A wooden or steel form used to hold concrete to the desired shape and size until it hardens.

FOOTLAMBERT: The unit of brightness of an evenly diffused surface emitting or reflecting light at the rate of one lumen per square foot. Footcandles and footlamberts are both expressions for lumens per square foot. Lumens measured at the surface gives footcandles. Lumens measured coming from the surface are footlamberts.

FRAMING: Wood skeleton of a building constructed one level on top of another.

FREQUENCY: The number of complete cycles per second of vibration.

FRIEZE: The flat board of cornice trim which is fastened to the wall.

FROSTLINE: The deepest level of frost penetration in soil. This depth varies in different climates. Footings must be placed below the frostline to prevent rupturing the foundation.

FUMES: Vaporous exhalation, usually odorous.

FUMIGATE: To destroy harmful insect or animal life with fumes.

FUNGICIDE: A substance poisonous to fungi; retards or prevents fungus growth.

FURRING: Wood or metal strips used to create a cavity within an outer wall to keep out dampness or to provide air space; this process itself is also known as furring.

FURRING STRIPS: Thin strips of wood fastened to walls or ceilings for leveling and for receiving the finish surface material.

FUSE: A strip of soft metal inserted in an electric circuit and designed to melt and open the circuit should the current exceed a predetermined value.

GABLE: The triangular end of a gable-roofed house.

GALVANIZE: A lead and zinc bath treatment to prevent rusting.

GAMBREL ROOF: A roof with two pitches, the lower slope steeper than the upper.

GARRET: An attic.

GELCOAT: A colored, polyester resin material used to form the surface of some fiberglass bathtubs or showers. Don't confuse with acrylic on fiberglass.

GIRDER: Heavy structural member supporting lighter structural members of a floor or roof.

GLARE: Excessive brightness within a viewer's field of vision that handicaps seeing even if sufficient light is present. Glare from a sun low in the sky or from a too bright window are familiar problems. Ceiling lights without proper lenses or louvers can be a source of glare as can veiling reflections (q.v.) coming from glossy surfaces. Lighting fixtures can be properly designed to avoid this.

GLAZING: Placing of glass in windows and doors.

GLOBE: An enclosing device of clear or diffusing material that protects the lamp, diffuses or redirects its radiant energy or modifies its color

GLUE-LAMINATED COLUMNS: Columns that are constructed of layers of wood laminated together with glue to provide more strength and stiffness than in a single wood member.

GPM: Gallons Per Minute. The rate of water flow by which faucets and showerheads are measured and regulated.

GRADE: The level of the ground around a building.

GRADIENT: The inclination of a road, piping, or the ground, expressed in percent.

GRAPHIC SYMBOLS: Symbolic representations used in drawing that simplify presentations of complicated items.

GRAVEL STOP: A strip of metal with a vertical lip used to retain the gravel around the edge of a built-up roof.

GREEN LUMBER: Lumber that still contains moisture or sap.

GRILLE: A louvered or perforated covering for an air-passage opening.

GROIN: The ridge or curved line where the soffits of two vaults intersect.

GROMMET: A hemp washer soaked in joining compound and fitted between the back nut and the socket of a connector to make a tight joint. Many other grommets exist.

240

GROUNDED: A term meaning connected to earth or some conducting body which serves in place of an earth connection.

GROUND-FAULT CIRCUIT INTERRUPTER (GFCI): An electrical device that breaks an electric circuit when an excessive leakage current is detected. Intended to eliminate shock hazards to people.

GROUNDS: Wood strips fastened to walls before plastering to serve as screeds and nailing base for trim.

GROUT: A thin cement mortar used for leveling and filling masonry holes.

GUSSET: A plywood or metal plate used to strengthen the joints of a truss.

GUTTER: A metal or wood trough for carrying water from a roof.

GYPSUM BOARD: Square-edged plasterboard available in standardized sizes replacing plaster and lath in modern wall construction; Sheet-rock; wall board; drywall.

HALF TIMBER CONSTRUCTION: A frame construction of heavy timbers in which the spaces are filled in with masonry

HAND: The feel of a carpet in the hand, determined by such factors as pile height, quality and kind of fibers, type of construction, type of backing, and dimensional stability.

HANDSHOWER: A showerhead designed with a handle that is connected to a water supply via a flexible hose.

HANGER: A metal strap used to support piping or the ends of joists.

HEAD: The upper frame on a door or window.

HEADER: In framing, the joists placed at the ends of a floor opening and attached to the trimmers. In masonry work, the small end of a masonry unit.

HEADER: (1) A brick laid across a wall to bond together the different parts of a wall, and, by extension, the exposed end of a brick. (2) The horizontal supporting member above openings that serves as a lintel. (3) One or more pieces of lumber supporting ends of joists. Used in framing openings of stairs and chimneys.

HEADROOM: The clear space between floor line and ceiling, as in a stairway.

HEADS: Horizontal cross member supported by the jambs.

HEARTH: The incombustible floor in front of and within the fireplace.

HEARTWOOD: The central portion of wood within the tree, which is stronger and more decay-resistant than the surrounding sapwood.

HEAT: The form of energy that is transferred by virtue of a temperature difference.

HEEL PLATE: A plate at the ends of a truss.

HERTZ: Unit of frequency measurement.

HID LIGHTING: Lighting using one of a number of gaseous discharge lamps as a source. The term stands for high intensity discharge since such sources generally have a high lumen output from a relatively compact bulb. HID lighting combines the globe-like form usually found in incandescent lamps with the high efficiency of fluorescent lighting. HID lamps are now available with varying color characteristics useful in differing situations. HID units require a warm-up time on starting and can not be restarted at once if turned off.

HIGH DENSITY: A term to describe a material with heavier than normal weight-per-unit volume.

HIGH-DENSITY FOAM: Rubber product applied as a liquid foam then cured, to form an integral part of the carpet back. The minimum standards are weight of 38 oz./sq yd.., thickness of 48 in. (3.2 mm), density of 25 lb./cu ft.

HIP RAFTER: The diagonal rafter that extends from the plate to the ridge to form the hip.

HIP ROOF: A roof that rises by equally inclined planes from all four sides of a building.

HIGH-TANK (TOILET): An antique style of toilet which is configured of a separate tank and bowl in which the tank is wall mounted above head height and is connected to the bowl by a flush pipe. (AKA, pull-chain toilet.)

HOSE BIBB: A water faucet made for the threaded attachment of a hose.

HOT MELT: A blend of polymer and filling applied in a heated state to a carpet back in order to lock in surface yarns and provide lamination.

HOUSE DRAIN: Horizontal sewer piping within a building which carries the waste from the soil stacks.

HOUSE SEWER: The watertight soil pipe extending from the exterior of the foundation wall to the public sewer.

HPDL: High-pressure decorative laminate.

HUMIDIFIER: A device, generally attached to the furnace, which supplies or maintains correct humidity levels in a building.

HUMIDISTAT: An instrument used for measuring and controlling moisture in the air.

HVAC: Heating, ventilating, and air conditioning.

I BEAM: A steel beam with an I-shaped cross section.

ILLUMINATION: The density of luminous flow of energy on a surface.

INCANDESCENT LAMP: A lamp within which a filament gives off light when sufficiently heated by an electric current.

INCIDENCE/REFLECTION: When a ray of light strikes a reflective surface at right angles it is reflected back to its source. If the ray strikes at an angle it is reflected at an angle. The angle between the perpendicular and the ray as it strikes the surface (incident) and the angle between the perpendicular and the reflected ray are equal. The angle as the ray strikes the surface is the angle of incidence and the angle as the ray bounces back is the angle of reflectance. The angle of incidence is equal to the angle of reflection.

INDIRECT LIGHTING: Lighting an area by reflecting the light from a diffusing source, such as the ceiling. The light source will not be visible.

INFILTRATION: Air flowing inward as through a wall, crack, etc.

INSULATING BOARD: Any board suitable for insulating purposes, usually manufactured board made from vegetable fibers, such as fiberboard.

INSULATING CONCRETE: Concrete with vermiculite added to produce lightweight, insulating concrete for subfloors and roofs.

INSULATION: (1) Materials for obstructing the passage of sound, heat, or cold from one surface to another. (2) A material used to cover conductors in order to prevent the metallic conductor from contact

INSULATION, SOUND: Accoustical treatment of parts of the mechanical system and equipment to isolate vibration or reduce transmission of noise

INTENSITY: (1) Light travels in a straight line. As it moves away from its source it spreads out. The greater the distance from the source, the less intense the fall of light on the surface. It can be shown that light from a point source varies inversely as the square of the distance from the source. (2) The rate of sound energy transmitted in a specified direction through a unit area.

INTERIOR TRIM: General term for all the finish molding, casing, baseboard, etc., applied within the building by finish carpenters.

IPS: Iron Pipe Size. Standard pipe threads. See also "FIP", "MIP".

ISOLATION, SOUND: The use of materials of construction that resist the passage of sound through them.

JACK RAFTER: A rafter shorter than a common rafter; especially used in hip-roof framing.

JACUZZI: The brand name of the original whirlpool tub. Often misused to mean any "whirlpool tub". See also, "Whirlpool Tub".

JALOUSIE: A type of window having a number of small, unframed yet movable pieces of glass.

JAMB: The vertical members of a finished door opening.

JERRY-BUILT: Poorly constructed.

JIG: A clamp or other device for holding work or guiding a tool so that repetitive jobs can be done accurately without repeating the marking.

JOINERY: A general woodworking term used for all better-class wood-joint construction.

JOINTS: The meeting of two separate pieces of material for a common bond.

JOIST: A horizontal structural member supported by bearing walls, beams, or girders in floor or ceiling framing.

JOIST HANGER: A metal strap to carry the ends of floor joists.

KALAMEIN DOOR: A fireproof door with a metal covering.

KERF: A cut or notch made with a cutting tool.

KEYSTONE: The wedged center stone at the crown of an arch.

KILN: A heating chamber for drying lumber.

KILN-DRIED LUMBER: Lumber that has been properly dried and cured to produce a higher grade of lumber than that which has been air dried.

KINGPOST: The center upright strut in a truss.

KIP: A unit of 1000 pound load.

KNEE BRACE: A corner brace, fastened at an angle from wall stud to rafter, stiffening a wood or steel frame to prevent angular movement.

KNEE WALL: A low wall resulting from 1-1/2-story construction.

KNOB AND TUBE: Electric wiring through walls where insulated wires are supported with porcelain knobs and tubes when passing through wood construction members

KNOCKED DOWN: Unassembled; refers to construction units requiring assembly after being delivered to the job.

LAITANCE: Undesirable surface water that forms on curing concrete.

LALLY COLUMN: A steel column used in light construction.

LAMINATED BEAM: A beam made of superimposed layers of similar materials by uniting them with glue and pressure.

LAMINATED GLASS: Breaks without shattering; glass remains in place.

LAMP: Man-made lighting source. An incandescent filament lamp is often referred to as a bulb and a fluorescent lamp is sometimes called a tube.

LANDING: A platform between flights of stairs or at the termination of stairs.

LAP JOINT: A joint produced by lapping two similar pieces of material.

LATH: A sawn or split strip of wood formerly used in new work as a base for plaster. More generally it is any material, such as fiberboard or plasterboard, used as a base for plaster.

LATH (METAL): Sheet-metal screening used as a base for plastering. Lath (wood) A wooden strip nailed to studding and joists to which plaster is applied.

LATTICE: Framework of crossed or interlaced wood or metal strips.

LAVATORY, LAVY, LAV: A fixed bowl or basin with running water and drainage for washing.

LEACHING BED: A system of trenches that carries wastes from sewers. It is constructed in sandy soils or in earth filled with stones or gravel.

LEADER: A vertical pipe or downspout that carries rainwater from the gutter to the ground or storm sewer.

LEAKS, SOUND: Any opening that permits airborne sound transmission.

LEAN-TO: A shed whose rafters lean against another building or other part of the same building.

LEDGER: A wood strip nailed to the lower side of a girder to provide a bearing surface for joists.

LEDGER STRIP: A strip of lumber fastened to the lower part of a beam or girder on which notched joists are attached.

LESSEE: The tenant who holds a lease.

LESSOR: The owner of leased property.

LEVEL, SOUND: A measure of sound pressure level as determined by electrical equipment.

LEWIS: A metal device used in the hoisting of masonry units; uses a dovetail tenon to fasten to a mortise cut into the masonry.

LIEN: A legal claim on a property that may be exercised in default of payment of a debt.

LIGHT: (1) A single pane of glass in a window or door (alt. spelling, lite). (2) Visually measured radiant energy. Light as energy exists in pure form. Since there is no artificial energy there can be no artificial light. Light in building is produced by electricity and is therefore called electric light.

LINEAL FOOT: A 1' measurement along a straight line.

LINEAR SOURCES: Light output from sources of relatively large dimension such as fluorescent lamps cannot be measured by the inverse square law. Data is supplied by the manufacturer of the equipment to determine lighting intensities.

LINTEL: A small beam over a door or window head, usually carrying the wall load alone.

LOAD-BEARING WALL: A wall designed to support the weight imposed upon it from above.

LOADS: Live load: the total of all moving and variable loads that may be placed upon a building. Dead load: the weight of all permanent, stationary construction included in a building.

LOGGIA: A roofed, open passage along the front or side of a building. It is often at an upper level, and it often has a series of columns on either or both sides.

LOOKOUT: A short wooden framing member used to support an overhanging portion of a roof. It extends from the wall to the underside surfacing of the overhang.

LOT LINE: The line forming the legal boundary of a piece of property.

LOUDNESS: The effect on the hearing apparatus of varying sound pressures and intensities.

LOUVER: An opening or slatted grill allowing ventilation while providing protection from rain.

LOW-BOY (TOILET): A slang term for a toilet style in which the tank height is lower than normal. Usually a one piece toilet. Occasionally a two piece toilet.

LOW-TANK (TOILET): An antique style toilet in which the tank is wall mounted slightly higher than the bowl. Tank water flows to the bowl via flush ell.

LUMEN: The unit of luminous flux which is equal to the luminous flow of energy on a surface all points of which are of uniform distance from a source of one candle. The measurement is made on one square foot of surface at a distance of one foot

LUMINAIRE: A complete lighting unit consisting of the lamp or lamps, elements that distribute the light, and connect the lamp or lamps to the power supply. The luminaire is sometimes termed a fixture.

MANSARD ROOF: A hip-type roof having two slopes on each of the four sides.

MANTEL: A shelf over a fireplace.

MARKET PRICE: The amount that property can be sold for at a given time.

MARKET VALUE: The amount that property is worth at a given time.

MASKING: The increase in threshold of audibility of a sound necessary to permit its being heard in the presence of another sound.

MASONRY: A general term for construction of brick, stone, concrete block, or similar materials.

MASTIC: A quick-setting waterproof pointing or plastering material containing litharge and linseed oil, now replaced by Portland cement.

MATTE FINISH: A finish free from gloss or highlights.

MEETING RAIL: The horizontal rails of a double-hung sash that fit together when the window is closed.

MEMBER: A single piece of material used in a structure.

METAL TIE: A strip of metal used to fasten construction members together.

METAL WALL TIES: Corrugated metal strips used to tie masonry veneer to wood walls.

METER: Unit of metric measure equal to 1.1 yard.

MILDEW: A mold on wood caused by fungi.

MILLWORK: Prefabricated doors, windows, panels, stairs, etc., made at the mill and partly fabricated there.

MINERAL WOOL: An insulating material made into a fibrous form from mineral slag.

MINI-WIDESPREAD: A special style of bathroom lavatory faucet having separate spout and handles. But designed small enough that it will fit 4" center-to-center faucet holes.

MIP: Male Iron Pipe. Standard external threads on pipe and fittings.

MITER: An angle joint between two members of a similar cross section. Each is cut at the same bevel -- 45 degrees for a right-angle corner so that the straight line of the joint is seen to bisect the angle.

MITER JOINT: A joint made with ends or edges of two pieces of lumber cut at a 45° angle and fitted together.

MODULAR CONSTRUCTION: Construction in which the size of all components has been based upon a standardized unit of measure.

MOISTURE BARRIER: A sheet material that retards moisture penetration into walls, floors, ceilings, etc.

MOLDING: A continuous projection or groove used as a decoration, to throw shadow, or sometimes to throw water, away from a wall.

MONOLITHIC: Concrete construction poured and cast in one piece without joints.

MONUMENT: A boundary marker set by surveyors to locate property lines.

MORTAR: A mixture of cement, sand, lime, and water used to bond masonry units.

MORTGAGE: A pledging of property, conditional on payment of the debt in full.

MORTGAGEE: The lender of money to the mortgagor.

MORTGAGOR: The owner who mortgages property in return for a loan.

MORTISE: (1) a rectangular slot cut in one member, in which usually a tenon from another member is glued or pinned, or a lock is fixed. (2) a rectangular sinking cut in a stone to receive a cramp or other locking device or a lewis.

MOSAIC: Small colored tile, glass, stone, or similar material arranged to produce a decorative surface.

MUD ROOM: A small room or entranceway where muddy overshoes and wet garments can be removed before entering other rooms.

MULLION: A vertical dividing member of a frame between the lights of a door or window, which may be further subdivided into panes by glazing bars.

MUNTIN: (1) a subsidiary vertical framing member in a door, framed into the rails and separating the panels; usually of the same width as the stiles. (2) a glazing bar or a mullion.

NARROW CARPET: Fabric woven 27 in. (68.6 cm) and 36 in. (9.4 cm) in width.

NEWEL: A post supporting the handrail at the top or bottom of a stairway.

NEWEL POST: The main post supporting a handrail at the bottom or top of a stairs.

NOISE: Any unwanted sound.

NOMINAL DIMENSION: Dimensions for finished lumber in which the stated dimension is usually larger than the actual dimension.

NOMINAL SIZE: The size of lumber before dressing, rather than its actual size.

NON-BEARING WALL: A wall supporting no load other than its own weight.

NONFERROUS METAL: Metal containing no iron, such as copper, brass, or aluminum

NOSE: (1) any blunt overhang. (2) the lower end of the shuttling stile of a door or casement.

NOSING: The rounded edge of a stair tread.

NRC: Noise reduction coefficient. The average percentage of sound reduction at various Hz levels.

OBSCURE GLASS: Sheet glass that is made translucent instead of transparent.

OIL STAIN: A coating material with an oil binder plus dyes or pigments, but formulated so that normal applications do not deposit an opaque film.

OIL VARNISH: A varnish which contains resin and drying oil as the basic film-forming ingredients and is converted into a solid film primarily by oxidation.

OLEORESIN: A vehicle for varnishes and paints consisting of drying oils and resins

ON CENTER: A method of indicating the spacing between framing members by stating the measurement from the center of one member to the center of the succeeding one.

ONE-PIECE (TOILET): An upgraded style of toilet which is configured of an integral tank and bowl which are formed as "one piece" during the manufacturing process.

OPEN-END MORTGAGE: A mortgage that permits the remaining amount of the loan to be increased, as for improvements, by mutual agreement of the lender and borrower, without rewriting the mortgage.

OPEN FRONT: A style of toilet seat rim where there is an open space about three inches wide at the front. Considered more sanitary in commercial applications where constant usage exceeds janitorial sanitation.

ORIENTATION: The positioning of a house on a lot in relation to the sun, wind, view, and noise.

OUTLET: Any type of electrical box allowing current to be drawn from the electrical system for lighting or appliances.

OVERHANG: The projecting area of a roof or upper story beyond the wall of the lower part.

PAINT: A pigmented liquid composition which is converted to an opaque solid after application of a thin layer. Generally considered as all coating materials used in the act of painting.

PALLET: A rugged wood skid used to stack and mechanically handle units of masonry.

PANEL: A flat, rectangular surface framed with a thicker material.

PANELBOARD: The center for controlling electrical circuits.

PARAPET: A low wall or railing; usually around the edge of a roof.

PARGE COAT: A thin coat of cement plaster applied to a masonry wall for refinement of the surface or for damp-proofing.

PARGING: A thin coat of plaster applied to masonry surfaces for smoothing purposes.

PARQUET FLOORING: Flooring, usually of wood, laid in an alternating or inlaid pattern to form various designs

PARTING STOP: Thin strips set into the vertical jambs of a double-hung window to separate the sash.

PARTICLE BOARD: Boards made from sawdust, wood chips, flax stalks, etc., under pressure with or without added adhesive.

PARTITION: A wall that divides areas within a building.

PARTY WALL: A wall between two adjoining buildings in which both owners share, such as a common wall between row houses.

PASSIVE SOLAR SYSTEM: An integral energy system using only natural and architectural components to utilize solar energy.

PATIO: An open court.

PEDIMENT: The triangular space forming the gable end of a low-pitched roof. A similar form is often used as a decoration over doors in classic architecture.

PEELABILITY: A quality which describes how a wallcovering from which the decorative surface may be dry-peeled from the substrate, leaving a continuous layer of the substrate on the wall, when the wallcovering has been installed and peeled according to the manufacturer's instructions.

PENNY: A term used to indicate the size of nails, abbreviated d. Originally, it specified the price per hundred nails, (i.e., 6-penny nails cost $.06 per hundred nails).

PERIPHERY: The entire outside edge of an object.

PERSPECTIVE: A drawing of an object in a three-dimensional form on a plane surface. An object drawn as it would appear to the eye.

PIER: (1) the load-bearing masonry in a building between two openings. (2) short buttresses on one or both sides of a wall, bonded to it to increase its stability.

PIGMENTS: Solid coloring agents used in the preparation of paint and substantially insoluble in the vehicle.

PILASTER: A rectangular pier, sometimes fluted, projecting from the face of a wall and having a capital, shaft, and base. It buttresses the wall.

PILES: Long posts driven into the soil in swampy locations, or whenever it is difficult to secure a firm foundation, upon which the foundation footing is laid.

PILLAR: A column used for supporting parts of a structure.

PINNACLE: Projecting or ornamental cap on the high point of a roof.

PITCH: (1) The slope of a roof usually expressed as a ratio. (2) The physical response to frequency of sound.

PLAN: A horizontal, graphic representational section of a building.

PLANKS: Material 2" or 3" (50 or 75 mm) thick and more than 4" (100 mm) wide, such as joists, flooring, and the like.

PLASTER: A mortar-like composition used for covering walls and ceilings. Usually made of portland cement mixed with sand and water.

PLASTERBOARD: A board made of plastering material covered on both sides with heavy paper.

PLASTER GROUND: A nailer strip included in plaster walls to act as a gage for thickness of plaster and to give a nailing support for finish trim around openings and near the base of the wall.

PLAT: A graphic description of a surveyed piece of land, indicating the boundaries, location, and dimensions. The plat, recorded in the appropriate county official's office, also contains information as to easements, restrictions, and lot numbers, if any.

PLATE: The top horizontal member of a row of studs in a frame wall.

PLATE CUT: The cut in a rafter that rests upon the plate. It is also called the seat cut or birdmouth.

PLATE GLASS: A high-quality sheet of glass used in large windows.

PLATFORM: Framing in which each story is built upon the other.

PLENUM: A method of air-conditioning a factory or large building by keeping the pressure in it above atmospheric pressure. Clean air is blown into the rooms near the ceiling level and foul air is withdrawn near floor level at the same side of the room, or allowed to escape through cracks in doors and windows.

PLENUM SYSTEM: A system of heating or air-conditioning in which the air is forced through a chamber connected to distributing ducts.

PLOT: The land on which a building stands.

PLOW: To cut a groove running in the same direction as the grain of the wood.

PLUMB: Said of an object when it is in true vertical position as determined by a plumb bob or vertical level.

PLYWOOD: A piece of wood made of three or more layers of veneer joined with glue and usually laid with the grain of adjoining piles at right angles.

P. O. PLUG: Plug Outlet. A style of drain outlet for lavatories. The drain outlet is closed by a rubber stopper, or "plug".

POCHE: The darkening in of areas on a drawing to aid in readability.

POINTING: Term for the finishing of joints in masonry; also, the material used for this purpose.

POINT SOURCE: A lighting source is considered as a point when its maximum dimension is less than one-fifth the distance from source to plane of measurement. Most incandescent lamps can be considered as a point source. The fundamental relationship for determining illumination in foot candles for a point source is the inverse square law in which E (illumination in foot candles at a point on a plane normal to the light ray) equals 1 (the candle-power directed at the point) divided by d (the distance in feet from source to point) or $E = 1/dz$.

POP-UP ASSEMBLY: The drain mechanism of a faucet installed on a lavatory. The drain stopper "pops" up and down.

PORCELAIN: A white ceramic ware that consists of kalin, quartz and feldspar. It is fired at high temperature on steel to make the surface of some bathtubs, kitchen sinks and bathroom lavatories.

PORCELAIN ENAMEL: Vitreous enamel.

PORCH: A covered area attached to a house at an entrance.

PORTICO: A roof supported by columns, whether attached to a building or wholly by itself.

PORTLAND CEMENT: A hydraulic cement, extremely hard, formed by burning silica, lime, and alumina together and then grinding up the mixture.

POST: A perpendicular supporting member.

POST-AND-BEAM CONSTRUCTION: A type of building frame in which roof and floor beams rest directly over wall posts.

POT: Slang for toilet. Possibly derived from "chamber pot".

PRECAST: Concrete units that are cast and finished at the plant rather than at the site of construction.

PREFABRICATED BUILDINGS: Buildings that are built in sections or component parts in a factory, and then assembled at the site.

PREHEATING: In air conditioning the heating of the air in advance of other processes.

PREPASTED: Wallcovering having a factory-applied adhesive on the back surface for adherence to a hanging surface after the adhesive has been activated.

PRESSURE BALANCE VALVE: A shower mixing valve that automatically maintains balance between incoming hot and cold water supplies by immediately regulating fluctuations in pressure. As a result the outlet temperature remains constant, though the outlet pressure may drop.

246

PRIME COAT: The first coat of paint that serves as a filler and sealer in preparation for finish coats.

PRINCIPAL: The original amount of money loaned.

PULL-CHAIN (TOILET): An antique style of toilet which is configured of a separate tank and bowl in which the tank is wall mounted above head height and is connected to the bowl by a flush pipe. Due to the height of the tank location, a chain is necessary to pull the trip lever to flush the toilet. (AKA, high-tank toilet.)

PURLIN: A horizontal member supporting the common rafters in a roof.

PVC: PolyVinyl Chloride. A white plastic used in the manufacture of water supply pipe.

PVD: Physical Vapor Deposition. A modern plating process used in faucet manufacturing. Vaporized zirconium reacts with nitrogen and another special gas to form a durable plated surface.

QUAD: An enclosed court.

QUARRY TILE: Unglazed, machine-made tile used for floors.

QUARTER ROUND: Small molding presenting the profile of a quarter circle.

QUARTER-SAWN OAK: Oak lumber, usually flooring, which has been sawed so that the medullary rays showing on end-grain are nearly perpendicular to the face of the lumber.

QUOINS: Large squared stones set in the corners of a masonry building for appearance's sake.

RABBET (OR REBATE): A groove cut along the edge or end of a board to receive another board producing a rabbet joint.

RADIANT HEATING: A method of heating with the use of radiating heat rays.

RADIATION: The transmission of heat by direct waves.

RAFTER: A roof structural member running from the wall plate to the ridge. There are jack, hip, valley, and common rafters. The structural members of a flat roof are usually called roof joists.

RAGLIN: The open joint in masonry to receive flashing.

RAKE JOINT: A mortar joint that has been recessed by tooling before it sets up.

RAKE MOLDING: Gable molding attached on the incline of the gable. The molding must be a different profile to match similar molding along the remaining horizontal portions of the roof.

RANDOM RUBBLE: Stonework having irregular shaped units and coursing.

RANDOM-SHEARED: Textured pattern created by shearing some of the top or higher loops and leaving others looped.

REFLECTING SURFACES: Room surfaces from which significant sound reflections occur.

REFLECTOR: A device for redirecting the radiant energy of a lamp by reflection in a desired direction.

REFRACTION: Refraction is caused by the bending of light rays as they pass from one transparent medium such as water to another medium of different density such as air. Although light travels in a straight line it travels more slowly in some media than in others depending upon the density of the medium involved. As a result the rays alter their direction when they reach the surface that separates the two mediums.

REFRIGERANT: A substance which produces a refrigerating effect.

REGISTER: Opening in air duct, usually covered with a grill.

REINFORCED CONCRETE: Concrete containing steel bars or wire mesh to increase its structural qualities.

RENDERING: The art of shading or coloring a drawing.

REPEAT: The distance from a point in a pattern figure to the same point where it occurs again, measuring lengthwise.

RESIN: A material, usually a solid or viscous liquid, used as part or all of the film-forming phase of paints, varnishes, and lacquers.

RESISTANCE: The reciprocal of thermal conductance.

RESONANCE: The natural vibration of a volume of air or a panel of material at a particular frequency as the result of excitation by a sound of that particular frequency.

RESTORATION: Rebuilding a structure so it will appear in its original form.

RESTRICTIONS: Limitations on the use of real estate building materials, size, or design styles.

RETAINING WALL: A heavy wall that supports an earth embankment.

REVEAL: The outer part of a jamb visible in a door or window opening and not covered by the frame. It is the visible part to a window or other opening.

REVERBERATION: The time in seconds required for a sound to decay to inaudibility after the source ceases.

RHEOSTAT: An instrument for regulating electric current.

RIBBON: A wood strip set into studs to support floor joists in balloon framing.

RIDGE: The top edge of a roof where two slopes meet.

247

RIDGEBOARD: The highest horizontal member in a gable roof; it is supported by the upper ends of the rafters.

RIDGE CAP: A wood or metal cap used over roofing at the ridge.

RIPRAP: Stones placed on a slope to prevent erosion. Also broken stone used for foundation fill.

RISE: The vertical height of a roof or stairs.

RISER: The vertical part of a step, or its height.

ROCKLATH: Paper covered gypsum sheets used as a plaster base.

ROCKWOOL: An insulating material that looks like wool but is composed of such substances as granite or silica.

RODDING: Stirring freshly poured concrete with a vibrator to remove air pockets.

ROLL ROOFING: Roofing material of fiber and asphalt manufactured in rolls.

ROUGH FLOOR: The subfloor on which the finished floor is laid.

ROUGH HARDWARE: All the concealed fasteners in a building such as nails, bolts, hangers, etc.

ROUGHING IN: Putting up the skeleton of the building.

ROUGH LUMBER: Lumber as it comes from the saw.

ROUGH OPENING: An unfinished opening in the framing into which doors, windows, and other units are placed.

ROUND FRONT: The standard shape of the front of a toilet bowl. About 2" shorter than the optional "elongated" bowl.

ROUT: To cut and smooth wood in a groove using a tool called a router

RUBBLE: Irregular broken stone.

RUN: The horizontal distance of a flight of stairs, or the horizontal distance from the outer wall to the ridge of a roof.

RUN: Sometimes called a making or batch. The collective rollage produced at one time on a single machine, all of which would be expected to have the same overall appearance and physical characteristics.

RUNNER: A horizontal member that carries the joists of the formwork under a concrete slab or the folding wedges of an arch.

R VALUE: Unit of thermal resistance in rating insulating materials; higher values are better insulators.

SABIN: A measure of sound absorption of a surface, equivalent to one square foot of a perfectly absorptive surface.

SADDLE: A small gable roof placed in back of a chimney on a sloping roof to shed water and debris.

SAFETY FACTOR: The ultimate strength of the material divided by the allowable working load. The element of safety needed to make certain that there will be no structural failures.

SAND FINISH: A final plaster coat; a skim coat.

SAP: All the fluids in a tree.

SASH: An individual frame into which glass is set.

SCAB: A short piece of lumber fastened to a butt joint for strength.

SCARFING: A joint between two pieces of wood that allows them to be spliced lengthwise.

SCHEDULE: A list of similar items and information about them, such as a window schedule.

SCRATCH COAT: The first coat of plaster. It is scratched to provide a good bond for the next coat.

SCREED: A guide for the correct thickness of plaster or concrete being placed on surfaces

SCRIBE: Mark and shape a member to fit an irregular surface.

SCRIM: Coarse canvas, or cotton or metal mesh, used for bridging the joints between board, sheet, or slab coverings before they are plastered, and as reinforcement for fibrous plaster.

SCRIM BACK: A double back made of light, coarse fabric, cemented to a jute, kraftcord, or synthetic back in tufted construction

SCRUBBABILITY: A quality of withstanding scrubbing with a brush and a prescribed detergent solution.

SCUTTLE: A small opening in a ceiling to provide access to an attic or roof.

SEALER: A paint, varnish, or resinous product used to prevent excessive absorption of finish coats by the substrate; also applied to prevent bleeding or bonding chalked masonry surface before painting.

SEASONING: Drying out of green lumber, either in an oven or kiln or by exposing it to air.

SECOND MORTGAGE: A mortgage made by a home buyer to raise money for a down payment required under the first mortgage.

SECTION: (1) A unit of land measurement usually one mile square. A section contains approximately 640 acres, and there are 36 sections to a township. (2) A drawing showing the cut-open view of an object.

SEEPAGE PIT: A pit or cesspool into which sewage drains from a septic tank, and which is so constructed that the liquid waste seeps through the sides of the pit into the ground.

SELF-RIMMING: A style of bathroom lavatory or kitchen sink with a rolled and finished edge, or rim. The fixture installs on top of a counter without the need for a metal sink rim.

SEMIGLOSS: The glossiness of a finish that is between eggshell and a high or full gloss.

SEPTIC TANK: A concrete or steel underground tank used to reduce sewage by bacterial action.

SERVICE CONNECTION: The electric wires to the building from the outside power lines.

SET: The hardening of cement or plaster.

SETBACK: A zoning restriction on the location of the home on a lot.

SETTLEMENT: Compression of the soil or the members in a structure.

SHAKE: A handsplit wood shingle.

SHEARING: The process in manufacture in which the fabric is drawn under revolving cutting blades as in a lawn mower, in order to produce a smooth face on the fabric.

SHEATHING: The rough boarding or covering over the framing of a house.

SHEATHING PAPER: A paper barrier against wind and moisture applied between sheathing and outer wall covering.

SHED ROOF: A flat roof slanting in one direction.

SHELLAC: A purified lac resin dissolved in an organic solvent (usually alcohol) and used to seal (fill) wood or as a varnish

SHIM: A piece of material used to level or fill in the space between two surfaces.

SHINGLES: Thin pieces of wood or other materials that overlap each other in covering a roof. The number and kind needed depend on the steepness of the roof slope.

SHIPLAP: Boards with lapped joints along their edges

SHOE MOLD: The small mold against the baseboard at the floor.

SHOP COAT OR SHOP PAINTING: Coating applied in the fabricating shop or plant before shipment.

SHORING: Planks or posts used to support walls or ceilings during construction.

SHRINKAGE: A decrease in dimensions occurring when a wallcovering is exposed to moisture.

SIDING: The outside finish covering on a frame wall.

SILL: The lowest horizontal member of a framed partition, of frame construction, or of a frame for a window or a door.

SINK: A stationary basin connected with a drain and water supply for washing and drainage.

SKELETON CONSTRUCTION: Construction where the frame carries all the weight.

SKID: A short length of wood used for packing walling stones to the correct height when laying them.

SKIM COAT: A very thin finishing coat usually of plaster usually applied to drywall.

SKYLIGHT: A window in a roof.

SLAB FOUNDATION: A reinforced concrete floor and foundation system.

SLEEPERS: Wood strips placed over or in a concrete slab to receive a finish wood floor.

SMOKE CHAMBER: The portion of a chimney flue located directly over the fireplace.

SOFFIT: (1) the under-surface of a cornice, stair, beam, arch, vault, or rib or the uppermost part of the inside of a drain, culvert, or sewer. Generally, it is any under-surface except a ceiling. (2) the lining at the head of an opening.

SOFTWOOD: Wood from trees having needles rather than broad leaves. The term does not necessarily refer to the softness of the wood.

SOIL STACK: The vertical pipe in a plumbing system that carries the sewage.

SOLAR HEAT: Heat from the sun.

SOLE: The horizontal framing member directly under the studs.

SOLEPLATE: The horizontal member of a frame wall resting on the rough floor, to which the studs are nailed.

SOUND: A vibration in a medium; usually in the frequency range capable of producing the sensation of hearing.

SPACING: The distance between structural members.

SPACKLE: To cover wallboard joints with plaster.

SPAN: The horizontal distance between supports for joists, beams, or trusses.

SPECIFICATIONS: The written instructions that accompany a set of working drawings.

SPIKE: A large, heavy nail.

SPLICE: Joining of two similar members in a straight line.

SQUARE: A unit of measure -- 100 sq ft. Commonly used in reference to the amount of roofing material to cover 100 sq ft.

STABILIZING: Treating a fabric so that it will not shrink or stretch more than a certain percentage.

STACK: A vertical pipe.

STAIN: A thin liquid composition, usually transparent, used to change the color of a surface without leaving a film of significant thickness.

STAIN RESISTANCE: A quality of showing no appreciable change in appearance after application and removal of certain specified materials.

STAKEOUT: Marking the foundation layout with stakes.

STEEL FRAMING: Skeleton framing with structural steel beams.

STEENING: Brickwork without mortar.

STILE: The vertical member on the door or panel.

STIRRUP: A metal U-shaped strap used to support the end of a framing member.

STOCK: Common sizes of building materials and equipment available from most commercial industries.

STOOL: Horizontal interior member of trim below a window.

STOP: A small strip to hold a door or window sash in place.

STOP MARKS: A mark across the width of tufted carpet caused by an off-standard feed relationship of either yarn or cloth feed or both on the start-up of the machine.

STORM DOOR OR WINDOW: An extra door or extra window placed outside an ordinary door or window for added protection against cold.

STORM SEWER: A sewer that is designed to carry away water from storms, but not sewage.

STRESS: Any force acting upon a part or member.

STRESS-COVER CONSTRUCTION: Construction consisting of panels or sections with wood frameworks to which plywood or other sheet material is bonded with glue so that the covering carries a large part of the loads.

STRIPPING: Removal of concrete forms from the hardened concrete.

STRETCHER: A brick or stone laid with its length parallel to the length of the wall.

STRETCHER COURSE: A row of masonry in wall with the long side of the units exposed to the exterior.

STRING: A sloping board at each end of the treads, housed or cut to carry the treads and risers of a stair.

STRINGER: he inclined structural member supporting the treads and risers of a stairs; sometimes it is visible next to the profile of the stairs.

STRIPPABILITY: A quality that describes a wallcovering which can be dry-stripped after having been installed and striped according to manufacturer's instructions, leaving a minimum of product residue on the wall, without damage to the wall surface.

STUCCO: A cement plaster finish applied to exterior walls.

STUDS: The vertical framing members of a wall.

SUBFLOORING: Any material nailed directly to floor joists. The finish floor is attached over the subflooring.

SUMP: A pit in a basement floor to collect water, into which a sump pump is placed to remove water

SUNSPACE: Glassed-in area for the collection of solar heat.

SURFACED LUMBER: Lumber that is dressed by running it through a planer.

SWALE: A drainage channel formed where two slopes meet.

TAIL JOIST: A relatively shorter joist that joins against a header or trimmer in floor framing.

TAMP: To ram and compact soil.

TAR: A dark heavy oil used in roofing and roof surfacing.

TEAR STRENGTH: A quality of resisting the propagation of an existing tear.

TEMPERATURE: The tendency to communicate heat. If no heat flows upon contact of two materials there is no difference of temperature between them.

TEMPERED: (1) Thoroughly mixed cement or mortar. (2) Method of turning regular glass into safety glass.

TENACITY: Stress applied to produce a particular elongation in a fiber. The breaking tenacity is the stress required to elongate a fiber to the breaking point.

TENON: An end of a rail or similar member, reduced in area at its end to enter a mortise in another member.

TENSILE STRENGTH: The greatest longitudinal stress a structural member can bear without adverse effects (breaking or cracking).

TERMITE SHIELD: Sheet metal placed over masonry to prevent the passage of termites into wood.

TERRA-COTTA: Baked clay and sand formed into masonry units.

TERRAZZO FLOORING: Wear-resistant flooring made of marble chips or small stones embedded in cement that has been polished smooth.

THERMAL CONDUCTIVITY: The measurement of heat flow through a material.

THERMAL CONDUCTOR: A substance capable of transmitting heat.

THERMOSTAT: A device for automatically controlling the supply of heat.

THERMOSTATIC VALVE: A shower mixing valve with automatic temperature control. When temperature fluctuations occur at the water inlets, a thermal actuator adjusts the hot and cold ratio to maintain the original temperature setting.

THRESHOLD: The beveled piece of stone, wood, or metal over which the door swings. It is sometimes called a carpet strip, or a saddle.

THROAT: A passage directly above the fireplace opening where a damper is set.

TIE: A structural member used to bind others together.

TIMBER: Lumber with a cross section larger than 4x6 (100 by 150 mm), for posts, sills, and girders.

TITLE: Legal evidence to the ownership of property.

TITLE INSURANCE: An agreement to pay the buyer for losses in title of ownership.

TOE NAIL: To drive nails at an angle.

TOLERANCE: The acceptable variance of dimensions from a standard size.

TON: Unit of Refrigeration A ton of refrigeration is the cooling effect obtained when one ton of ice at 32 degrees F melts to water at 32 degrees F in 24 hours. The cooling effect or rate of one ton of refrigeration (2000 lbs.) is taken as 288,000 BTU per day of 24 hours or 12,000 BTUH (BTUH is BTU per hour). The required capacity of a refrigerating machine in tons may therefore be found by dividing the total heat gain in a building in BTUH by 12,000.

TONGUE: A projection on the edge of wood that joins with a similarly shaped groove.

TOTAL RUN: The total of all the tread widths in a stair.

T-POST: A post built up of studs and blocking to form the intersection of the framing of perpendicular walls.

TRANSMISSION: The propagation of a vibration through various media.

TRANSMISSION LOSS: The decrease in power during transmission from one point to another

TRANSOM: A horizontal beam, particularly the stone or timber bar separating the lights of a window or a door from the fanlights over it.

TRAP: A U-shaped pipe below plumbing fixtures to create a water seal and prevent sewer odors and gases from being released into the habitable areas.

TREAD: The horizontal part of a step, or its length.

TRIM: A general term given to the moldings and finish members on a building. Its installation is called finish carpentry.

TRIMMER: The longer floor framing member around a rectangular opening into which a header is joined.

TRIMMERS: Single or double joists or rafters that run around an opening in framing construction.

TRIP LEVER: The flush handle and actuating arm on a toilet tank. Also the lever that opens and closes the drain on a bathtub waste & overflow.

TROMBE WALL: A passive heating concept consisting of a south-facing masonry wall with glazing in front. Solar radiation is absorbed by the wall, converted to heat, and conducted and radiated into the building.

TRUSS: A frame, today generally made of steel, used to carry a roof or other load and built up wholly from members in tension and compression. Trusses are usually spaced about 3 m. apart, but their spacing is fixed by the design of the purlin.

TWO-PIECE (TOILET): A standard style of toilet which is configured of a separate tank and bowl which are connected.

UNDERCOAT: In a multicoat system, any intermediate coat or a first or primer coat.

UNDERPINNING: A foundation replacement or reinforcement for temporary braced supports.

UNDRESSED LUMBER: Lumber that is not squared or finished smooth.

UNIT CONSTRUCTION: Construction that includes two or more preassembled walls, together with floor and ceiling construction, for shipment to the building site.

VACUUM BREAKER: An anti-siphon device which prevents the backflow of non potable water into the water supply system. For example, if a handshower were left extended into a bathtub of dirty water, and a siphon effect were to occur, a vacuum breaker would prevent the tub water from traveling back into the water supply system.

VALLEY: The internal angle formed by the two slopes of a roof.

VALLEY JACKS: Rafters that run from a ridgeboard to a valley rafter

VALLEY RAFTER: The diagonal rafter at the intersection of two intersecting sloping roofs.

251

VALVE: A device that regulates the flow of material in a pipe.

VANITY: A bathroom storage cabinet beneath the counter.

VAPOR BARRIER: A watertight material used to prevent the passage of moisture or water vapor into and through walls.

VARNISH: A liquid composition which is converted to a transparent or translucent solid film after application as a thin layer When a varnish is pigmented, it is usually called an "enamel.

VEHICLE: The liquid portion of a paint. Anything dissolved in the liquid portion of the paint is part of the vehicle.

VELOCITY: The time rate of change of position of a reference point moving in a straight line.

VENEER: A thin covering of material over a core material.

VENEERED CONSTRUCTION: Type of wall construction in which frame or masonry walls are faced with other exterior surfacing materials.

VENT: A screened opening for ventilation.

VENTILATION: The process of supplying and removing air by natural or mechanical means to or from any space.

VENT STACK: A vertical soil pipe connected to the drainage system to allow ventilation and pressure equalization.

VERGEBOARD: The board that serves as the eaves finish on the gable end of a building.

VESSEL: A style of basin that installs partially into the counter rather than fully into the counter. The portion of the fixture rising above the counter has a finished exterior.

VESTIBULE: A small entrance room.

VIBRATION: An alternation in pressure or direction of motion.

VITREOUS: A surface material on some plumbing fixtures derived from or consisting of glass. It is low in porosity and is translucent.

VITREOUS CHINA: A clay material with a vitreous surface used to manufacture some plumbing fixtures such as toilets and lavys.

VOLUME: The amount of space occupied by an object. Measured in cubic units.

WAINSCOT: The surfacing on the lower part of an interior wall when finished differently from the remainder of the wall.

WALLBOARD: Large sheets of gypsum or fiberboard that are usually nailed to framing to form interior walls.

WALLCOVERING: A flexible product designed to cover walls and ceilings for decorative and/or functional purposes.

WALL TIE: A small metal strip or steel wire used to bind tiers of masonry in cavity-wall construction, or to bind brick veneer to the wood-frame wall in veneer construction.

WARRANTY DEED: A guarantee that the property is as promised.

WASHABILITY: A quality of withstanding occasional sponging with a prescribed detergent solution to remove surface soil.

WASH: The slant upon a sill, capping, etc., to allow the water to run off.

WASTE & OVERFLOW: The drain assembly for a bathtub. The outlet at the top removes the "overflow" water during tub filling and the drain at the bottom removes "waste" water when the tub is drained.

WASTE STACK: A vertical pipe in a plumbing system that carries the discharge from any fixture.

WATER CLOSET: Toilet.

WATER COOLING TOWER: An enclosure for evaporating cooling water by contact with air.

WATER HAMMER: A destructive, high-pressure surge in a water supply piping system accompanying the quick closure of valves or faucets on the system. The surge causes a shock wave which vibrates the pipes causing them to bang, knock or "hammer" against the wall or floor.

WATERPROOF: Material or construction that prevents the passage of water.

WATER-TABLE: A horizontal member extending from the surface of an exterior wall so as to throw off rainwater from the wall. Water level below ground.

WATT: A unit of electrical energy.

WAVE, SOUND: A disturbance that is propagated in a medium in such a manner that at any point in the medium the displacement is a function of the time.

WEATHERING: The mechanical or chemical disintegration and discoloration of the surface of exterior building materials.

WEATHER STRIPPING: A strip of fabric or metal fastened around the edges of windows and doors to prevent air infiltration.

WEEP HOLE: Small holes in masonry cavity walls to release water accumulation to the exterior.

WEIGHTING: Finishing materials applied to a fabric to give increased weight.

WELL OPENING: A floor opening for a stairway.

WHIRLPOOL TUB: A bathtub with a whirlpool system added. The whirlpool system recirculates the tub water and mixes in air to create hydro therapy via jet inlets.

WIDESPREAD: A style of bathroom lavatory faucet having separate spout and handles. Usually 8" from center of handle-to-handle. Some widespread faucets can be set with handles up to 12" apart.

WIDTH: The cross-direction measurement after trimming for hanging.

WINDER: The radiating or wedge-shaped treads at the turns of some stairs.

WYTHE: Pertaining to a single-width masonry wall.

ZONING: Building restrictions as to size, location, and type of structures to be built in specific areas.

"ALTERNATE GLOSSARY"

(Terms found in several websites; search "construction humor")

BID: A wild guess carried out to two decimal places.

BID OPENING: A poker game in which the losing hand wins.

COMPLETION DATE: The point at which liquidated damages begin.

CONTRACTOR: A gambler who never gets to shuffle, cut or deal!.

CRITICAL PATH METHOD: A management technique for losing your shirt under perfect control.

DELAYED PAYMENT: A tourniquet applied at the pockets.

ENGINEER'S ESTIMATE: The cost of construction in Heaven.

LIQUIDATED DAMAGES: A penalty for failing to achieve the impossible.

LOW BIDDER: A contractor who is wondering what he/she has left out.

OSHA: A protective coating made by half-baking a mixture of fine print, split hairs, red tape and baloney - usually applied at random with a shot gun.

PROJECT MANAGER: The conductor of an orchestra in which every musician is in a different union.

STRIKE: An effort to increase egg production by strangling the chicken.

WIDOW MAKER: A poorly constructed scaffolding or staging platform.

ORDER FORM

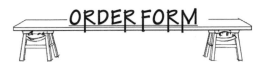

Please ship (___) copies of the book to:

NAME _____

COMPANY _____

ADDRESS _____

CITY, STATE, ZIP _____

PHONE (Day): _____ PHONE (Evening): _____

E-MAIL: _____

CREDIT CARD: [ ] Visa # _____ Expiration: ____/____

[ ] MasterCard # _____ Expiration: ____/____

Each Book = $34.95+S/H. Quantity Discounts Available (call 503-761-7294 for information).
SEND ORDER FORM TO: D. P. Design
P. O. Box 305, 9610 SE 82nd Avenue
Portland, OR 97266

ORDER FORM

Please ship (___) copies of the book to:

NAME _____

ADDRESS _____

ADDRESS _____

CITY, STATE, ZIP _____

PHONE (Day): _____ PHONE (Evening): _____

E-MAIL: _____

CREDIT CARD: [ ] Visa # _____ Expiration: ____/____

[ ] MasterCard # _____ Expiration: ____/____

Each Book = $34.95+S/H. Quantity Discounts Available (call 503-761-7294 for information).
SEND ORDER FORM TO: D. P. Design
P. O. Box 305, 9610 SE 82nd Avenue
Portland, OR 97266